A BILL OF ASSERTIVE RIGHTS

I: You have the right to judge your own behavior, thoughts, and emotions, and to take the responsibility for their initiation and consequences upon yourself.

II: You have the right to offer no reasons or excuses for justifying your behavior.

III: You have the right to judge if you are responsible for finding solutions to other people's problems.

IV: You have the right to change your mind.

V: You have the right to make mistakes—and be responsible for them.

VI: You have the right to say, "I don't know."

VII: You have the right to be independent of the goodwill of others before coping with them.

VIII: You have the right to be illogical in making decisions.

IX: You have the right to say, "I don't understand."

X: You have the right to say, "I don't care."

YOU HAVE THE RIGHT TO SAY NO, WITHOUT FEELING GUILTY

Bantam Books by Manuel J. Smith, Ph.D.

KICKING THE FEAR HABIT
WHEN I SAY NO, I FEEL GUILTY

When I Say No, I Feel Guilty

How to Cope— Using the Skills of Systematic Assertive Therapy

MANUEL J. SMITH, Ph.D.

*This low-priced Bantam Book
has been completely reset in a type face
designed for easy reading, and was printed
from new plates. It contains the complete
text of the original hard-cover edition.*
NOT ONE WORD HAS BEEN OMITTED.

WHEN I SAY NO, I FEEL GUILTY

*A Bantam Book | published by arrangement with
The Dial Press*

PRINTING HISTORY

*Dial Press edition published January 1975
5 printings through July 1975*

Bargain Book Club edition | December 1974

Literary Guild Book Club edition | June 1975

Bantam edition | November 1975

2nd printing .. November 1975	9th printing .. December 1976
3rd printing .. December 1975	10th printing ...... March 1977
4th printing .. December 1975	11th printing ...... August 1977
5th printing ...... January 1976	12th printing ...... August 1977
6th printing .... April 1976	13th printing .... January 1978
7th printing .... July 1976	14th printing .... May 1978
8th printing .. September 1976	15th printing .... March 1979

ISBN 0–553–12553–2

Published simultaneously in the United States and Canada

PRINTED IN THE UNITED STATES OF AMERICA

To Mankind,
the one animal species
I truly care about,
and its following members:
Dennis
Evelyn
Fred
Gladys
Hal
Ian
Irv
Jennie
JoAnn
Joe
Mannie
Phil
Sue
and
The Turk

The author wishes to acknowledge the work of Dr. Bruce Leckart towards formulating the concepts and writing the first draft of this manuscript.

Preface

The theory and verbal skills of systematic assertive therapy are a direct outgrowth of working with normal human beings, trying to teach them something about how to cope effectively with the conflicts we all have in living with each other. My initial motivation for developing a systematic approach for learning to cope assertively began with my appointment as a Field Assessment Officer at the Peace Corps Training and Development Center in the hills near Escondido, California, during the summer and fall of 1969. During this period, I observed with dismay that the traditional techniques—fancifully known as the "armamentarium"—of the clinical psychologist (or of any theraputic discipline for that matter) were quite limited in that training setting. Crisis intervention, individual counseling or psychotherapy, and group process including sensitivity training or growth-encounter group methods did little to prepare relatively normal Peace Corps trainees for coping with the everyday human interaction problems that most veteran volunteers had met overseas in their host countries. Our failure to help these enthusiastic young men and women became apparent after twelve weeks of intensive training and counseling when, for example, they were given their first dry-run demonstration of a portable insecticide sprayer. Squatting on their heels in a dusty field to simulate a group of rural Latin American farmers were a motley bunch of PhDs, psychologists, a psychiatrist, language instructors, and veteran volunteers dressed in straw hats, shorts, sandals, GI boots, tennis shoes, or bare feet. As the trainees proceeded with their field demonstration, the ersatz farmers showed little interest in the insecticide sprayer and great interest in the strangers coming to their village fields. While the trainees could adequately answer questions on agronomy, pest control, irrigation, or fertilization, not one gave a believable answer to questions that the people they wanted to help would probably ask first: "Who sent you down here to sell us this machine? Why do you want us to use it? Why do you come all the way from America to tell us this? What's in it for you? Why do you first come to our village? Why do we have to grow better crops?" And so forth. As each trainee tried, in exasperation, to talk about the insecticide sprayer, the ersatz farmers kept asking questions about the trainee's reasons for coming to them. Not one trainee, as I recall, assertively responded with something like: *"Quien sabe . . .* Who knows the answers to all your questions? I don't. I only know that I wanted to come to your village and meet you and show you how this machine can help you grow more food. If you want to grow more food, maybe I can help you." Without such a *nondefensive attitude and assertive verbal response* when they found themselves in the *indefensible* position of being interrogated for suspicious motives, most of the trainees had an unforgettable, embarrassing experience.

While we had taught them adequate language, cultural, and technical skills, we had not prepared them at all for assertively and confidently dealing in public with a critical personal examination of their motives, wants, weaknesses, even their strengths—in short, an examination of themselves as persons. We had not taught them to cope in a situation where the trainee wanted to talk about agronomy and the ersatz farmers (as the real *campesinos* would) wanted to talk about the trainee. We had not taught them how to respond in such a situation because we didn't then know what to teach them. All of us had vague ideas about the situation but none of us helped much. We did not teach the trainee how to assert himself without having to justify or give a reason for everything he does or wants to do. We had not taught the trainee how to say simply: "Because I want to . . ." and then leave the rest up to the people he was going to try and help.

In the few weeks remaining before they took their oaths and departed, I experimented with all sorts of theraputic training variations and improvisations with as many of the trainees as were receptive. As the final week drew nearer, the number of trainees who avoided me grew. None of the ideas off the top of my head showed any results then or even any promise, but I did make one important observation: the trainees who coped least well with critical personal examination behaved, in dealing with other people, as if they could not admit failure—they seemed to feel they had to be perfect.

This same observation was made again during my clinical appointments in 1969 and 1970 at the Center for Behavior Therapy in Beverly Hills, California, and at the Veterans Administration Hospital in Sepulveda, California. In treating and observing patients whose diagnoses ranged from normal or mild phobias to severe neurotic disorders, and even with schizophrenics, I found that many of them had the same inadequacy in coping as did the young Peace Corps trainees, although to a much greater degree. Many of these patients seemed incapable of coping with critical statements or questions about themselves from other people. One patient in particular showed such a marked resistance to talking about anything to do with himself that four months of traditional psychotherapy produced only a few dozen sentences from him. Because of his mute withdrawal from other people and his obvious anxiety at being around other people, he was diagnosed as a severe anxiety neurotic. On a hunch that he was simply an extreme case of the Peace Corps trainee syndrome, I switched from "talking" about him to talking about the people in his life who gave him the most trouble. Over a period of weeks, I learned that he was both terrified of and hostile toward his stepfather, a person who related to him in one of two ways—he either criticized or patronized. Our young patient, unfortunately, knew no other way to relate to his stepfather except as the object of criticism or patronage. Consequently, in the presence of this authority figure, the patient was all but mute. His almost involuntary silence, produced by his fear of being criticized and his knowledge that he was unable to defend himself, became generalized and was employed with anyone else who had the least amount of self-assuredness. When I asked this fearful young man if he would be interested in learning how to cope with his stepfather's criticism, he began to talk to me as one person to another. We worked experimentally on *desensitizing him to criticism* from his stepfather, his family, and people in general. Within two months, this "mute neurotic" was discharged, after leading a group of other young patients out on a drinking spree and then generally raising good-natured hell on their ward when they returned. At last report, he was enrolled in college, dressing as he pleased, doing much of what he wanted to do in spite of any protests from his stepfather, and with a good prognosis of not being rehospitalized.

After this successful but novel treatment, Dr. Matt Buttiglieri, Chief Psychologist of the Sepulveda VAH, encouraged me to try these treatment techniques with similar patients and to develop a systematic treatment program for nonassertive people. During the spring and summer of 1970, the assertive therapy skills described in this manuscript were clinically evaluated both at the Sepulveda VAH and at the Center for Behavior Therapy with that master clinician and colleague, Dr. Zev Wanderer. Since that time, these systematic skills have been expanded and used by myself, my students, and my colleagues to teach nonassertive people how to cope effectively with other people in a variety of settings. These assertive skills have been taught in university, county, and private outpatient clinics, university training programs and classes, graduate and undergraduate psychology programs, weekend training seminars, and professional workshops, as well as in probation, social welfare, prison, rehabilitation, and public school training programs, and the results have been reported on in professional meetings.

Whether we choose to call the people who can benefit from systematic assertive therapy everyday people who have difficulty in coping verbally with others, as in the case of the Peace Corps trainees, or neurotic, as in the case of the young "mute" patient, is to me irrelevant. What is relevant and important is learning how to cope with life's problems and conflicts and the people who present them to us. That, in a nutshell, is what systematic assertive therapy is all about and why this book was written. The assertive skills described in this work are based on five years of my own and my colleagues' clinical experiences in teaching people to cope. By writing about the theory and practice of systematic assertive therapy it is my aim to help give as many people as possible a better understanding of what often happens when we feel at a loss in coping with one another . . . and what we can do about it.

M.J.S.
Westwood Village
Los Angeles

Acknowledgments

The colleagues, students, and learners who contributed to the final production of this manuscript and the development of systematic assertive therapy as a body of clinical and practical knowledge have my sincere thanks for letting me describe our experiences together.

In particular, I would like to thank the following persons for their constructive criticism, advice, and review of the manuscript: Ms. Susan F. Levine, M.S.W., my close colleague at Los Angeles County Mental Health, for her critical appraisal of each portion of the manuscript as it was written from a clinical, yet warm and human viewpoint, and for her gutsy and sparkling ways of teaching systematic assertiveness even after many classes and workshops; Dr. Irving M. Maltzman, Chairman of the Department of Psychology, University of California at Los Angeles, for reading early drafts which he prompted me to expand into book form, and for his review of the first technical draft; Mr. Fromme Fred Sherman, M.S., my old Peace Corps colleague, for reviewing the first draft and making valuable suggestions for improving it, as well as for his quick mind and wit when teaching assertive workshops and later, for his delightful renditions of Tevye after eight hours of work; Dr. Zev Wanderer, Director of the Center for Behavior Therapy, Beverly Hills, California, for his advice, counsel, and critique of the therapy techniques described in the manuscript and his encouragement to publish them. Although these reviewers contributed to the final content and writing of the manuscript, I myself must take full responsibility for any errors or inaccuracies that remain.

I also want to thank Nancy Stacy and Jennifer Patten Smith, those assertive typist-editors who insured that what I wrote made sense; thanks are especially due to Jennifer, who could always tell when what I had in mind wasn't coming out on paper.

Very special thanks are due to Ms. Joyce Engelson, Executive Editor at The Dial Press, New York; I thank that exceptionally literary drill sergeant whose hard work and tender loving care with this manuscript made a significant difference.

Table of Contents

Do you want to assert yourself or do you want to control other people?

What happens to society if a lot of us become more assertive and less manipulable?

Table of Dialogues

assert, *v. t.* Vindicate a claim to (rights);
—one*self,* insist upon one's rights;
declare. Hence -able, -ive, aa., -ively (-vl-)
adv., -iveness (-vn-) *n.* [f. L AS (*serere*
sert- join) put one's hand on slave's head
to free him (whence obs. sense "free" in
English) or claim him, claim, affirm]
The Concise Oxford Dictionary

—to assert is to state positively with
great confidence but with no objective
proof.
Webster's Dictionary

1

Our inherited survival responses; coping with other people by fight, flight, or verbal assertiveness

Almost twenty years ago, in college just after being discharged from the army, I met an honest, gutsy man. Joe was a young professor then and I was one of his students. He taught psychology when I met him, and still does. He taught it in a tough, opinionated, open style. He left his students none of their naïve notions about the discipline of psychology. He refused to give the expected explanations for morbidly interesting aberrations or even for mundane normalities of the human mind, behavior, or motivating spirit. In place of complicated theories on why we behave in a certain way, he stressed simplicity. For him, it was enough to describe how things worked psychologically, and that they did work, using simple assumptions, urging us to let it go at that. He held the firm, scholarly belief that 95 per cent of what is pandered as scientific psychological theory is sheer garbage and that it will be a long time before we really know our basic mechanics well enough to explain completely most of what we see.

The merit of Joe's argument is as compelling now as it was twenty years ago . . . and I agree with it! Long-winded technical or mystical explanations are often intriguing and even literary, but not only are they unnecessary, they actually complicate without adding a jot to our understanding. To *use* what psychology does have to offer, it is more important to know *what will work*, not why it will work. For example, in treating patients, I find that it is typically useless to concentrate a lot on *why* a patient is in trouble; that tends to be academic masturbation and can go on for years with no beneficial results. It may even be harmful. It is much more beneficial to concentrate on *what* the patient is going to do about his behavior rather than to understand why he behaves as he does!

Joe even took away any notion we had about psychologists being the new, all-knowing high priests of human behavior by grumbling in class, "I hate students who ask questions I can't answer!" As you might guess, Joe's character out of the classroom wasn't too much different, and in spite of being an expert in human behavior, he had his share of problems with other people. Joe had enough problems besides those I caused him to grouse at me with gusto each semester after assigning grades: "These students always complain about having too many personal problems to study. They can't cope with problems? If you haven't had problems, you haven't lived yet!"

As I came to know Joe over the years as a close friend and a fellow expert on human behavior, it turned out that he had the same problems with other people that I did, and in about the same proportion. As I gradually got to know more and more experts on human behavior in psychology and psychiatry, I found that they too had problems in coping. The title of "Doctor" and the knowledge that went with it did not exempt us from experiencing the same problems we saw in our relatives, neighbors, friends, and even in our patients, no matter what their occupation or education. Like Joe, like other psychologists and nonpsychologists, we all have problems with other people.

When our husbands, wives, lovers are unhappy about something, they have the ability to make us feel guilty without even talking about it. A certain look does it, or a door closing a bit too loud announcing an hour of silence, or a frosty request to change the television station. Joe once complained to me, "I'll be damned if I know how they can do it, or why I respond that way, but somehow I finish up feeling guilty, even when there's nothing to feel guilty about!"

Problems are not limited to those provided by our mates. If parents and in-laws want something, they have the power to make their grown sons and daughters feel like anxious little children, even after they have children of their own. You and I know too well what the gut response is to a mother's silence over the phone; or an in-law's disapproving look; or a prompt from Mom or Dad like, "You must be very busy lately. We never see you any more," or "There's a nice apartment for rent in our neighborhood. Why don't you come over tomorrow night and we'll all look at it."

As if having to cope with those stomach-knotting conflicts was not enough to make us wonder about ourselves, we also have problems with people outside our families. For example, if the auto mechanic does a poor repair job on your car, the garage manager has the knowledge to explain in great detail why your radiator still overheats after you paid $56 to have it fixed. In spite of his ability to make you feel ignorant about your car and rotten for somehow not taking better care of it, there is still the nagging uneasiness that an honest day's work for a day's pay does not apply here. Even our friends cause problems. If a friend suggests something to do for an evening's entertainment that doesn't appeal to you, the almost automatic response is to make up an excuse, you have to lie so your friend doesn't get his feelings hurt, at the same time feeling like a guilty sneak for doing so!

No matter what you or I do, other people can cause problem after problem. Many of us have the unrealistic belief that having to live with problems day after day is an unhealthy or unnatural lifestyle. Not so! Life presents us all with problems. It is entirely natural. But very often, as a result of the unrealistic belief that a healthy person has no problems, you may feel the lifestyle we are all caught up in is not worth living. Most of the people I get to know well from therapy sessions develop this negative belief. But it is not the result of having problems, it is the result of feeling inadequate to cope with our problems and the people who present them.

In spite of similar feelings in myself when I cope poorly, the sum of all my experience as a psychologist rebels at the idea that human beings are some genetically obsolete species designed for an earlier age when things were simpler. Rubbish! I do *not* accept that we are losers who cannot happily live our everyday lives and cope adequately in this industrialized, urbanized, sanitized space age. Instead, I have a different, more hopeful outlook from my own experience; from my professional reading; from what I was taught and my own teachings; from my research in the laboratory and in the clinic; from training people to cope with life's problems; from going out into the community and having to hospitalize hundreds of people against their will simply because they did not know how to cope with other people; and from clinically treating the mildest to the most bizarre and dangerous psychiatric disorders. Placing all these experiences in perspective with a naturalistic observation of the thousands of other humans encountered in my lifetime prompts a sounder and more realistic conclusion: *not only is it natural to expect that we will have problems in living, it is also natural to expect that we all have the ability to cope adequately with these problems.*

If we did not have an inherited ability to cope with all sorts of problems, human beings as a species would have died out long ago. Contrary to what some doomsday prophets tell us, we humans are the most successful, most adaptive, smartest, and toughest biological organisms ever to come off nature's evolutional drawing board. If we can believe the evidence and general conclusions that anthropologists, zoologists, and other scientists place before us, we can see that eons ago, a long evolutional struggle took place on this earth. In this struggle, the genetic family of our human and animal ancestors competed with other species for survival under the harsh terms laid down by the ecological forces of nature. Not only did our ancestors survive under these competitive conditions, they flourished. We have survived and prevailed while other species have died out or are facing extinction because we are physiologically and psychologically built for survival under all conditions. Our primitive ancestors survived, not in spite of problems, but because of them. We have developed as humans from a series of animals who evolved the ability to cope successfully with problems in harsh times and a harsh environment. With this ability, not only have we conquered our earth, our environment, and found no other life form that could compare with us in terms of our grand capacity for coping with difficulties, we are beginning a process of preserving our earth and the other species on it for the survival of future generations.

What are these inherited coping abilities that have produced the success of humans? What have you and I in common with dying animal species and what have we that is uniquely human? If you observe the major coping behaviors of the subhuman species, particularly the vertebrates, whenever there is conflict between two animals of the same species, you can usually see a fight or flight response on the part of at least one of the pair. Both fighting and running away are very efficient ways for animals to deal with each other. These types of coping seem to be almost automatic, pre-programmed responses with great survival value for the lower animals. You and I do fight and run from each other too, sometimes not of our choice, sometimes freely, occasionally openly, more often in ways disguised from each other. We fight or we run as a result of evolving from prehuman ancestors who successfully used these same innate coping responses. In our present human form, however, we have no fighting teeth, no sharp claws, no specialized muscles to efficiently back up our inherited aggressive or flight behavior as primary ways for dealing with each other. You and I can't even produce a decent growl that would frighten off a mugger, and though I trust my running ability in a tight spot, I wouldn't want to rely on it very often.

Although we have fight and flight in common with the lower animals who survive now only by our sufferance, what distinguishes us from the other species most is our great *new* verbal and problem-solving brain that has been added evolutionally in layers over our more primitive animal brain. Roughly about a million years ago, it is thought, evolution and competition for survival weeded out our ancestral cousins who could not add something more efficient to their primitive coping portfolio of fight or flight. At the same time, evolution genetically strengthened the verbal and problem-solving ability for each generation of our ancestors who survived and produced us as their descendants. Our new problem-solving brain enables us to communicate and work together when there is a conflict or a problem. This verbal communication and problem-solving ability is the key survival difference between humans and those species who have either died out, face extinction, or worse, have been domesticated.

While the nonhuman animal species have only those two major inherited survival coping behaviors—fight or flight—in common with us, thanks to our more successful ancestors we have *three* major survival coping behaviors—fight, flight, and a verbal problem-solving ability. Fighting and running away from danger are the responses inherited from our *pre-human* ancestors. Verbally communicating with one another and working out our problems in an assertive manner instead of fighting or running away is that part of our evolutional inheritance passed down from our early *human* ancestors. In short, while you have the inherited ability to either fight or run to survive, you are not instinctively forced to do either. Instead, you have the human option to talk with others and in that way to cope with what is bothering you.

When you or I try to cope with conflict in this modern, civilized world by aggression or flight, typically we do not do it openly. There is very little external payoff in acting out on these feelings. As a child, I was taught that I should not fight, I should not punch other children in the nose. I was also taught that I should be brave and not openly run away from people who frightened me. Most middle-class children in Western society are similarly taught by their parents. We are trained to cope with conflict in a passive way. "Do not fight back," "Stand there and take it"—these are both passive modes. When someone makes us mad, for example, we rarely show it openly. Instead, we silently grit our teeth and make the empty vow of later revenge. This was the typical pattern shown by one of my patients, Diane, a twenty-nine-year-old clerk-typist. Diane tried to cope with demands she didn't like made by her boss through passive aggression. Instead of either talking to her boss about her dislikes or acting out her anger by jumping up and shouting at him "Go to hell!" or something similar, Diane would drag her feet on what her boss wanted. Whenever it was her turn to make the office coffee she made a botch job of it; she spilled it, made it too weak or very strong—in short, made a poor showing, as anyone does who is passively fighting something. If she was asked to work late for a short rush job, she made many typographical errors and took twice as long to do it. Instead of open aggression, Diane used passive aggression; her boss could not put his finger on any fight behavior, but she still frustrated his goals as much as she could. As you would guess, Diane's passive aggression caused her more problems than it caused her boss.

Like Diane, if you or I passively aggress, *we* clean up the coffee mess, or make it over, or work twice as late by dragging our feet, *not the boss!* Even worse, if we passively aggress in this way, our boss is likely to make the same request again and again and we are as frustrated tomorrow in coping with it as we are today. Passive aggression usually works poorly for us and doesn't get us what we want.

Diane, like many of us, also coped with some problems through passive flight. When someone presented her with a problem, she avoided that person as long as possible. For example, Diane came into therapy with a breakdown of marital relations and a possible divorce as her presenting problem. While they were separated, she saw her husband almost daily. Both worked in the same office building. At times during these chance meetings, her husband was cool toward her. His attitude was, in part, understandable since he blamed her for most of their marital troubles. Diane had difficulty coping with his coolness, especially when it happened in public. She reported at the time that she was still fond of Bob and felt like crying when he acted that way. Diane didn't know what to do when Bob was cool. She tried to cope by spending a great deal of effort in avoiding him. When Bob tried to call her about the disposition of their common property, she avoided his telephone calls for weeks. Diane carried her flight behavior to the point of walking away from her desk phone when it rang, even if she didn't know who was calling. In carrying her flight to this extreme, she couldn't be comfortable even in her own apartment for fear Bob was going to call. When Diane told me of this problem, we set up coached sessions to teach her to *assertively cope* with Bob's behavior in place of her passive flight coping. With practice, Diane was able to telephone Bob, settle the property division, and most importantly, to set up a lunch date for discussion of what she didn't like about their chance meetings.

If Diane's passive flight had continued, it would also have continued to fail as an effective method of coping (just as her passive aggression with her boss did). She was required to face the issue of property settlement ultimately, or really run away from both Bob and the divorce process. Later in therapy, Diane was able to trace many of her marital problems to her methods of passive aggression and passive flight in conflicts between Bob and herself. As Diane found out the hard way, if you or I passively flee continuously from someone during conflict, it is likely that person will become disgusted, give up, and break off the relationship.

When we interact only through aggression or flight, we also feel terrible since these modes of behavior always have the unpleasant emotions of anger or fear associated with them. If we cope in these ways, not only do we get angry or afraid but we usually lose the battle—and there are real battles in life, to be won or lost—with other people; we get frustrated and eventually sad or depressed. The triad of anger, fear, and depression is our basic set of inherited survival emotions and the common emotional denominator that prompts troubled people to seek professional psychotherapy.

The patients I see in therapy get angry and aggressive toward other people too often for their own liking, or continually fear and then retreat from other people, or are fed up with losing and being depressed most of the time. Most people seen by therapists are seeking help as a result of over-reliance on fight or flight in various, sometimes bizarre forms. All of us have felt the emotions of anger, fear, and depression associated with aggression, flight, and frustration. If you feel angry, afraid, or depressed, that does not mean you are necessarily sick in any sense, even if you decide to get help because of these emotions. You and I get angry, fearful, or depressed because we are physiologically and psychologically constructed to feel these ways. We are built the way we are because this particular arrangement of nervous tissue, muscle, blood, bone, and the behavior following from it, allowed our ancestors to survive under harsh conditions.

The negative emotions of anger, fear, and depression have survival value in the same way physical pain has survival value. When you touch a hot object, your hand will automatically retract. Your nervous system is constructed so this reaction will occur automatically; no thinking is required. When you sense an unpleasant emotion, you really sense the physiologic and chemical changes ordered by the primitive "animal" parts of your brain to ready your whole body for some behavioral response. In the case of anger, you are sensing your body's preparation for an attack toward some person or animal. Not only can we feel this preparation for aggression in ourselves but we can see its results in the behavior of other people. For example, how many championship football teams have been upset in the big game because the underdog team physically outplayed their traditional rivals after the coach insulted and abused them in the locker room? We are not nature's favored children when it comes right down to physically defending ourselves. Even so, if we get angry, we have a better chance to survive by aggressively defending ourselves when there is no chance to escape or to talk our way out of a dangerous situation.

Whenever you feel afraid, on the other hand, you sense a physiochemical change ordered by your primitive brain that automatically prepares your body for running away from danger as fast as possible. Our chances for survival are better if we can run away from a danger that cannot be dealt with by talking. If a mugger approaches you with an open switchblade knife on a dimly lighted street, the panicky feeling you sense in your breathing, gut, and limbs is not cowardice but a natural feeling of arousal automatically triggered by your brain centers preparing your body for flight.

Even though we have a third human alternative to aggression and flight—verbal problem-solving—at times all of us are going to feel angry or nervous and afraid, no matter what we do. When the careless driver cuts in front of me at 70 mph on the freeway, it doesn't help me one bit to try to be assertive and keep my hands from trembling, that close to disaster I get shaky and there is nothing I can do to prevent it. When a dent mysteriously appears in the fender of my brand-new car, it doesn't help me to be assertive to someone who isn't there; I get mad as hell no matter what I tell myself! If my wife comes home frustrated and grouchy and vents her feelings by kicking me instead of the dog, we go six rounds occasionally and really get into the spirit of it! If things like these happen, our inherited psychophysiology allows us no choice; we are going to feel afraid or angry. But when you *can* assertively interact with other people and, by doing so, have a chance of getting at least part of what you want, automatic anger or fear is less likely. If, on the other hand, we are frustrated by something we cannot change, or we fail to use our innate verbal ability to cope with something we can change, we are likely to feel emotionally depressed.

Although depression would appear to have little or no survival value today, its worth to our ancestors becomes clear if we look at how you or I typically behave when we become depressed. In fact, we hardly behave at all! We do little or nothing except maintain our essential body functions. We usually don't make love or enjoyably explore things like going to the movies, learn anything new, solve many problems, or get much done at home or at work. If we look at how we get depressed, we can observe that when we are mildly depressed or sad, we miss something we are used to or we have been mildly frustrated. When we are deeply depressed, we have suffered an emotional loss or we have been very much frustrated. When you feel depressed, you sense the result of messages sent by the primitive parts of your brain to slow down much of the normal functioning of your body physiology needed for most common, everyday activities.

For our early ancestors, depression was a beneficial state when they had to put up with a period of harsh conditions in their environment. When things got rough, they really had to withdraw to retrench. Our early ancestors who got depressed and just sat around during very frustrating times were more likely to conserve their resources and energy. In doing so, they increased their chances for survival until better times came along. We probably see an indication of this primitive emotional residue in ourselves on a cold, overcast, wintery Saturday when, for no reason we can put our finger on, we find it difficult to do anything besides snacking, napping, and moping around the house. The common depression you and I often experience may last from several hours to several days. We feel miserable, but with time and some positive experience our depression lifts.

In the relatively affluent society we live in today, depression and withdrawal have no apparent survival benefits. For most of us, conditions are not so physically harsh and demanding as they were for our early ancestors. So this psychological "hibernation" mechanism of depression, evolved by our ancestors for successfully waiting out harsh periods in the environment, does nothing for us. Our frustrations today do not come from the environment but from the action of other people. Patients that I, and other therapists, have seen for long-term depression have a history of being frequently frustrated.

Clinical experience in treating persons for temporary or even long-term depression suggests that it is more beneficial to help the depressed person to get his or her feet moving again and reconnected with positive life experiences than to sit out the course of the depression. The treatment of Don, a thirty-three-year-old divorced bookkeeper with recurrent phases of long-term depression, illustrates this concept. Don was reared by a mother and father who constantly frustrated what he wanted to do. When he was a young child, the typical interaction between Don and his parents was for him to receive little or no thanks for performing his tasks around the house, but to be severely punished and made to feel guilty whenever he did anything poorly. When he wanted his first bicycle, for example, Don was given all sorts of reasons why bike riding at his age was dangerous—bikes were expensive, and he was reminded that a careless child like himself probably would not take care of a bike if he were given one. He never got one. When he wanted to learn to drive, he was told that teenagers are bad drivers and he would have to wait. He learned to drive in college, away from home.

Don married a woman he described as similar to his mother. His wife never praised him and always seemed able to find something to bitch about. Three years before treatment, Don's wife divorced him with his consent. Shortly after their separation, Don began experiencing depressed periods that became longer with each occurrence. At the time of treatment, Don had been given antidepressant "mood-elevating" medication for several months with little effect. The treatment of choice, in Don's case, was to discontinue his medication since it had no effect on his depression but did have the side effect of making him nervous and irritable. In place of this medication, I told Don to make up a list of things he enjoyed doing when he was not depressed. His job, then, was to indulge himself in at least two of these activities each week, to force himself if necessary, no matter how depressed he was. In addition, whenever he sensed he was doing something poorly at work or socially, he was not to repeat his past habit of fleeing from the situation by rehearsing his depressed feelings and withdrawing into himself or going home, but was to finish the job at hand or to continue the activity he was engaged in, even if his own immediate feeling was that he didn't want to. With this therapeutic program in effect, Don's chronic depression of five months lifted within four weeks.

While our neurophysiologic coping mechanisms of anger-aggression, fear-flight, and depression-withdrawal are not in themselves signs of sickness and maladaptive coping, they just aren't of much use to us. They seldom work, they rarely even help. Most of our conflicts and problems come from other people and in dealing with other people, our primitive responses are insignificant in comparison with our uniquely human coping ability of verbal assertive problem-solving. Anger-fight and fear-flight, however, actually interfere with this verbal coping ability. When you become angry or afraid, your primitive lower brain centers shut down much of the operation of your new human brain. The blood supply is automatically rerouted away from your brain and gut to your skeletal muscles to prepare them for physical action. Your human problem-solving brain is inhibited from processing information. When you get angry or afraid, you just don't think clearly or efficiently. You make mistakes. To an angry or frightened man, two plus two no longer add up to four.

For our ancestors and sometimes for ourselves, this inhibition of our new human brain by our lower primitive brain presents no problem. If we can do nothing but physically fight or run to survive, we don't have to be fancy about it. That we fight as hard as we can or run as fast as we can is enough, and our inherited psychophysiology insures that we will. But our usual dealings with people require neither fighting nor fleeing. And, in fact, these primitive responses also interfere with our verbal problem-solving ability in a second way. Most of us verbally assert ourselves with other people only when we have had enough frustration to become irritated and angry. Not only does anger make you less effective in dealing with the issues in conflict, but when you are angry, other people tend to put your grievances down to: "He's just blowing off steam. When he calms down, he'll be okay. Just forget it." Our primitive coping responses are less than useless: they usually cause us more problems than they solve.

If this evolutional view of three major coping behaviors, two animal and one human, is correct, why do so many of us get angry or fearful and resort to aggression and flight when other people give us problems and conflict? If our entirely human coping alternative of verbal assertive problem-solving is so valuable for survival, how come so many of us use it so poorly? The purpose of this introductory chapter is to help provide an answer to this perplexing and important question. An answer to it will help us understand why so many of us need *to rediscover the natural verbal assertiveness* we are born with but so often lose somewhere along the way. To begin to answer why most of us use primitive responses that are useless and compound our problems, let us look at what happens to us during childhood.

As infants, we are naturally assertive. Your first independent act at birth was to protest the treatment you were receiving! If something happened which you didn't like, you let others know immediately by verbal assertion—whining, crying, or screaming at all hours of the day or night. You were also very persistent. You rarely stopped letting everyone know you were displeased until they did something about it. As soon as you could crawl, you persistently and assertively did what you wanted whenever you wanted to do it. You crawled into, over, and under anything you wanted to explore. Unless infants are physically restrained or sleeping, they generally create havoc for the people around them. Hence the invention of the crib, playpen, halter, and babysitter to allow parents freedom to do other things besides worry about chasing after babies.

These devices work well for a while in controlling infantile assertive activities but soon a baby matures into a young child. You could walk and talk and understand what your parents told you. At this point, it was no longer appropriate to physically restrict your behavior if you were ever to progress beyond the infant stage. The control your parents exerted over you changed from physical to psychological. As soon as you could learn to speak, the word that rolled from your tongue most assertively was an emphatic "No!" You would even give up a favorite treat sometimes to be able to say "No!" While this obstinacy may have driven Mom up the wall, it was only an extension of your innate assertiveness into the verbal sphere. To psychologically control your behavior while you were learning and exploring this fascinating verbal ability, as soon as you could understand what your parents told you, you were trained to feel anxious, ignorant, and guilty.

These feelings are simply conditioned or learned variations of our basic survival emotion of fear. Once we have learned to feel anxious, ignorant, or guilty, we will do a lot of things to avoid feeling these ways. Our parents train us to feel these negative emotions for two important reasons. First, playing upon our negative emotions is a very efficient way of controlling our natural, annoying, and sometimes explosive childish assertiveness. In using our emotions for controlling behavior, our parents are not necessarily uncaring, lazy, or insensitive to our wants. Instead, our assertiveness at that young age is readily mistaken by them for the innate, aggressive fight-coping we do show when we are frustrated. Second, our parents use this psychological control method because our grandparents taught *them* to feel anxious, ignorant, and guilty.

Our parents accomplish this emotional training in a very simple way. They teach us ideas and beliefs about ourselves and the ways people behave that produce feelings of anxiety, ignorance, and guilt. For example, place yourself in the shoes of a young child, your own child perhaps, or yourself when you were young, and look at the training you undergo. This training is given by both parents, but Mom usually has to do most of the "dirty work" since she is with you much more than Dad. When you clean up your room and put all the toys away, Mom usually says things like: "That's a good boy." When she doesn't like the job you do—if you do it at all—she usually says things that sound like: "What kind of kid are you? Only naughty children don't clean up their room!" You soon learn that "naughty," whatever that means, applies to you. Whenever it is used, Mom's voice and mood tell you that something scary and unpleasant *may* happen to you. She also uses words like bad, terrible, awful, dirty, willful, unmanageable, and maybe even words like wicked or evil, but they all describe the same thing: You! What you are: small, helpless, and not knowing much. And what you "should" feel: dumb, nervous, perhaps frightened, and certainly guilty!

In training you to attach emotionally loaded ideas like *good* and *bad* to your minor actions, Mom is denying that she has any responsibility for making you do what *she* wants, like cleaning up your room. The effect upon you as a small child of using such loaded ideas as good, bad, right, and wrong to control what you do is the same as if Mom had said: "Don't make that sour face at me. It's *not me* who wants you to clean up your room. *God* wants you to clean up your room!" By using good-bad statements to control your behavior, Mom shifts the responsibility off her shoulders for making you do something. With external statements like right and wrong that have nothing to do with your interaction with her, she blames your discomfort at doing what *she* wants onto some external authority that made up all the rules we "should" obey.

This is nonassertiveness. This way of controlling behavior, i.e., "That's a good-bad boy," is very efficient, but it is manipulative, under-the-table control and not an honest interaction in which Mom *would assertively, on her own authority,* tell you what *she* wants you to do, and stick to it. Instead of asserting her wants to an assertive young child until he responds to her wishes (and he will), Mom finds it easier to make you struggle through bad and good with God, the government, the sanitation and safety department, the old man with the white beard, the police chief, or whoever else you childishly perceive as the one who decides what is good and what is bad. Mom rarely tells you: "Thank you. I like it very much when you clean up your room," or even "It must really bug you when I make you do your room over, but that's exactly what I want you to do." With statements like these, Mom teaches you that whatever Mom wants is important simply because *she* wants it. And that is the truth. She teaches you that nobody else is checking up on you but her. And that too is the truth. You are not led into feeling anxious or guilty or unloved because you don't like what Mom wants. You are not taught that what Mom likes is good and what she dislikes is bad. If she uses simple assertive statements of "I want," there are no implications or unspoken threats that "good" children are loved and "bad" ones are not. *You don't even have to like what Mom wants you to do; you only have to do it!*

What a happy situation: being able to bitch and grumble to Mom and Dad to get things off your chest and know they still love you. Using psychological guilt to manipulate your behavior, on the other hand, is the same thing as teaching you that you have to like the taste of aspirin before it will cure your headache. Thankfully, when parents assertively assume themselves to be the authority on what their child can and cannot do, they then teach the assertive concept that when you grow up, not only can you do what you want, *just like Mom and Dad,* but you will also have to do some things you don't care for so that you can do other things you do want, just like Mom and Dad.

Children unfortunately are taught to respond to psychological control of their learned emotions of anxiety, ignorance, and guilt in many childhood situations. For example, if you are playing with your dog in the living room and Mom wants to take a nap on the couch, she teaches you to respond to manipulative emotional control by saying: "Why are you always playing with Rover." You then must come up with an answer as to why you are always playing in the living room with Rover. Not knowing any reason why except the fact that you like to and it is fun, you feel ignorant, because if Mom asks for a reason, there must be one. She wouldn't ask for something that didn't exist, would she?

If you honestly but sheepishly reply: "I don't know," Mom counters with: "Why don't you go play in your sister's room with her?" Lacking a "good" reason why you prefer to play with the dog than with your sister, you are again induced to feel ignorant for not knowing why. Searching awkwardly for a reason, your mumbled reply is cut off by Mom: "It seems like you never want to play with your sister. She wants to play with you." Feeling guilty as hell by now, you remain silent as Mom delivers the coup de grace: "If you never want to play with your sister, she won't like you and want to play with you." Now feeling not only ignorant and guilty but also anxious about what your sister might think of your attitude, you depart with Rover on your heels to take up your rightful station in life beside Sis and out of Mom's hearing.

Ironically, all the tortuous finagling Mom goes through to convince you that you "should" like to play with Sis is more harmful to your natural assertive initiative than if she showed you her down-to-earth, obviously human grouchiness and said: "Get the hell out of the living room while I'm trying to sleep and take that mangy mutt with you!" Even with statements like this, she is exposing you to the hard realities of living with other humans. Sometimes the people you love and care for are going to treat you rottenly, because they are human. They can love and care for you and still get angry with you. Living with people is never just peachy all the time, so with occasional episodes of anger, tempered by everyday love, Mom prepares you emotionally to cope with this human paradox.

Manipulative training of learned negative emotions is reinforced and carried on when you are out of the home. Older children who have been trained themselves this way use manipulative emotional control to get other children to do what they want. Teachers in school pick up where the mother leaves off and use manipulative emotional control as a very efficient means to run their classrooms with less work on their part. Eventually, when you are very well trained in being controlled through your learned negative emotions and effectively blocked from being assertive, you begin to use passive aggression, passive flight, or countermanipulation in an effort to gain some control over your own behavior.

Your own early manipulations, for example, sound like: "Mommy, how come Sis always sits in her room playing when I have to clean up the yard?" critically suggesting that Mom is playing favorites. At this young age, you haven't yet learned enough about manipulation to be a match for Mom. You won't be that facile until you are a teen-ager and want your own car, or the use of one, to stay out late on dates, or any one of a hundred other things. By then you are slick enough to play on your parents' learned feelings of anxiety and guilt with barbs like: "Ron's father bought him a car, aren't you as rich as him?" or "Jennifer's mom has a maid. Why can't you have one to clean up the house?" But in the meantime, your first manipulative attempts are quite sufficient to make Mom feel defensive and protective of herself. Your criticism implies that she is not being fair or sticking to the external rules she taught you. In the same manipulative spirit that you offered your veiled criticism of her, Mom replies with something like: "Your sister helps me around the house. It's only fair that she shouldn't have to do the yard work too. You should do *something* around here! Girls clean up the house and boys clean up the yard." Here again, safely hidden behind the curtain of her manipulation, Mom subtly implies that not only are you perilously close to being a useless loafer, but that it is not by her wishes that you have a displeasing task. Mom implies that she's only following some complex set of rules which she didn't make up and which you don't fully understand yet. (You, incidentally, will later also use these rules, but *never* fully understand them, since each of us, like Mom, improvises our own details of the rules as we go along, selectively uses the rules when it suits us and conveniently ignores them when

that serves our purpose.) Faced with this formidable
verbal tangle, you find it easier to retreat to the yard
for a long session of grumbling and passively dragging
your rake. Not only does Mom's manipulative control
of your emotions and behavior train you further in the
arbitrary use of ideas like right and wrong, or fairness,
but with the same words, Mom is conditioning you to
think according to vague general rules that "should" be
followed.

The flaw in this conditioning process is that these ab-
stract rules are so general they can be interpreted in
any way desired, in the same circumstances. These
rules are external to your own judgment of what you
like and dislike. They tell how people "should" feel and
behave toward each other, regardless of the relationship
between them. They are often dogmatically and provin-
cially interpreted to the point of training you for a totally arbitrary sexual lifestyle that has nothing to do
with survival or reproduction. Why should boys do
yards and not their sisters, for example?

Mom does have the more promising option, however,
of dealing *assertively* with manipulative statements
from her children. More hopefully she uses verbal
assertion in her response, and in doing so, she neither
punishes nor countermanipulates her child. In coping
with your criticism of her job assignments, for example,
she can assertively and empathically respond with:
"I can see that you feel it's unfair that you do the
yard while your sister is playing. That must upset you,
but *I still want you to rake the yard now.*" By her assertive response in the unpleasant job of coping with
your manipulation, Mom is telling you a lot of emotionally supportive and reassuring things. She tells you
that even though you are going to do something you
don't like, you are entitled to feel the way you do and
she's not insensitive to you; despite the way you see
your ordered, fair world crumbling, things are still
going the way Mom wants them, and most reassuring
of all, disaster is not lurking around the next turn be-

cause Mom is smart enough not to be "conned" by an insignificant little kid like you or your sister.

The mothers I see in my teaching all express similar uncomfortable feelings about the job of coping with young children. They have two main sources of worry. First, they are confused about the different methods used over the years for rearing children. Spock tells them one thing. Gesell told them something different, Patterson something else. Second, *all* the mothers erroneously assume that if they decide to assertively take charge, they will only have two options: either being tyrannical bastards or indulgent jellyfishes with their kids. They see no meaningful middle ground between these two extremes. Faced with such a distasteful choice, they fall back upon the efficient, emotional manipulation taught them by their parents instead of assuming the frank, honest responsibility of taking authority: *"I want you to . . ."*

Taking this authority and using it to make themselves and their children feel better about the stresses of growing up is simple behaviorally, but not easy emotionally. One mother, for example, asked me, with a tinge of hostility, "How do *you* break a promise to a child?" The feeling tone that accompanied this question suggested that this mother, like many others, felt it was imperative that she always be on top of things and present at least the illusion of a super-competent mom to her daughter—someone who never breaks a promise, for example.

As I talked to her later it turned out that my analysis was correct. She was in the bind of having to be perfect, not to make mistakes, and above all not appear dumb to other people. As I like to describe it, she had set herself up in a "sucker's play." In trying to be perfect and a supermom to her daughter, she was an odds-on favorite to lose. Eventually she was going to have to break promises either because she could not or did not want to keep them. If she could drop her need to be perfect and her pretense that she was, she could break a promise to her daughter in an assertive way that would minimize *both* their uncomfortable feelings. She could say, for example, "I know it's dumb of me to make you a promise that I can't keep, but we are going to put off going to Disneyland on Saturday. You didn't do anything wrong and it's not your fault. Let's see when we can go again, okay?" With this *assertive* negative statement, she would be giving her daughter the message that even Mom does dumb things now and then, but even more important she serves as a model for her daughter, showing that if Mom doesn't have to be perfect, neither does daughter. She models this important part of being human while she makes the reality clear: for whatever reason, Mom has decided that they will not go this time, *and they are not going*.

In summary, you and I and most of the rest of the population are trained to be responsive to manipulative emotional control as soon as we are able to speak and understand what other people tell us. These psychological puppet strings that our parents attach to us through *learned* feelings of nervousness or anxiety, ignorance and guilt, control our childish assertiveness. They effectively and efficiently keep us out of real and imagined danger as children and make the lives of the adults around us a lot easier. These emotional strings, however, have an unfortunate side effect. As we grow into adults and are responsible for our own well-being, they do not magically disappear. We still have feelings of anxiety, ignorance, and guilt that can be and are used efficiently by other people to get us to do what *they* want, irrespective of what we want for ourselves. The subject of this book is the reduction, at least, if not the elimination of these learned emotions in coping with other people in the ordinary experiences of our lives. In particular, the following chapters deal with (1) the nonassertive beliefs we acquire because of our feelings of anxiety, ignorance, and guilt, and how these beliefs allow other people to manipulate us; (2) the rights we have as human beings to assertively stop the manipulation of our behavior by others; and (3) the systematic verbal skills easily learned in everyday situations that allow us to enforce our human assertive rights with family members, relatives, parents, children, friends, fellow employees, employers, repairmen, gardeners, salesclerks, managers; in short, other human beings, no matter what their relationship to us is.

2

Our prime assertive human right
—how other people violate it

Each of us, at times, gets into situations that confuse us. A friend, for example, asks you to pick up his aunt flying in from Pascagoula at 6:00 P.M. The last thing in the world that you relish is fighting the traffic rush to the airport and then trying to make bumper-to-bumper conversation with someone you know zero about, without giving her the idea you wish she had stayed in Mississippi. You rationalize with: "Well, a friend's a friend. He would do the same thing for me." But other nagging thoughts intrude: "But I never asked him to pick up anybody for me. I always did it myself. Harry never told me why he couldn't pick her up. How come his wife couldn't do it?"

In situations like this, all of us feel like saying: "When I say 'No,' I feel guilty, but if I say 'Yes,' I'll hate myself." When you say this to yourself, your real desires are in conflict with your childhood training and you find yourself without cues that would prompt you in coping with this conflict. What can you say? If I say "No," will my friend feel hurt or rejected? Will he not like me anymore? Will he think I am self-centered, or at least not very nice? If I don't do it, am I an uncaring son of a bitch? If I say "Yes," how come I'm always doing these things? Am I a patsy? Or is this the price I have to pay to live with other people?

These internal questions on how to cope are triggered by an external conflict between ourselves and another person. We want to do one thing, and our friend, neighbor, or relative assumes, hopes, expects, wishes, or even manipulates us into doing something else. The internal crisis comes about because you'd like to do what you want but are afraid that your friend may think what you want is wrong; you may be making a mis-

24

take; you may hurt his feelings and he may reject you because you did what you wanted; perhaps you fear that your reasons for doing what you want are not "reasonable" enough (you don't have a broken leg and the Feds aren't looking for you so why can't you go to the airport?). Consequently, when you try to do what you want, you also allow other people to make you feel ignorant, anxious, or guilty; the three fearful emotional states you were trained as a child to feel when you don't do what someone else wants you to do. The problem in resolving this conflict is that the trained manipulated part of us accepts without question that someone else "should" be able to control us psychologically by making us feel these ways. With the innately assertive part of us suppressed by our training in childhood, we respond by countermanipulation to the frustration of being manipulated. Manipulative coping, however, is an unproductive cycle. Manipulatively dealing with another adult is not like manipulatively dealing with a little child. If you manipulate adults through their emotions and beliefs, they can countermanipulate you in the same way. If you again countermanipulate, so can they, and so on. For example, in trying to get out of picking up your friend's aunt, the words and phrases you use would be much more subtle but still boil down to something like this short segment of a manipulative dialogue:

YOU: God, Harry! I'm so tired at that time of day. [Trying to induce guilt in Harry by implying, "How could anybody ask a tired friend to fight the traffic at that time of evening," even though Harry's telling himself, "Hell! I fight the same traffic every evening at five."]

HARRY: Little old ladies can get really scared arriving in a strange airport with no one to meet them. [Trying to induce guilt in you by implying, "What kind of fellow would make a little old lady go through that just because he is a little tired," while you're thinking, "Where did all this fragile-old-lady business come from? After fifty years of living with the Pascagoula mosquitos she must have the endurance of a horse!"]

YOU: Well, I'd really have to go out of my way . . . [Trying to induce guilt by implying, "I will really suffer if you make me do this," while Harry says to himself, "It's a pain in the neck, but you've done it before and it won't kill you."]

HARRY: If I had to pick her up, I wouldn't even get there until seven thirty. [Suggesting that you are ignorant of the facts by implying, "My trip would be much longer and harder than yours," except you think, "Where and what would he be coming from? He's probably closer to the airport than I am!"]

The farce of this manipulative-countermanipulative interchange is that who goes to the airport, you or Harry, does not depend upon what you want but upon whoever can make the other one feel guiltier. As a result of these types of manipulative interactions with other people you are more likely to finish up frustrated, irritated, or anxious, in spite of your best efforts to avoid feeling these ways. Without an adequate, mature, and assertive outlet, these feelings eventually are expressed by you in verbal fighting or by running away from someone. The end result of this unresolved internal coping conflict between our natural wants and our childhood belief and habit training leaves us with some really dismal choices: we can do what someone else wants, be frustrated very often, get depressed, withdraw from people, and lose our self-respect; we can do what we want angrily, alienate other people, and lose our self-respect; or we can avoid the conflict by running away from it and the people who cause it, and lose our self-respect.

As a first step in becoming assertive, you have to realize that *no one can manipulate your emotions or behavior if you do not allow it to happen.* In order to stop anyone's manipulation of your emotions or behavior, you need to recognize how people do try to manipulate you. What do they say, how do they act, or what do they believe that controls your emotions and behavior? To make yourself as effective as possible in stopping manipulation you also need to question the childish attitudes and ideas many of us have been reared with which make us susceptible to manipulation by other people. Although the words and ways people use to manipulate us are infinite, in my clinical experience in treating nonassertive people, I have observed that there is a most common set of manipulative expectations that many people have about themselves and each other. The manipulative behavior prompted by these expectations can also be seen in the general nonclinical population. These childish expectations and their consequent behavior deny us much of our dignity and self-respect as human beings. If we have the same expectations about ourselves as our manipulators do, we surrender to them our dignity and self-respect, the responsibility for governing our own existence, and the control over our own behavior.

This and the next chapter deal with the common set of childish assumptions on how we all supposedly "should" behave in order to avoid resorting to our primitive coping of anger-aggression and fear-flight. Such beliefs are the basis for most of the ways other people manipulate us into doing what they want us to do. They directly contradict our assertive rights as healthy, emotionally stable individuals. In this and the next chapters, I describe these beliefs along with each of our assertive rights: the rights that we and other people violate daily in a futile attempt to keep aggression or flight out of our relationships with each other.

Our assertive rights are a basic framework for each individual's healthy participation in any human relationship. These assertive individual rights are the framework upon which we build positive connections between people, such as trust, compassion, warmth, closeness, and love. Without this basic assertive framework that allows each of us to express our individual selves to each other, trust gives way to suspicion, compassion evolves into cynicism, warmth and closeness disappear, and what we called love acquires an acid bite. Many people are afraid to show their true feelings

of love and closeness because they think they may be
trod upon and will have no way to cope with rejection.
If they were confident that, yes, in fact there probably
will be difficulties to iron out, but that they can assertively cope with these difficulties, even with rejection,
there would be less fear in showing tenderness,
closeness, and love. I like to think that being assertive
means being confident of yourself and your abilities!
"No matter what happens to me, I can cope with it."

The Bill of Assertive Human Rights presented herein
is composed of statements about ourselves as humans,
statements about our true responsibilities for ourselves
and our own well-being, and statements about our acceptance of our humanness which set practical limits on
what other people can expect of us. Let's examine,
first, our prime assertive right—from which all the
other assertive rights are derived: *our right to be the ultimate judge of all we are and all we do.* Then let's see
how we let people manipulatively violate this right in
different types of relationships.

ASSERTIVE RIGHT I
**You have the right to judge your
own behavior, thoughts, and
emotions, and to take
the responsibility for
their initiation and
consequences upon
yourself**

*You have the right to be the ultimate judge of your-
self:* a simple statement that sounds so much like common sense. It is a right, however, that gives each of us
so much control over our own thinking, feelings, and
behavior that the more manipulatively trained and
nonassertive we are, the more likely we are to reject it
as the right of other people or even ourselves.

Why should this be? Why should such a simple
statement—that each of us has the right to be the ultimate judge of ourselves—generate any controversy at
all? If you exercise this assertive right, you take the re-

sponsibility for your very existence upon yourself and away from other people. To those who are fearful of what others may do, and therefore feel that people must be controlled, your independence from their influence is quite disturbing, to say the least. Those who are disturbed by independence feel that the people they relate to must be controlled because they themselves are powerless. This feeling of helplessness is a result of their failure, because of nonassertive attitudes, beliefs, and behavior, in attempting to cope with other people. If someone they relate to is not controlled by some external standard of behavior, they feel that their own goals, their very happiness, will be subject to the whim and mercy of the uncontrolled person. When we truly doubt that we are the ultimate judge of our own behavior, we are powerless to control our own destiny without all sorts of rules about how each of us "should" behave. The more insecure we are, the more fearful we become when there is no superabundance of arbitrary rules for behavior. If we are very insecure and disturbed by a lack of guidelines in any particular area of behavior, we will invent enough arbitrary rules until we again feel comfortable and unthreatened. For example, there are no laws in most municipalities specifically controlling each individual's bodily waste elimination, a matter with serious public health consequences. If you voided your bowels at high noon at Wilshire and Westwood Boulevards, you might be arrested for littering, but not specifically for that act of waste elimination. There are also no rules on how we all "should" *behave* while eliminating the waste products from our bodies. Yet our behavior in this area does not vary much from person to person even though there are a great number of ways we could behave. In a public rest room, is it all right to converse with the person in the booth next to you? What would he think? I don't really know, but my guess is that he would think I was some kind of nut if I did. No one has ever talked to me in that circumstance. When standing up at a crowded public urinal, is it permissible to be curious about what the guy next to you is doing? What would he think if he saw you looking at him? Is it allowed to trace out your initials on the porcelain? What's the approved way to get rid of that last drop of urine? A nervous snap? An insolent flip? A dignified shake? If there are no rules, and I have never been told or read of any, how come all the other men in there with me behave identically and none of us engage in these finer nuances of elimination? If they are like me, then they too have invented an arbitrary set of rules on what they "should" or "should not" do while performing this function. Although this example describes an unimportant pattern of our behavior, the behavior observed is very regulated.

The same concept of personal insecurity prompting us to invent rules to control behavior applies to other more significant things. What is the "right" way to have sex? The standard missionary position? How about the things they describe in the Kama Sutra? If those are okay too, how come it was not published in most countries until a few years ago? In other areas of living, how do you tell your mother to stop bugging your wife? What are the rules on how mothers and daughters-in-law "should" behave to each other? How come your wife doesn't take care of this problem herself? Are only sons "supposed" to deal with mothers? Where did all these arbitrary ways of "properly" doing things come from? The answer is a simple one. All of us invent the rules as we go along, using the beliefs taught us in childhood as an outline. We then manipulatively use them with other people to control their behavior, through violation of their assertive rights, and thereby relieve our feelings of personal insecurity about not knowing what to do and how to cope. But when we act as if we are the ultimate judge of our own behavior and someone's arbitrary rules must first be approved by us before we follow them, we will severely threaten this arbitrary structured order that nonassertive people use to cope with us. Consequently, the nonassertive person will be loath to grant other people any assertive rights and powers to influence their relationship with him. As a self-protective measure, he will psychologically manipulate you with rules and standards of right and wrong, fairness, reason, and logic to control behavior that may be in conflict with his own personal wants, likes, and dislikes. The manipulative person will invent this type of external structure or assume it already exists in a relationship in order to control your behavior. The tragedy of this manipulative coping is that the manipulator is unaware that the only justification he really needs to negotiate a change in anything is *the fact that he wants a change*. He does not need external structure or arbitrary rules as a manipulative backup for what he wants. To negotiate his wants with you, all he need do is to make a judgment that his likes and dislikes are sufficient justification for the effort he will expend in negotiation.

Does the manipulator's use of structure, i.e., the way he determines and tries to convince you of the "right, wrong, fair, or logical" way of doing something mean that all structure is manipulative? Does it mean that if you rely on rules and structure to make your relationships a bit simpler and easier, you open yourself to manipulation? These questions are difficult to answer with a simple yes or no. An answer more in touch with the reality of how structure can be used is *"probably yes,"* depending upon how the structure in the relationship was worked out and what type of relationship exists between the people in conflict. How can structure in a relationship work for you or against you? What are the important things about structure and relationships that allow you to make the distinction between structure used to manipulate and structure (workable compromises) used to make things easier, more stable, and less chaotic? First, all structure or rules in any interaction between two people is arbitrary. If one particular blueprint on how things will operate can be designed, you can usually find a half dozen other ways that will more or less produce the same results. For example, if you and your business partner design a scheme whereby you handle the office while he meets the public, that is not the only way you could have arranged things. You could have shared the bookkeeping or hired a part-time bookkeeper or any of a number of things that would produce the same result, i.e., a successful business with you doing more of what you want. If you take care of the kids while your husband works, that is only one arbitrary arrangement. You can share the responsibility with him, hire a babysitter, use a day-care center, drop them off at Grandma's, get a job yourself, or any of a number of arbitrary possibilities —none laid down in heaven.

Second, to better understand how structure can be used either to make things easier or to violate your right to judge what you will or will not do, it is convenient to classify all your relationships with other people into three gross categories: (1) commercial or formal relationships, (2) authority relationships, and (3) equality relationships. How you categorize a particular interaction between yourself and someone else depends upon how much of the interaction between the two of you is regulated by rules from the outset, perhaps even before you and the other person meet. For example, in spite of what you may first think, of all your interactions, commercial dealings have the most structure imposed upon them before the interaction even starts. This structure may even be in the form of a legal code or contract. Both parties in buying and selling merchandise, for example, know or spell out exactly what all their commercial behavior toward each other will be. One usually selects and pays for merchandise and the other usually receives money, delivers the goods, and backs up performance of what is sold. Problems arise in commercial relationships when one of the parties (usually the seller) brings in external manipulative structure that has not been mutually agreed upon in advance and does not allow you to be your own judge of what you will do. For example, "We've got nothing to do with the repair of your radiator. That was subcontracted out to the radiator shop. You'll have to go see them about that." (Implying: "You dummy! Don't you know how we do business around here at Ripoff Motors?")

The middle category (2), involving relationships with some sort of authority figure, is only partially structured beforehand. Not all the behavior that people in this relationship show each other is covered by mutually agreed-upon rules. You will observe defined roles and organization imposed upon both people from the start, but not all their behavior is regulated as in a commercial relationship. One example that fits this category is the interaction between a boss and an employee. In my dealings with my boss, not all the rules have been spelled out and mutually agreed upon in advance. I may know specifically how to deal with him on the job, but what do I do when we get together after work? Who buys the drinks? Or who chooses the bar? Or even on the job, for instance, what do you do when your boss brings in something out of left field that you haven't seen before, like taking on more responsibility, working odd shifts, or covering overtime without more money? In this type of interaction you can see problems occur when manipulative structure is arbitrarily imposed in areas where no mutually agreed upon rules exist and this structure does not allow you to be your own judge of what you will do. For example, your boss at work is not your boss on the tennis court (thank God!), so how come you are always making all the arrangements when you play tennis together? How did that one come about? Your boss during working hours is not your boss after 5:00 P.M. on your way home, so how come you are dropping his suit off to be cleaned? Even more galling than the tennis situation, you resent being his flunky, but still don't say anything about it to him! This is the sort of thing that *will* happen to you when arbitrary structure is introduced into areas of your relationships with other people which do not require structure for *mutual convenience*. When structure is imposed unilaterally, its effect and *intent* are to control your behavior, and this violates your own right to judge what you will or will not do.

Another good example of the authority type of relationship exists between young children and their parents. Here you can observe that the parent starts out with the authoritarian roles of mother-father, helper, teacher, nurse, protector, provider, model, disciplinarian, decider, and judge. You can also see that the child begins with the roles of dependent, learner, patient, petitioner, etc., etc. Over the years as the child grows up and assumes more and more self-responsibility for his welfare, the initial reality-imposed parent-child structure requires modification. Less and less structure and fewer and fewer rules are required since the child has to be allowed more and more freedom of choice if he is ever to take the initiative for managing his own life. As you may remember from your own experiences, when the roles between parent and child become more equal, both parents and their children can share some of their personal feelings, goals, and problems with each other. Usually this sharing does not reach the level of closeness that characterizes the relationship between equals. Too often, due to ignorance or insecure clinging to the old, safe, but obsolete structure, parents allow their children adult freedom but do not surrender their initially imposed roles as all-knowing father-mother, thus violating their children's assertive right to be their own judge. The result of this resistance to inevitable change is an unnecessary distance between parents and their children.

This unfortunate circumstance was evident in one case between a mother and her forty-year-old daughter, before the daughter came in for therapy. In reaction to being constantly frustrated, this nonassertive daughter found at least some satisfaction in life from eating, and eating, and eating! Consequently, she was often on a strict diet. On one occasion while she was dieting, she went shopping with Mom. At the end of the trip, they stopped in a coffee shop to relax. Mom promptly proceeded to talk her daughter into having something besides a cup of coffee, on a "Mother knows best" basis. Although the daughter pleaded that she knew what she was doing, she ended by eating, even though she didn't want to. And until assertive therapy was completed, this patient never dared or desired to shop with Mom again. Mom manipulated her daughter (who knows why?—and for our purposes, it doesn't matter) by bringing in structure from a previous situation (childhood) that had no current basis between two women, one aged sixty and the other aged forty. At the same time, this mother was having severe difficulties in her own home life. Her husband was physically disabled and she was making a mess of things financially and organizationally by undertaking projects she was just not suited or experienced for. Her daughter wanted to help but avoided getting involved since she realized that Mom probably wouldn't trust her judgments or advice. She also had her fill of Mom's continual manipulative shenanigans and simply did not want to be around her. *Parents like this have failed to work out new adult-to-adult roles with their sons and daughters that would be more appropriate to the unique, and hence more wonderful, relationship which parents can have with their grown children.*

In sharp contrast to this example of children still being children-to-parents at age forty and parents still being parents-to-children at age sixty is the relationship between another mother and daughter I know well. These women also had severe disruption in their lives, but at an earlier age. When this daughter was entering puberty, her father died. In spite of all the problems naturally encountered by a family in such a situation, through trial and error over the years, this mother and daughter evolved a mutual respect for each other's choices and decisions. At present, Mom is fifty-six and living alone while her daughter is thirty-one and married with two children. Each is a source of good feeling, support, and counsel for the other. This mother told her daughter recently about her problems in living alone and commented: "I really like talking to you about my problems. You aren't judgmental about my boy friends. You don't cut them up and try to tell me what to do. You just listen and give me an opportunity to get things off my chest. I really appreciate it." And not only is this mother able to accept help and counsel from her daughter, she is also able to respect the limits her daughter places on her when interacting with her grandchildren and son-in-law.

In the third category of relationships—between

equals—there is no initial structure imposed upon either person's behavior beforehand. All structure in this type of interaction is evolved as the relationship progresses, through compromises that work. These mutually agreed-upon compromises (structure) are practical ones; they allow the business of the relationship to be carried on without daily negotiation of who does what and when. People I have taught to be more assertive often naïvely insist that these compromises should be fair ones. They often seem a bit shocked when I respond to them with: "Compromises don't have to be fair to be useful. All they have to do is work! Where did you ever read that life is fair? Where did you ever get that crazy idea? If life were fair, you and I would be taking turns visiting the South Pacific, the Caribbean, and the French Riviera with the Rockefellers! Instead we're in this crummy classroom trying to learn to be assertive!"

Examples of equal relationships are those between friends, neighbors, roommates, co-workers, dates, lovers, adult family members, cousins, in-laws, brothers, sisters; relationships where you have the most freedom to work out what you want as well as having the most chance for getting hurt. The most obvious example is between spouses in a marriage. In those effective, equal marriages that you know of, you will see both partners collectively work, and expect to rework, the compromise structure they require through frequent communication with each other of what they want and are capable of giving to one another. There is no fear of appearing odd or selfish in their own eyes or violating some sacred set of rules on how husbands and wives "should" behave. With this assertive sharing ability, the partners lay down a minimum of renegotiable, workable compromises on each other's behavior, thus keeping their marriage structure as flexible as humanly possible to deal with the real problems of life instead of the self-frustrating, manipulative ones.

Problems in this type of equal relationship come about when one or both of the partners, due to personal insecurity or perhaps ignorance, have entered the situation with preconceived ideas on how friends, roommates, or husbands and wives "should" behave. For example, if you look at the troubled marriages you know, you will probably see that one or both spouses have definite roles in mind for themselves and each other. These imposed rules do not allow the other spouse to be the judge of his or her own behavior in the marriage. But imposed rules do not work in reality: the details of each of their roles must be worked out *as they go along* if they are to pull together and create a happy life for themselves. The more personally insecure either of the marriage partners may be, the more arbitrary and manipulative a structure she or he tries to impose on their mates and themselves as soon as possible. The insecure person copes best in a very structured situation where there are very few unknowns to deal with. The insecure husband may impose arbitrary structure upon his wife simply in order to deal with his fear of coping poorly with her. He may, for instance, insist that wives should not work, should stay home, take complete care of the children, or not be allowed to manage money. He may even feel wives should be punished or at least made to feel guilty if they have other ideas about such an artificially imposed way of dealing with marriage. He may do this even at the same time that he is mouthing platitudes about fairness and give-and-take.

Such a husband was married to one of my patients of several years ago. This unfortunate couple had had no social or sexual experience with anyone else before marriage. The only close, equal relationship they ever had was with each other. They were completely devoid of any other experience in coping on a close, equal level. The husband's arbitrary structure was dominant in their interactions from the start, and this young woman was not assertively independent enough to challenge it. Consequently, the only coping styles she had at her disposal were passive aggression, passive flight, or a manipulation that was second-rate in comparison to her husband's. After six years of marriage, they came into therapy, all their coping problems piled on a psychic wheelbarrow with a flat tire which she pushed around and called "my sexual problem." Unable to assertively cope with his manipulations in their everyday life, she gradually withdrew from him in all ways, including sexually. After four years of unsuccessful sexual relations, she complained of orgasmic dysfunction (frigidity), vaginitis (vaginal irritation), vaginismus (involuntary contractions of the vaginal opening preventing sexual intercourse), dyspareunia (deep vaginal pain typically reported in sexual malingering) as well as not being turned on sexually by her husband. Denying that she was nonassertive and insisting that their marital coping outside of the sexual area was satisfactory, she started treatment for the sexual dysfunction. Vaginismus typically takes three weeks to correct with behavioral methods. For her, it took three months. After several of these foot-dragging attempts to rectify her specific sexual difficulties, general exploratory psychotherapy was initiated with no results. Both spouses could not see or accept that their sexual problems were in any way connected to their general behavior toward each other. When she was questioned on why she wanted to rid herself of her sexual difficulties, she responded truthfully with: "So Chuck will be happy," while saying nothing about her own sexual gratification. She did not realize that having difficulty in being sexually turned on by your husband is a nifty way to cut him up and express your frustration in being married to him without being caught at it! Who can kick back at an invalid? This couple discontinued this type of psychotherapeutic help shortly after its inception and showed no later interest in resuming it. At last report, they were contemplating a divorce.

A personally insecure wife, on her side, may also impose manipulative structure into the marriage in order to deal with her own fears of not being able to cope with the unknown. She may violate her husband's assertive right to be the judge of what he does by subtly, even condescendingly, treating him as if he were an irresponsible little boy. She will allow him the freedom of working for a living, but in not trusting him, she will try to control everything else he does and make him feel guilty if he does not agree with her rigid methods of coping. As with the manipulated wife, this husband must believe that it is okay for his wife to do this to him before he can be manipulated. He must believe that he is not his own judge before the structure imposed by her can have a manipulative effect. If he doesn't accept it, she can't impose it on him.

One patient I saw recently had this type of interaction with his wife. Prior to therapy, he was employed as a manager in a chain store. With his promotion to manager, he was subjected to various pressures both from the public he dealt with and from the district management of his firm. Because of his nonassertive belief system, he did not draw firm limits on what he would do for his customers and also did not insist on definite commitments of support from his firm. Consequently, he did not last very long in his job as manager. During the time he was unemployed, he felt he had to lie to his wife about having a job rather than tell her he was drawing unemployment insurance. When he was offered a temporary low-pressure job as a warehouseman, he avoided taking it because he dreaded a confrontation with his wife on what her relatives would think about his being a blue-collar worker. This poor fellow clearly did not believe he was the ultimate judge of his own behavior and therefore showed a primary coping style of passive flight instead of verbal assertiveness.

A common source of problems in any of these three ways you relate to other people—commercially, authoritatively, or equally—exists when you have more than one type of interaction with the same person. For instance, when you enter into a commercial relationship with a friend, each of you may have difficulty in keeping your commercial behavior with each other from interfering with your equal, friendly interactions or vice-versa. Your friend may manipulate you by imposing previously agreed-upon ways of doing things as friends that have nothing to do with your commercial dealings. He may, for instance, begin to borrow your car for business purposes since both of you have extended this courtesy to each other in the past. He may try to borrow larger sums of money since a previous arrangement of lending small amounts has worked well. If you and your friend have not yet worked out a true, equal interaction that is free of manipulative structure, your friend will probably make the same manipulative assumptions about how friends "should" behave toward each other in your commercial dealings with him, i.e., "How could a friend put pressure on just to meet a deadline?" These examples of mixed relationships resulting in manipulation have a parallel in the commonsense folk saying, "Friends and business don't mix." As my cousin Edgar from Hawaii emphatically pointed out when we talked about these problems, "When I need some business done, I want to start out simply, with a clear understanding that if my associate doesn't do what he said he'd do, I'm gonna come down on him hard! I don't want to have to act tough with my friends. I've got better things to do with them." While Cousin Edgar's solution to the problem of mixing relationships has great appeal, you may find yourself in the position of having no choice but to deal on two different levels with the same person. Like getting into a bar room brawl, after you are involved it doesn't much matter if you slipped and fell into it, jumped in willingly, or were shoved and dragged into the fray. Does it matter how it came about that your friend totaled your car, or wants you to help him out by investing in Magic Moment Wart Remover? You still have to cope with what's going on. If you cope with manipulation in mixed relationships by assertively being your own judge, deciding yourself what *you* want, and spelling out compromises you are willing to accept each step of the way, you can do business with a friend and maintain the friendship.

In any of these three types of interaction with other people, manipulation of your behavior occurs when extraneous rules are imposed upon you that you have not previously agreed to and which therefore violate your assertive right to judge how you do things yourself. If any of us were to verbalize the primary childish belief we have learned that makes manipulation possible, each of us might use different words or phrases, but the meaning would still be approximately as follows: *You should not make independent judgments about yourself and your actions. You must be judged by external rules, procedures, and authority wiser and greater than yourself.* Basically, then, manipulation is any behavior prompted by this belief. You are being manipulated when someone reduces, by any means, your ability to be your own judge of what you do. The external rules and authority which this belief refers to have profound implications for the control and regulation of all you do, feel, and think. For example, in one class of eighty-five people learning to be assertive, when I asked about this primary childish belief: "How many of you *really believe* it?" only three people raised their hands. But when I asked them: "How many of you *behave as if you believe* it?" the whole class raised their hands.

The right to be the final judge of yourself is the prime assertive right which allows no one to manipulate you. It is the assertive right from which your other assertive rights are derived. Your other assertive rights are only more specific everyday applications of this prime right. The other rights are important since they provide you with the details for coping with the most common ways that other people psychologically manipulate you, violate your personal dignity and self-respect. Examples of the ways other people try to manipulate you by setting up themselves or some arbitrary standard as the ultimate judge of your behavior are given with each of the specific assertive rights that follow. For the moment, however, let's briefly examine some of the consequences of exercising your basic assertive right to be your own ultimate judge.

When you become the judge of yourself, you learn how to work out independently your own ways for judging your behavior. The judgments you make through your own experience of trial and error are less like a system of "rights and wrongs" and more like a system of "this works for me, that doesn't." Your independent judgments are a loose system of "I like—I

don't like," not a system of "I should—I shouldn't,"
"you should—you shouldn't." The particular judgment
each of us makes about ourselves may not be systematic, logical, consistent, permanent, or even sensible to
everyone else. They will, however, be judgments that fit
our particular personality and lifestyle.

For many of us, the prospect of having to be one's
own judge can be frightening. Being our own ultimate
judge, without a lot of arbitrary rules, is like traveling
in a strange, new country without a tourist guide to
point out what we should see, or even more worrisome,
without a road map to tell us how to get there. Having
to make up one's own rules for living *as we go along* is
no easy task, but faced with the alternatives of frustration, aggression, and flight brought about by allowing
manipulation of our feelings, what other choice do we
have? We have to rely upon our own judgment because
the truth is—whether we wish to face it or not—only
we have responsibility for ourselves.

The responsibility incumbent upon each of us for in-
itiating and accepting the consequences of all we do
cannot be avoided by denying or ignoring its existence.
You cannot assume the responsibility of someone else
for his happiness, nor can you automatically shunt the
responsibility for your own happiness onto someone
else. You cannot avoid your responsibility for the way
you live your life with presumably rational reasons
meant to show that you have been forced to do one
thing or another. *It is your life, and what happens in it
is up to you, no one else.* Many people deny that they
are the judge of their own behavior. Refusing to take
responsibility for it, they are apt to offer excuses, justifi-
cations. Examples of such denials of responsibility are
usually some rephrasing of the classical Nuremberg de-
fense: "I was only following orders." One of several assertive alternatives in place of such a denial by the ac-
cused German soldiers could have been: "I chose to do
what I am on trial here today for, instead of choosing
to be reprimanded, reduced in rank, court-martialed,
sent to the Russian front, or being killed myself."

As a final step leading to the examination of our

other, more specific assertive rights—all based on the central one—let us clarify just how our behaving assertively relates to external authority such as moral and legal systems.

Morals are arbitrary rules people adopt to use in judging their own and other people's behavior. The way we adopt and use moral systems is very much like the way we would behave backpacking in the Sierras after our surefooted guide tripped over a log and broke his neck. Each of us is then faced with the difficult task of finding our way home and the frightening possibility that we may not know enough to survive. As each of us finds a trail, we tell ourselves and the others: "This is the right way." Our fear of being lost in the wilds and not knowing what to do is relieved by finding any sign of civilization, even though it may lead us farther into the forest. We refuse to worry about coping again by considering the possibility that there may be other trails out of the forest, some better than the one we choose. By rigidly declaring our trail as the right way, we dump the responsibility for getting home off our own shoulders and onto the arbitrary path we choose. If this trail doesn't get us home, we can always blame the dumb people who made it instead of ourselves! This allegory is used to point out that there is no absolute "right or wrong" moral way to behave; there isn't even any technically correct way to behave. There are only the personal ways each of us chooses to behave, which enrich or befoul our lives. For example, the assertive backpacker in the Sierras might choose to follow none of the paths found by the rest of his group, but instead to follow his own nose, using any information available; the path of the sun and stars, the position of light-sensitive plant growth, landmarks he remembers, and also his best guess on where highway 99 is from looking at his Standard Oil map.

Legal systems are arbitrary rules society has adopted to provide negative consequences for behavior that society wishes to suppress. Just as with moral systems, laws have nothing to do with absolute "right and wrong." Systems of right and wrong are used to psychologically manipulate people's feelings and behavior. Legal codes are set up to limit behavior and to settle disputes between people. But you always have the assertive judgment to break a law and face the consequences. How many of us can say that we have never chosen to break driving and parking ordinances and pay the fine if we were caught? We take the responsibility for the choice and for its consequences. Many of us, however, confuse systems of right and wrong with legal codes. Most legislators, judges, and law officers get as confused about right and wrong as the rest of us. Legal and judicial problems in controlling right and wrong courses of behavior demonstrate this confusion. The coupling of legal codes with systems of right and wrong turns laws into instruments of manipulative emotional control. A right-and-wrong system can be incorporated within the body of law as in the case of the United States Supreme Court's mind-bending phraseology, "socially redeeming" pornography. Does the Supreme Court mean that you can read pornography that has socially redeeming value and not feel guilty because of your prurient interest? If a book's characters who participate in a literary sex orgy do not later suffer the fires of hell or, even worse, repent and become social workers, does that mean you "should" feel guilty reading it?

The concepts of right and wrong may also be wrapped around a law and used in an attempt to punish "wrong" behavior in the streets by police officers. "Legal" manipulation of this sort was attempted on me recently by a traffic officer of a Los Angeles area police department. After being stopped and ticketed for going 63 mph in a 65 mph zone on the freeway by this middle-aged, mustachioed, pot-bellied centurion in baggy khakis, I was then supposed to feel guilty too: "If you want to be a *putz* (Yiddish for male genitals) in the slow lane, that's okay. But if you are a *putz* in the fast lane, that's wrong so don't do it again!" Not only did he want me to pay a fine for going too slow, but he also expected me to feel like a "*putz*" (guilty) because of his judgment of me. He seemed a bit disappointed over my lack of emotion, but was able to recover his poise once he mounted his Yamaha and drove off.

When systems of right and wrong are used, psychological guilt results. When laws are used to induce psychological guilt, these laws, or their enforcers, violate your human assertive right to be the ultimate judge of your own emotions. Such *emotionally used* laws are radically different in their effect from other laws. If you decide to assert yourself in the face of an ordinarily enforced law, you can break the law and face the legally prescribed consequences, i.e., a civil judgment against you, a fine, or a jail sentence. That is your own decision. It may or may not be wise in someone's view, but it is your decision, just as the consequences, positive or negative, are yours. If you decide to break an "emotional law," you not only face legal consequences but are also expected, irrespective of your own judgment, to feel psychological guilt for breaking such a law. A very clear though extreme example of an emotional law can be seen in the case of conscientious objectors to the draft. Men with sincere beliefs that war is a tragic waste of man's efforts and who will have nothing to do with war have been routinely sentenced by courts to several years of menial work like cleaning out bedpans in hospitals in lieu of a jail sentence. While cleaning out things like bedpans may not sound attractive, that part of the court sentence is trivial. What is important is that the freedom of the conscientious objector to go home at night depends greatly upon the system of rights and wrongs held by the hospital staff, or even upon their whims. If the staff does not like the C.O., they fire him and he may go to jail. In plain language, when a judge sets up this sort of arrangement, he is really telling the C.O., "You are sentenced to several years of licking someone else's boots to stay out of jail. You will not be your own judge, but I am making them the judge of all you do." The C.O.'s choice is clear: go to jail or renounce your right to be your own judge of yourself. Such an arrangement, if not successful in making the C.O. feel guilty by seeing his "error," at least punishes him for using his own judgment in not "defending" his country. He is made to agree to give up his assertive right to judge himself in other areas for several years.

These examples of legal manipulative emotional control point out the ultimate misuse of the consent of the governed. No government can be democratic if it attempts to regulate or manipulate the emotional state of its people. In my reading of the American Constitution and the Declaration of Independence of the American Colonies from Great Britain, for example, I can find no section that would empower the American government to engage in the punishment of legal offenses by controlling the emotions of the offender. I do read, however, that we are entitled to certain inalienable rights, among them, the right to life, liberty, and the pursuit of happiness. If you do not exercise your assertive right to be the ultimate judge of yourself, then the right to life, liberty, and the pursuit of happiness are just words printed on paper.

Now, let us look at your other assertive rights, all derived from your basic right to be your own ultimate judge. We'll also take a look at the most common ways other people manipulatively violate these rights.

3

Our everyday assertive rights— the common ways other people manipulate us

Being your own judge has a great number of implications for your behavior and thoughts about yourself and other people. But how do you translate this one overall statement about yourself into common language that relates meaningfully to your everyday living. How can you tell when you are being manipulated, when your assertive human right is being violated? One way we all know, unfortunately, is after the fact; when you say to yourself: "I don't know how it happened, but I've got that uncomfortable, queasy feeling that I've been had." This after-the-fact feeling, again unfortunately, is not much help to you for future coping except that we tend to avoid people who are consistently associated with our "being had." To help you recognize *that* you are being manipulated *when* you are being manipulated, this chapter lists the most common ways other people will use to manipulate you and your everyday assertive rights in those situations.

ASSERTIVE RIGHT II
You have the right to offer no reasons or excuses to justify your behavior.

As with the remaining assertive rights listed in this chapter, the right not to give reasons for what you do is derived from your prime assertive right to be the ultimate judge of all you are and do. If you are your own ultimate judge, you do not need to explain your behavior to someone else for them to decide if it is right, wrong, correct, incorrect, or whatever tag they want to use. Of course, other people always have the assertive option to tell you they do not like what you are doing. You then have the option to disregard their preferences, or work out a compromise, or respect their preferences and change your behavior completely. But if you are your own ultimate judge, other people do not have the right to manipulate your behavior and feelings by demanding reasons from you in order to convince you that you are wrong. The childish belief that underlies this type of manipulation goes something like this: *You should explain your reasons for your behavior to other people since you are responsible to them for your actions. You should justify your actions to them.* An everyday use of this manipulative belief is seen, for example, when a salesclerk asks a customer who is returning a pair of shoes: "Why don't you like these shoes?" (Unspoken: it seems unusual for someone not to like these shoes.) With this question the salesclerk is making a judgment for the customer that she should have a reason for not liking the shoes that is satisfactory to him. If the customer lets the salesclerk decide that there must be some reason for not liking the shoes, she will feel ignorant. Feeling ignorant, the customer will likely feel compelled to explain why she doesn't like the shoes. If she does give reasons, she allows the salesclerk to give her equally valid reasons why she should like them. Depending upon who can think up the most reasons, she or the salesclerk, she will probably finish by keeping a pair of shoes she doesn't like, as the following manipulative dialogue points out:

SALESCLERK: Why don't you like these shoes?

CUSTOMER: They're the wrong shade of magenta.

SALESCLERK: Nonsense, dear! This is just the color you need to match your toenail polish!

CUSTOMER: But they are too loose and the heel straps keep falling down.

SALESCLERK: We can fix that by putting in arch pads. They are only $3.95.

CUSTOMER: But they are too tight in the instep.

SALESCLERK: Simple to fix! I'll take them in the back right now and stretch them a little.

If the customer makes her own decision on whether or not she requires an answer to the "why" question, she is more likely to respond simply by stating the facts of the situation: "No reason, I just don't like the shoes."

People whom I teach to be assertive, invariably ask, "How can I refuse to give reasons to a friend when he asks for them? He won't like that." My answer is a series of provocative questions in reply: "How come your friend is requiring you to give reasons to explain your behavior?" "Is that a condition of his friendship, that you allow him to make decisions about the appropriateness of your behavior?" "If you don't give him a reason for not lending him your car, is that all that is required to end your friendship?" "How valuable is such a fragile friendship?" If some of your friends refuse to acknowledge your assertive right to halt manipulation by being your own judge, perhaps these friends are incapable of dealing with you on any other basis but manipulation. Your choice in friends, like anything else, is entirely up to you.

ASSERTIVE RIGHT III
You have the right to judge whether you are responsible for finding solutions to other people's problems.

Each of us is ultimately responsible for our own psychological well-being, happiness, and success in life. As much as we might wish good things for one another, we really do not have the ability to create mental stability, well-being, or happiness for someone else.

You have the ability to please someone temporarily by doing what he or she wants, but that person has to go through all the work, sweat, pain, and fear of failure to arrange his own life in a way that makes him healthy and happy. In spite of your compassion for the troubles of others, the reality of the human condition is that each of us must come to terms with the problems of living by learning to cope on our own. This reality is expressed in one of the first principles of modern psychotherapy. Practitioners of this healing art have learned that the process of therapy does not solve problems for the patient, but helps the patient gain the ability to solve his own problems. Any of us can help temporarily by giving advice or counsel, but the person with the problem has the responsibility to solve it himself. Your own actions may even have been directly or indirectly the cause of their problems. Nevertheless, other people have the ultimate responsibility to solve their own problems, no matter who or what the cause may be. If you do not recognize your assertive right to choose to be responsible only for yourself, other people can and will manipulate you into doing what they want by presenting their own problems to you as if they were your problems. The childish belief underlying this type of manipulation goes something like this: *You have an obligation to things and institutions greater than yourself which groups of other people have set up to conduct the business of living. You should sacrifice your own values to keep these systems from falling apart. If these systems do not always work effectively, you should bend or·change, not the system. If any problems occur in dealing with the system, they are your problems and not the responsibility of the system.* Examples of manipulative behavior produced by this childish belief abound in our common dealings with people. You may see wives or husbands manipulate each other by saying: "If you don't stop irritating me, we are going to have to get a divorce." Statements like this induce guilty feelings by implying that the marriage contract and relationship are more important than the individual desires and happiness of either partner. If their mates also have this childish belief, they have the option (1) to do what they want individually and feel guilty for placing their own wants above the marriage relationship, or (2) to do what their spouses want and be frustrated, angry, aggressively cause more friction, or get depressed and withdraw. If the marriage partner threatened with divorce nonassertively responds with a defensive posture that divorce is not a possible alternative solution to their problems, he or she may be manipulated into doing what the spouse wants, as pointed out in the following dialogue:

MATE ONE: If you don't stop irritating me with all your excuses for not doing anything around here, we might as well get a divorce!

MATE TWO: (in frustrated anger) Don't be silly. You don't really want a divorce!

MATE ONE: I do! Don't you care about our marriage and what I'll have to go through being single again?

MATE TWO: (feeling guilty) Of course I care! What kind of person do you think I am? I do a lot of things for us!

MATE ONE: You only do things that *you* care about. Why are you so stubborn? If you really cared about our marriage, you would try to make things a bit easier for me! I do all these things and what do you do?

If, on the other hand, the spouse threatened with the prospect of divorce assertively makes his or her own judgment on where the problem and responsibility for solving it lies (on the spouse threatened with divorce or on the marriage relationship), he or she is likely to reply: "If you truly feel that you can't cope with the way I am, perhaps you're right. If we can't work it out, maybe we should consider a divorce."

In commercial dealings you can see other everyday examples of people manipulatively trying to get you to place the well-being of ineffective systems of doing things above your own well-being. Salesclerks may often try to get a determined customer (you) to stop complaining about defective merchandise by saying: "You are holding up the line. All these other people want to be served too." In making this statement, the clerk is manipulatively inducing guilt in you by implying that you have some responsibility to see that the store is able to serve other people without making them wait. The judgment made by the salesclerk *for you* is that if the store's system of processing complaints does not work well in processing your complaint, the responsibility for solving the problem lies with you and not with the store. But if you were to make your own decision on where the responsibility lies, you would simply state the facts of the situation; for example: "That's true, I am holding up the line. I suggest you satisfy my complaint quickly or they will have to wait even longer."

When you try to get adequate repairs on defective merchandise, or a refund, you will often observe salesclerks and managers saying things like: "Your problem is not with us. You have a problem with the manufacturer (or the body shop, or the factory, or the main office, or the importer, or the shipping line, or the insurance company, etc.). The manufacturer won't give us a refund for defective merchandise, so we can't give you one." This type of statement is a manipulative evasion of responsibility. If you allow the clerk or manager to make the decision for you that you must provide a solution to the store's problem of staying in business and not losing money on defective merchandise, you are forced into the ludicrous position of: (1) ceasing to press your claim of value for money paid; (2) accepting the childish notion that you should not cause problems for the employees or the company; and (3) having the frustration of not knowing how to get what you want without causing problems for others. If, on the other hand, you make your own decision on whether or not you need to be responsible for finding a solution to the store's problems with the manufacturer you can assertively reply: "I am not interested in your problems with the manufacturer (or the radiator shop, etc.). I am only interested in getting acceptable repairs (or a refund for defective merchandise)."

My favorite summary of the concept of defining your own responsibility for the problems of others was given in a joke, current several years ago. After being surrounded by 10,000 hostile Indians, the Lone Ranger turned to Tonto and remarked, "I guess this is it, Kimo Sabe. It looks like we have had it," whereupon Tonto, surveying the impending disaster, turned and replied, "What do you mean *we, white man?*"

ASSERTIVE RIGHT IV
You have the right
to change your
mind.

As human beings, none of us is constant and rigid. We change our minds; we decide on better ways to do things; we even change the things we want to do; our interests change with conditions and the passage of time. Each of us has to recognize that our choices may work for us in one situation and against us in another. To be in touch with reality, to promote our own well-being and happiness, we have to accept the possibility that changing our minds is healthy and normal. But if you do change your mind, other people may resist your new choice by manipulation based on any of the childish beliefs we have seen, the most common of which goes something like this: *You should not change your mind after you have committed yourself. If you change your mind, something is wrong. You should justify your new choice or admit that you were in error. If you are in error, you have shown that you are irresponsible, likely to be wrong again, cause problems. Therefore you are not capable of making decisions by yourself.*

When returning merchandise you will frequently see examples of behavior produced by this manipulative belief. Recently I returned nine gallons of house paint to one of the largest retail department stores in the country. In filling out the credit slip, the clerk came to the space marked "Reason for returning merchandise" and asked why the paint was being returned. I replied, "When I bought it, I was told that I could return any cans of unopened paint. I tried a gallon of it, didn't like it, and changed my mind about using it." In spite of the official policy of the store, the clerk could not bring himself to write "changed mind" or "didn't like it" in the blank space and persisted in asking for a reason why the paint was being returned, such as a defect, poor color, wrong consistency, etc. In effect, the clerk was asking me to invent a reason to satisfy him or possibly his superiors, to be dishonest, to find something I could blame as an excuse for the irresponsible behavior of changing my mind. I was tempted at that point to say it upset my dog Wimpy's sex life and let him figure that one out! Instead I persevered and told the clerk that there was nothing wrong with the paint. I simply changed my mind and decided not to use this particular paint on my home. Since the management had said that I could return any unopened cans, I was returning them and wanted my account credited. Apparently unable to conceive how any person, particularly a man, could simply change his mind and still feel comfortable with himself, the clerk had to confer with his supervisor before he would issue a refund. I could have let the clerk make a judgment for me that changing my mind was wrong. In that case if I could not find something to blame as a justification for my new decision, I would either have to be dishonest or keep the paint. As it turned out, I made my own judgment on the appropriateness of changing my mind, told the clerk that I just wanted a refund, and got it.

ASSERTIVE RIGHT V
You have the right to make mistakes—and be responsible for them.

"Let he who is without sin cast the first stone." I cite this particular piece of wisdom attributed to Jesus not so much for the compassion and tolerance he urges us to have for other people's fallibility, but for the more practical observation he forces upon us; none of us is perfect. To err is part of the human condition. Our assertive right to make errors *and be responsible for them* simply describes part of the reality of being human. However, we are susceptible to manipulation by other people for their own ends if we do not recognize that errors are simply that; just errors. We allow manipulation of our behavior and emotions if we believe that errors are somehow "wrong" and "should" not be made. Many of us feel that since errors are "wrongdoing," they must be atoned for and somehow a "right" behavior must be engaged in to make up for the error. This demand for atonement of errors which other people tack onto the tail end of our mistakes is the basis on which they manipulate our future behavior through our past mistakes. The childish belief underlying this manipulation is approximately as follows: *You must not make errors. Errors are wrong and cause problems to other people. If you make errors, you should feel guilty. You are likely to make more errors and problems and therefore you cannot cope properly or make proper decisions. Other people should control your behavior and decisions so you will not cause problems; in this way you can make up for the wrong you have done to them.* Again, as with our other childish beliefs, you can see this one expressed in our everyday behavior. As a result of this belief, husbands and wives, for instance, commonly try to control behavior in each other that is totally unrelated to their errors. This is done by implying that the mistakes of the spouse are "wrong" and therefore must somehow be atoned for (usually by doing something else the "offended" party wants done). For example, while balancing the family checkbook, a nonassertive husband may tell his wife with some emotion that she again forgot to write down the information on a check she wrote last month. Instead of coming right out assertively and saying, "I don't like it and want you to be more careful," the husband implies with his emotional tone that his wife did something "wrong" and she owes him something because of it—perhaps at that moment only some visceral squirming as a token of guilty feelings to be made up for later on!

If the wife is nonassertive enough to let her husband make judgments about her behavior for her, she is likely to (1) deny the error; (2) give reasons why she could not make the entry; (3) pooh-pooh the importance of the error, forcing her husband either to suppress his feelings about her error, thereby resenting her, or to escalate the conflict into a fight to express his nonassertive angry feelings; or (4) apologize for making an error that inconvenienced him and feel resentfully obligated to make it up to him. If, on the other hand, his wife is assertive enough to make her own judgment about her errors, she would likely reply to his raising of the issue by saying: "You're right. That was a dumb thing for me to do again and cause you all that extra work." It's a brief comment, raises no future problems, and says a lot: I did make a mistake, the mistake made trouble for you, I'm not afraid to admit it. Like everyone else, I make mistakes too.

In trying to help modify the automatic feeling of guilt, anxiety, or ignorance that we experience in making an error, I instruct students learning to be assertive never to say they are sorry (at least in class; *later,* out in the world, they can decide whether and when to add "manners" to their behavior *once they have learned to be assertive*). Instead, I prompt them to simply state the facts of the situation. For example: "You're right, I am late," without apologizing for that behavior. My only problem with this teaching method is that most of my students, including those over sixty, report the facts of their errors to me in class *gleefully* with broad grins on their faces. This teaching method does help however, since, outside the class, most of them do take their errors unemotionally as well as assertively, without much gut squirming.

ASSERTIVE RIGHT VI
You have the right
to say, "I don't
know."

Another of your assertive rights is the ability to make judgments about what you want without needing to know everything before you do something. You have the right to say, "I don't know" without having an immediate answer for questions people may ask you. Indeed, if you asked yourself what every possible outcome of your actions would be, before they occur, you are unlikely to accomplish much of anything, a condition probably much desired by the person manipulating you. If someone else behaves toward you as if you "should" know specific results of what would happen when you do what you want, he is assuming you have the following childish belief: *You should have answers to any question about the possible consequences of your actions, because if you don't have answers, you are unaware of the problems you will cause other people and therefore you are irresponsible and must be controlled.* You can see common instances of manipulation based upon this belief in any of your different relationships with other people. Students learning to be assertive relate numerous incidents where other people accuse them of being irresponsible because of the consequences of being generally assertive. One manipulative husband tried to make his assertive wife return to her former submissive, readily controlled state by asking her: "What do you think would happen to this country if everybody decided to be his own judge?" In asking this question, her husband was trying to make his assertive wife feel ignorant and therefore incapable of making decisions for herself. His wife made her own decision on the importance of having an answer to this question and replied: "I don't know. What would happen?"

In another case, a couple in their late fifties came to me for a mental health consultation on an involuntary hospitalization. As their story developed, it was apparent that the husband wanted his wife committed to a mental hospital because she was refusing to live with him anymore and wanted her own little apartment where she could take care of her own needs and not have to put up with his constant harassment. In so many marital counseling cases, one of the spouses is dragged into therapy by the other in order to have the doctor tell the identified patient that he or she is guilty of misbehaving, doing the wrong thing, etc. When it became apparent to the husband that I was not going to help him in the control of his wife's behavior and goals, or involuntarily hospitalize her because she wanted to be independent of him, he then tried to manipulate me. With contempt in his voice, he said; "Doctor! What would happen if every wife decided to have her own place and see who she wanted and run around with other men?" Resisting a sudden unprofessional urge to tell him my best guess on what might happen to his wife if she were to leave him, what chance she would have to become a real person again, I responded only to his question: "I really don't know. What would happen?" Ignoring my lack of upset in answering him, he countered with, "Doctor, would you think it was right if your wife told you what she is telling me?" With complete candor, I replied: "Frankly, I would be less concerned about the right or wrong of what she's wanting and more concerned about why she isn't getting what she wants from me." Perhaps unwilling to explore this approach to their difficulties as an alternative to locking up his wife, he took her in hand and left. Psychotherapy cannot be jammed down someone's throat. It's been tried many times and it won't work if forced. This poor fellow was interested only in controlling his wife's behavior and not improving their way of relating to each other. A sad circumstance, but unfortunately for many people, so often true.

Manipulation based upon the childish belief that you are required to know the answer to any question asked of you may be blatant, as in the previous examples, or very subtle. In whatever form, it usually can be recognized by phrases like "What would happen if ...?"; "What do you think . . .?; "How would you feel if ...?"; "What kind of friend, person, wife, son, daughter, parent, etc., would do ...?" In dealing with such manipulation, you don't have to know what would happen if ... No one can know all and, perhaps at times, *any* consequences of his own behavior. If the manipulator needs to speculate, let him!

ASSERTIVE RIGHT VII
You have the right to be independent of the goodwill of others before coping with them.

"No man is an island unto himself," said John Donne, and this makes a lot of sense. Taking it one step further and saying that all men are my brothers and friends, however, exceeds the most gross literary license as well as common sense. No matter what you or I do, someone is not going to like it, someone may even get his feelings hurt as a result. If you assume that in order to adequately cope with anyone you first need his goodwill as a brother or a friend, you leave yourself open to as much manipulative leverage as your need for goodwill dictates. Contrary to this common assumption, *you do not need the goodwill of other people to deal with them effectively and assertively.* Paraphrasing John Donne, we humans don't make very good isolated islands when we cut ourselves off from everybody, but we make damned fine peninsulas by being realistically sensitive only to the needs of those relatively few people in our lives to whom we are very close. People we deal with commercially or authoritatively may remove their goodwill toward us permanently, but we still have the ability to do business with them without their liking us. My students frequently object to this point of view, saying that they don't like to make a waiter or a salesclerk uncomfortable by being assertive when something goes wrong. I usually respond to their objections with statements like: "Gee, I don't understand. It sounds like the waiter invited you over for a free meal from the way you are talking and he is offering you a poor gift but it's all he has," or "It sounds like the salesclerk was donating all his salary to charity when he sold you the ten-speed bike that only operated in four gears. Is that correct?" and "Correct me if I'm in error, but it seems that in these situations either you or the waiter is going to feel uncomfortable. Which one would you rather it be—you or him?"

In our equality relationships, a lack of goodwill from someone else also in no way affects our realistic coping ability to resolve a conflict. Spouses, for instance, may routinely remove their goodwill when there is a conflict. This temporary lack of goodwill does not mean the marriage is on the rocks, or the weekend is spoiled, or that very evening cannot still be enjoyable. In discussing the removal of goodwill with my editor, Ms. Joyce Engelson, she neatly summed up my years of clinical experience with this problem: "People get so damned frightened if someone threatens not to like them or doesn't like them. They get paralyzed and don't function to their own benefit on jobs, with friends, spouses, lovers, dates, etc. Sometimes one feels like telling people: *You'll never be loved if you can't risk being disliked!*"

My clinical and personal observations have demonstrated to me that people only remove their goodwill toward you (assuming some existed to start with) if there is a payoff to them for doing so. If you respond as if your mate's withdrawal of goodwill affects your behavior, its withdrawal is a potent manipulative device for the other person and he or she will use it again. If you do not respond to the withdrawal of goodwill as a manipulative device, there is no payoff for it, except for venting anger (a transient state), and its frequency of use will diminish. Because of its possible potency, if the people you deal with are as nonassertive as most of us, they will probably try to manipulate you into doing things their way by consistently threatening to remove their goodwill toward you; they threaten directly or subtly to dislike you, or even reject you. Our childish belief, which people use as the basis for this type of manipulation, expresses itself like this: *You must have the goodwill of people you relate to or they can prevent you from doing anything. You need the cooperation of other people to survive. It is very important that people like you.* Examples of manipulation based on this belief are everyday occurrences, particularly in close relationships, but also in the authority relationships of work and school. For example, you may notice that you become anxious and susceptible to manipulation by other people when you automatically believe what other people hint at when they say: "I'll remember that," "You'll be sorry you did that," or "It'll be a cold day in hell before I . . .," or even more subtle cues like "hurt" or "cold" looks. Statements like these are similar in meaning and intent to those used when we were conditioned to become automatically anxious as children. When we did things that annoyed adults and older children, to control our behavior they told us things like: "If you keep that up (unspoken: if you still annoy me), the boogie man will get you (unspoken: I won't like you anymore and won't protect you from him)." When told, "I'll remember that (I won't like you anymore and maybe I'll get back at you someday)," the anxious adult makes a judgment that conditions are still the same as when he was a helpless child and required the goodwill and friendship of everyone else to be safe and happy. If, in coping with these intimidating hints of possible future reprisals, you make your own judgment on whether or not you need the goodwill of everyone else to be happy, you are more likely—sensibly and assertively—to reply: "I don't understand, why will you remember that?" or "I don't understand, it sounds like you won't like me anymore." Your behavior does not have to be liked or admired by those you deal with, *nor do you have to be anxious because you may not be liked;* all that counts is getting across the finish line. You get no points for form and style. You still get the prize no matter if you fall, slip, trip, or dash proudly through the wire!

Many of us seem to have great difficulty in simply saying "No" to requests made of us or even invitations to us. Somehow we assume—whether we are aware of it or not—that either the other person is too weak to cope with our refusal and will be offended, or a relationship is impossible to maintain without 100 per cent mutual agreement. Daily examples of the results of this nonassertive belief can be seen when other people invite you out to join them in some social activity. How comfortable do you feel in assertively revealing your true state by saying simply and openly: "No, I just don't feel like it this weekend. Let's try it another time?" Instead you invent "good" reasons that will not allow the other person to get irritated, feel rebuffed, and possibly dislike you. Most of us follow this inane behavior pattern because of our childish belief that we cannot function properly if we do things that cause other people to remove their goodwill toward us, even a little bit. Although generalizations are suspect and typically useless, our behavior in this area is sufficiently childish to prompt me to make this observation: one cannot live in terror of hurting other people's feelings. Sometimes one offends. That's life in the big city!

ASSERTIVE RIGHT VIII
You have the right to be illogical in making decisions.

Logic is a reasoning process all of us can use sometimes to help in making our judgments about many things, including ourselves. Not all logical statements are true, however, nor can our logical reasoning always predict what will happen in every situation. In particular, logic is not much help in dealing with our own and other people's wants, motivations, and feelings. Logic and reasoning generally deal with yesses or noes, black or white, and all or nothing as an input to the logical process. But in fact, our wants, motivations, and emotions are usually not apparent to us in terms of all or nothing. Often we have mixed emotions about things and people. Our emotions are felt in different degrees at different times and places. We may even want different things at the same time. Logic and reasoning don't work easily in dealing with such "illogical" gray areas of our human condition. Logical reasoning may not help us much in understanding why we want what we want or in solving problems created by conflicting motivations.

On the other hand, logic is a great help to other people in dealing with your behavior if they want to talk you into changing it. If I were asked to explain to a small child what the word "logic" means, I would not be too far off the mark in telling him: "Logic is what other people use to prove that you're wrong," and he would understand what I meant. Logic is one of the external standards that many people use to judge their own as well as your behavior. In spite of the misuse of logic in human relationships, many of us have the trained childish belief that "good" reasons must be given to justify our desires, our goals, and our actions, that the keen intellectual razor of reasoning and logic will slice through personal confusion and expose the proper course to follow. Many people will use logic to manipulate us into doing what they want us to do. The basis for this manipulation is our childish belief which says: *You must follow logic because it makes better judgments than any of us can make.* Examples of logic-bred manipulation are seen in our everyday relationships. In college, for example, some faculty advisors use logic to manipulate student choice of classes. Advisors manipulate with logic to keep the student "on schedule" and to keep the student from taking "unnecessary" classes in another department which may interest that student. This is done by reminding the student that he wants to graduate, wants to go to graduate school, or wants a good job when he graduates. The advisor then points out logically that unnecessary classes in Egyptological pornoglyphic sarcophagi (graffiti on mummy cases), for example, will not help the student graduate on time, go to graduate school, or get him a good job. It is never pointed out to the student, however, that graduating as fast as possible with a maximum of courses from the advisor's department benefits the advisor's department in terms of funding and teaching positions. If the student lets the advisor "logically" make his judgments for him he is likely to queue up like another sheep for departmental processing. If he *assertively* makes his own decision on what is more important to him—taking extra classes that interest him or possibly graduating a semester or quarter earlier —he is more likely to respond to his advisor's logical manipulation by saying: "That's true, I may spend more time in school this way, but I still want to take some of the classes that interest me."

You can observe many other examples of manipulation by logic in your everyday experience. Spouses commonly point out to each other that they shouldn't do one thing or another because, "We will get tired," or "We have to get up early the next day," or "Cousin Mildred is due in tomorrow night," or a hundred other possible negative consequences which may result from doing what we want to do. This manipulation is done in a helpful, altruistic, logical way without the manipulator coming right out and saying what he or she wants to do in place of what was proposed. This logical manipulation cuts off the potential negotiation of conflicting wants between husband and wife as well as making the manipulated spouse feel ignorant or guilty for even suggesting such illogical behavior.

One of the first things I learned in graduate school was that in order to survive, it was necessary to keep the electronic equipment in the laboratories working for the professors. The second thing I learned, consequently, was that after you wasted your time by going through all the logical steps in the maintenance manual to figure out what was wrong with a piece of apparatus, you still had to turn the damned thing upside down and randomly jiggle its wiring to make it work! Being logical does not necessarily mean that you will solve your problem. Being logical does mean you will limit what you will work with only to those things you completely understand, while, in fact, the solution to your problem many times will be outside these limits. Sometimes you just have to guess, no matter how crude, even inelegant that intellectual process is.

ASSERTIVE RIGHT IX
You have the right
to say, "I don't
understand."

Socrates observed that true wisdom comes to each of us when we realize how little we understand about life, ourselves, and the world around us. His observation aptly describes one aspect of being human. Not one of us is so quick-witted, so perceptive as to fully understand even most of what goes on around us. Yet we seem to survive in spite of these limits placed on our capabilities by the human condition. We learn what we do by experience, and experience with other people teaches most of us that we do not always understand what another person means or wants. Few of us read minds at all, none of us can read minds very well, and yet many people try to manipulate us into doing what they want us to do by hinting, implying, suggesting, or subtly acting as if they expected us to do something for them. The childish belief we've been trained to hold and which makes this type of manipulation possible goes like this: *You must anticipate and be sensitive to the needs of other people if we are all to live together without discord. You are expected to understand what these needs are without causing problems by making other people spell out their needs to you. If you do not understand without being constantly told what other people want, you are not capable of living in harmony with others and are irresponsible or ignorant.* Examples of manipulation prompted by this infantile belief can be observed frequently in your relationships with people you see every day. Members of your family, fellow employees, roommates, etc., who have such a belief may try to manipulate you into changing your behavior toward them with "hurt" or "angry" looks and silences. These manipulative attempts usually follow a conflict between yourself and the "injured" party where you have done something that the other person does not like. Instead of verbally asserting themselves in an attempt to gain at least part of what they want through a compromise, they make the judgment for you that (1) you are in the "wrong," (2) you "should" intuitively understand that they are displeased with your behavior, (3) you "should" automatically understand what behavior displeases them, and (4) you "should" change that behavior for them so they will no longer be "hurt" or "angry." If you allow the other person to make your own judgment for you that you "should" automatically understand what is bothering him, you are likely to change your behavior for their convenience and also do other things to relieve their "hurt" or "angry" feelings toward you. If you allow this kind of manipulation, you end up not only blocked from doing what *you* wanted to do, but doing something else to make up for wanting to do it in the first place.

You can also see the manipulation prompted by the childish belief that *you have to understand* on the part of people in commercial settings. For example, when you go to some private physician's offices for medical treatment, the time it takes to fill out the forms he wants before he will see you, concerning income, job security, insurance coverage, etc., can take longer than the medical consultation. Sometimes I get the impression that the physician thinks a loan is being asked for instead of medical treatment. I'm sure my impression is faulty, but more than once, I have felt that the behavior shown by medical staffs implies that the treatment is for free and I owe them something else besides money.

When I recently went for osteopathic treatment, the straw that broke the camel's back for me (no pun intended!) was the request for my social security number. At that, I drew the line and stopped filling in the card. It's a good thing that it was the last question or he wouldn't have known whom he was treating. In looking over the nonmedical information form, the nurse told me that a social security number was required before I could see the osteopath. When I said that I didn't understand how my social security number was necessary to treat my elbow, the nurse told me the number was necessary. The patronizing look on her face also said I "should" know why social security numbers are required. Still unable to read minds after all my fine psychological training, I again replied that I didn't understand how the number was connected to my elbow. Changing character, the nurse then explained that many cases were referred by workman's compensation and other disability agencies. The office staff routinely asked for the social security number of all patients to make things easier when communicating with these agencies. This (by then very assertive) prospective patient made his own decision on the necessity of giving his social security number to people he was paying money to for services rendered. I received excellent treatment from a hell of a nice guy even with the last space on my biographical card empty. A petty victory over one of my petty peeves—IBM binary minds. Even so, I don't understand why it was worth the bother at the time for me not to give my social security number upon demand. If you are like me and can't even read your own mind fully, how can you expect to perform this service for other people?

ASSERTIVE RIGHT X
You have the right to
say, "I don't
care."

You can see a lot of overlap in all of the assertive rights described since they are only detailed derivatives of your primary right: to be your own ultimate judge. There is also much overlap in the most common beliefs that underlie manipulation of your behavior by other people, since they are only different ways of saying one thing: you are *not* your own ultimate judge. One common thread that runs through all the nonassertive beliefs and devices that other people use to manipulate your behavior is the assumption that as a human being, even if you are not perfect, you "should" strive for perfection, and if, heaven forbid, you cannot improve yourself, you "should" at least *want to* improve your human, ungodlike ways of doing things. If you go along with this way of looking at yourself, you are open and ready for the thousands of ways in which your behavior can be manipulated, limited only by other people's ingenuity. If you were to verbalize this belief, it would sound something like this: *Because of your human condition, you are base and have many flaws. You must try to make up for this humanness by striving to improve until you are perfect in all things. Being human, you will probably fail in this obligation, but you still must want to improve. If someone else points out how you can improve yourself, you are really obliged to follow his direction. If you do not, you are corrupt, lazy, degenerate, and worthless, and therefore unworthy of respect from anyone, including yourself.* This belief, in my opinion, is the ultimate "sucker's play." If you set yourself up to be perfect in anything (even in being assertive!), you will be disappointed and frustrated. You have the assertive right, however, to say that you don't care to be perfect according to anyone's definition including your own, since one man's perfection is likely to be another's perversion.

You can see manipulation in many of your relationships, based upon this belief that you "should" want to improve yourself. If your marriage is like many others, your spouse may try to control your sloppy behavior by saying, for instance, "You are always leaving your clothes draped around the house! Don't you ever want to improve (or do things better, or learn what's important, or become civilized, or be a decent human being, or stop being a slob, etc., etc., etc.)?" If you fall into the manipulative trap that you "should" want to improve your behavior (according to someone else's arbitrary choice of what constitutes improvement), you are then forced into giving reasons why you left your clothes draped around so casually—you were late last night, or you were too tired, or you just forgot, or you really don't do it very often, or any number of other childish responses. If, on the other hand, you assertively make your own judgment on your own wish to improve or not, you are likely to respond more realistically to the situation, such as, "I realize that I should want to keep things neat, but sometimes I just don't care. I know it upsets you, but let's see if we can work out some compromise. If you don't try to cut me up when I do something that you don't like, I'll try not to cut you up when you upset me! Just tell me when I do something that's bothersome and I'll do the same for you." No beating around the bush! Just straightforward communication!

At work, you can often observe people telling each other how they can improve their performance, how it would be easier or more efficient or more esthetic to change things. A case in point is that of Sid, a nonassertive store manager who had learned from experience how best to set up his merchandise displays. At the time of therapy, he was quite depressed because certain new members of his staff kept manipulating him into letting them set up displays, instead of waiting on customers as he wanted them to do, by continually pointing out how his way of doing things could be improved. Sid did not know how to cope with this manipulation except by finally letting his repressed anger erupt at his salesmen, with negative consequences for the operation of his store. After several weeks of systematic assertive therapy, Sid was able to cope calmly with this type of manipulative interference without disrupting things. He also felt, at least initially, quite smug in his discovery that not only did he not have to be perfect, he didn't even have to want to improve!

The manipulation produced by believing that you "should" want to improve yourself is, in many situations, the kind of manipulation that can be the subtlest and hardest to cope with. The only sure way you can halt this manipulation is to ask yourself if you are really satisfied with your own performance or yourself and *then make your own judgment on whether or not you wish to make a change.*

Many learners, after beginning the process of becoming more assertive, state that they often become confused in distinguishing between manipulation of their behavior and what they want to do themselves. They often say things like: "I want to do this or that, but I think, 'I can't do that!' No one else is manipulating me. Am I manipulating myself?" Using a quick rule of thumb to help them clarify what they are doing, I often ask them to phrase their internal conflict in any of three categories: "I want," "I have to," or "I should." The *I want* category is straightforward, i.e., I want to have steak for dinner three times a week, I want to go to the movies instead of watching TV, or I want to spend the rest of my life living on the beach in Tahiti. From these wants, certain *I have to*s or contingencies follow. The *I have to*s are compromises that you work out within yourself and with other people. If *I want* steak three times a week, I have to get the money to afford steak three times a week. If I have to get this money (and I also want to stay out of jail), I have to work at a job that pays enough money so I can afford steak three times a week (or some other compromise that works!). If *I want* to go to the movies tonight, *I have* to forgo watching my favorite TV program. If I want to spend the rest of my life lounging on the beach in Tahiti, I will have to get used to "tropical lunch" (whatever you can mooch). All these contingencies on what you do because you want certain things are quite simple. You simply decide if the *I want*s are worth the *I have to*s. Many people, however, confuse the *I have to*s with the *I should*s and muddy the clear waters of their thinking. *Should*s, as a rule of thumb, can be categorized as manipulative structure used to get you to do what someone else wants or arbitrary structure you have imposed upon yourself to deal with your own insecurity concerning what you "can or cannot" do. For instance, *I should* work because everybody *should* be productive, not just because I want meat on the table three nights a week; *I should* get out in the evening because *I shouldn't* watch TV all the time; *I shouldn't* want to go to Tahiti because no one *should* be a beach bum. Whenever you hear yourself or someone else say "should," extend your antimanipulative antennae up as far as possible and listen carefully. In all likelihood, some message that says, "You are not your own judge," will follow.

4

The first thing to learn in being assertive: persistence

After digesting all the material about your assertive human rights, you may find yourself in the position of the learner who said: "I've secretly felt that way about myself and other people all my life. But whenever I expressed it, I was always told that way of thinking was wrong. . . . That I shouldn't feel that way. I'm glad that other people think I have a right to my own thoughts and ways of doing things. I understand everything you say. Great! But . . . I still don't know how to be assertive. What do I do now?" If you ask this same question, the answer is a simple one: "Do nothing. . . . Yet." To be assertive, you need to know your assertive rights and also learn how you can enforce them. One is a philosophy and the other is a set of assertive behaviors. As I pointed out in the introduction to this book, our human alternative to primitive fight-or-flight coping in a conflict situation is our great verbal problem-solving ability that allows us to communicate with others to work things out. A significant part of this ability is our assertive verbal behavior: what we do when we assert ourselves. Just talking about our assertive rights is insufficient to enforce them. That your assertive rights exist, that you accept them as part of yourself, does not mean that other people will either respect or understand them, or change their manipulative behavior, even if you explained your rights to them. For example, if you were in an auto parts store and responded to the clerk's attempted manipulation with: "Stop manipulating me!" he would probably reply: "What manipulation? I never laid a hand on you! Did anybody see me touch her? Did you see me manipulate her, Harry?" Or if you said: "I am my own ultimate judge," in response

72

to his manipulation, he would probably think: "What kind of a nut is this? I'm trying to explain something about our carburator exchange policy and he wants to talk philosophy!" Or if you were to explain your assertive right to your mother when she manipulatively tries to get you to see her more often, she would likely think that not only are you willful and spoiled as an adult, just like you were as a child, but now you have some crazy ideas too. She, like the auto parts clerk, may not be interested in your assertive rights at all, or she may just brush them aside with something like: "That's nice to know, dear, I'm glad I insisted you go to college. When are you coming over to see me again?"

To enforce your assertive rights and to halt manipulation of your behavior, you need to change your own behavior in response to manipulation—the behavior that allows you to be manipulated. The rest of this manuscript deals with learning a set of assertive verbal skills that are effective in enforcing your assertive rights in your relationships with other people.

BROKEN RECORD

In introducing students to the first systematic assertive skill, BROKEN RECORD, I begin by asking them: "Why do you usually lose in a conflict with the auto mechanic about correcting the sloppy repairs he made on your car?" Their answer to this question is typically a profound silence. Having thus established that the class doesn't know any more than I do—why they keep getting frustrated—I offer the following opinion: "You don't know why? I'll tell you why! Because you usually give up after you hear the first 'No.' He tells you 'No' and you say 'Okay' or mumble under your breath something less than flattering about his possible sexual habits and walk away. You lose because you give up too easily. This guy (like many other people) has only a few 'Noes' in his bag. If he's got three 'Noes,' you only need four. If he's got six 'Noes', you only need seven. It's that simple!" At this point, one of the students typically says: "But I can't do that. I can't ignore someone when he tells me 'No.'" My response: "What do you mean, you *can't*? I don't see any hand-cuffs or ball and chain on you that keeps you from doing anything. I'll respect that you *don't want to,* but I won't respect that you *'can't.'* And if you don't want to, my guess is that you are trained like the rest of us: you should be nice and listen to the poor garage mechanic when he says 'No.' Right? After all, he is only trying to make a living like the rest of us. Right? (Here the class usually picks up the litany with a sar-castic chorus of "Right!" including the one bearded left-winger present in all classes who adds an uplifted clenched fist to his "Right on!") He's got six kids he's trying to feed and educate just like you. Right? If he loses money in his business, he won't be able to support them in the manner to which they would like to be-come accustomed. Right? But where does it say that if he screws up the job on your car, you should keep him in business and let him make a profit by subsidizing his sloppy work?"

If you are like this student and many others, you need to learn to be more persistent in asserting your-self. *One of the most important aspects of being ver-bally assertive is to be persistent and to keep saying what you want over and over again without getting an-gry, irritated, or loud.* Most often, to communicate ef-fectively in a conflict situation, you have to be persis-tent and stick to your point. Nonassertive people tend to get bogged down in excess verbiage and give up eas-ily when someone tells them "why," shows them "logi-cally," or gives them "reasons" for not doing what they want to do. In learning how to be persistent, the nonas-sertive person must not give reasons or excuses or ex-planations as to "why" he wants what he wants; he needs to ignore guilt-inducing statements. One verbal skill that teaches people how to accomplish all of this simultaneously is a technique first used in assertive therapy by my close colleague Dr. Zev Wanderer, who gave it its descriptive title: BROKEN RECORD. By practicing to speak as if we were a broken record, we learn to be persistent and stick to the point of the discussion, to keep saying what we want to say, and to ignore all side issues brought up by the person we assert ourselves to. In using BROKEN RECORD, you, the learner, are not deterred by anything the other person may say, but keep saying in a *calm, repetitive voice* what you want to say until the other person acceeds to your request or agrees to a compromise. The purpose of BROKEN RECORD training and rehearsal is not to teach you to speak like a broken record, but to teach and reward persistence, no matter what words you use. To see how you can accomplish this result, let's look at a very simple real life BROKEN RECORD dialogue in a commercial situation.

Dialogue #1
Carlo and the
supermarket
clerk

The following BROKEN RECORD dialogue is one reported by Carlo, a Chicano community relations worker. Carlo received instruction from me as part of a staff development program in effective communication. During the fourth session, Carlo reported that on the previous Saturday he had done the week's marketing for his wife and when he returned home, he could not find his meat purchases. Since his father was at the house for dinner, Carlo asked if he would like to accompany him to the supermarket to get his meat purchases back.

Setting of the dialogue: Upon entering the supermarket with his father in tow, Carlo spoke to the clerk at the checkout counter about his missing purchases.

CLERK: Yes?

CARLO: When I was here earlier, I bought three steaks, a roast, and two chickens with my other groceries and when I got home, the meat was missing. I want my meat.

CLERK: Did you look in your car?

CARLO: Yes, *I want my meat.* [BROKEN RECORD]

CLERK: I don't think I can do anything about it. [Evasion of responsibility]

CARLO: I understand how you might think that, *but I want my meat.* [BROKEN RECORD]

CLERK: Do you have your cash register receipt?

CARLO: (Handing receipt to clerk) *Yes, and I want my meat.* [BROKEN RECORD]

CLERK: (Looking at the receipt) You have six meat purchases here.

CARLO: That's right, and *I want my meat.* [BROKEN RECORD]

CLERK: Well, I don't have anything to do with the meat department. [Evasion of responsibility]

CARLO: I understand how you feel, but you're the one I paid my money to and *I still want my meat.* [BROKEN RECORD]

CLERK: You will have to go to the back and see the meat manager. [Evasion of responsibility]

CARLO: *Will he give me my meat?* [BROKEN RECORD]

CLERK: He's the one to take care of it. [Evasion of responsibility]

CARLO: What's his name?

CLERK: Mr. Johnson.

CARLO: Call him up here, please.

CLERK: Just go in the back, you'll find him. [Evasion of responsibility]

CARLO: I don't see anyone there, *please call him up here.* [BROKEN RECORD]

CLERK: Go in the back, he'll be there soon. [Evasion of responsibility]

CARLO: I don't want to go in the back and wait around forever. I want to get out of here quick like, *please call him up here.* [BROKEN RECORD]

CLERK: You're holding up the line, all these people want to be served. [Guilt induction: don't you care about other people?]

CARLO: I know they want to be served, just like I

want to be served. *Please call the meat manager up here.* [BROKEN RECORD]

CLERK: (Looks at Carlo curiously for a few seconds, walks over to the girl in the check-cashing booth, speaks to her and walks back to Carlo) He'll be here in just a minute.

CARLO: Okay.

After a few minutes, the meat manager, Mr. Johnson, walks up to the checkout counter and taps the checkout clerk on the shoulder.

CLERK: This customer lost his meat purchase.

JOHNSON: (To Carlo) Where did you lose it?

CARLO: Here, I never got it from you, and *I want my meat.* [BROKEN RECORD]

JOHNSON: Do you have the cash register receipt?

CARLO: (Handing it to him) Yes, and *I want my meat.* [BROKEN RECORD]

JOHNSON: (Looking at the slip) There are six items from the meat department.

CARLO: Right, three steaks, a roast, two chickens, and *I want my meat.* [BROKEN RECORD]

JOHNSON: Did you look in your car to see if they fell out of the bag? [Ignorance and guilt induction: you have to be checked up on and are not responsible.]

CARLO: Yes, and *I want my meat.* [BROKEN RECORD]

JOHNSON: Is there any other place you could have dropped them? [Ignorance and guilt induction: you are careless.]

CARLO: Yes, here. And *I want my meat.* [BROKEN RECORD]

JOHNSON: I meant besides here.

CARLO: No, and I *want my meat.* [BROKEN RECORD]

JOHNSON: Most people who say they lost their purchases remember later that they left them somewhere else. Why don't you come back in tomorrow if you can't find them? [Ignorance and guilt induction: you don't have a good memory and made a mistake!]

CARLO: I understand why you feel that way, but *I want my meat.* [BROKEN RECORD]

JOHNSON: It's getting late and we're ready to close the store. [Guilt induction: you are keeping me from going home on time.]

CARLO: I understand how you feel, but *I want my meat.* [BROKEN RECORD]

JOHNSON: Well, I can't do anything about this myself. [Evasion of responsibility]

CARLO: Who can?

JOHNSON: The store manager.

CARLO: Okay. *Call him over here.* [BROKEN RECORD]

JOHNSON: He is very busy right now. Why don't you come back on Monday and talk to him? [Guilt induction: he is a busy, important person and you shouldn't bother him with a little problem like this.]

CARLO: I understand how you feel, but I'm very busy right now myself. *Call him over here.* [BROKEN RECORD]

JOHNSON: (First silently looking at Carlo for a few seconds) I'll go talk to him and see what I can do.

CARLO: Okay. I'll be here waiting for you.

Mr. Johnson walks to the back of the store, disappears in a doorway, and then reappears a few moments later in the window of a business office overlooking the merchandise displays. He starts a conversation with a man seated behind a desk. The man behind the desk says something. Mr. Johnson shakes his head and points to Carlo. The man stands up, looks at Carlo, and speaks again. Mr. Johnson replies, shaking his head. The man speaks again and goes back to his desk. Mr. Johnson disappears from the window and moments later walks up to Carlo.

CARLO: Well?

JOHNSON: We are very sorry this happened. Why don't you go back to the meat counter and pick out what you lost.

CARLO: Right, thank you.

JOHNSON: Next week we are having a sale in the meat section. Some very good buys.

CARLO: I'll tell my wife about it, thanks.

While picking out the meat replacements, Carlo's father expressed his approval of the way Carlo had dealt with the supermarket staff. He kept saying with amazement in his voice, "If that were me, I would have been looking for the meat in my pockets, underneath the seat in the car, in the closet at home and in the attic!" Driving home, Dad asked Carlo how he was able to do what he did. With some modesty, but no lack of confident self-respect, Carlo replied; "It's just something I picked up in a course on being assertive at work. If you want, I'll teach you it."

In Carlo's dialogue with the supermarket clerks, you can see how he repeatedly told them, via BROKEN RECORD, what he wanted, his main goal, the replacement of his meat purchases. When other minor goals arose in the discussion, Carlo did not hesitate to use BROKEN RECORD to communicate his immediate wants to the clerks. For example, when told to stand around and wait until they got to his problem, Carlo repeatedly asked that the person who could resolve the problem be brought to him. The purpose of BROKEN RECORD, Carlo had learned, is to transmit a message repeatedly to the person he asserts himself to: "I will not be put off, I can do this all day if necessary"—no matter what manipulative ploys the other person may come up with. The idea of persistently, verbally asserting ourselves, which BROKEN RECORD teaches us, goes hand in hand with most of the remaining verbal skills described. As you will see in the dialogues to come, the things said in being assertive are said over and over again until the desired result—the cessation of someone's manipulation, a material goal, a workable compromise, a therapeutic effect upon ourself, or the regaining of our self-respect—is achieved.

In first teaching students and patients how to get the most benefit from their practice of BROKEN RECORD, I have them role-play (in groups of four—one assertor, one manipulator, and two student coaches) the following situation: a door-to-door salesman tries to sell encyclopedias by making the assertive customer feel anxious or guilty. In Carlo's real-life dialogue, he responded voluntarily to everything that the manipulative clerk or manager said or asked of him. Each of his responses was well thought out, however. Carlo was only saying what he wanted to say. But in the BROKEN RECORD dialogues which Carlo first role-played to learn to be persistent and nonmanipulable, I had him and his fellow trainees literally speak as if they were broken phonograph records. No matter what the other person said, Carlo responded with: "I understand (how you feel), but I am not interested (in buying an encyclopedia)," *spoken in a low-level, relaxed voice.* This procedure was followed to help Carlo to break the belief and habit pattern that makes what he says dependent upon what someone else says first. For example:

Dialogue #2
Learning how
to say "No,"
persistently

SALESMAN: You do want your children to learn faster, don't you?

CARLO: I understand, but I'm not interested in buying.

SALESMAN: Your wife would want her children to have them.

CARLO: I understand, but I am not interested.

SALESMAN: It's awful hot out here, do you mind if I come in for a drink of water?

CARLO: I understand, but I'm not interested.

SALESMAN: You mean you won't give me a drink?

CARLO: I understand how you feel, but I'm not interested.

SALESMAN: You don't understand or you would want to buy these for your children.

CARLO: I understand how you feel, but I'm not interested.

SALESMAN: You just keep saying I understand. Can't you say anything else?

CARLO: I understand, but I'm just not interested.

SALESMAN: Let me ask one question. How old are your children?

CARLO: I understand, but I'm not interested in buying.

SALESMAN: Won't you even tell me how old your children are?

CARLO: I understand how you feel, but I'm not interested.

SALESMAN: Let me put it this way, how many children live on this block?

CARLO: I understand, but I'm not interested.

SALESMAN: You mean you won't even answer one question I ask you?

CARLO: I understand, but I'm not interested.

SALESMAN: If you don't want to talk to me, I'll leave.

CARLO: I understand, but I'm just not interested.

SALESMAN: Do you think your neighbor, Mr. Jones would be interested?

CARLO: I understand how you feel, but I'm just not interested.

With stereotyped BROKEN RECORD training dialogues like this one, Carlo and his colleagues learned how to change this compulsive habit of answering any question or responding to any statement put to them. This habit is based upon our belief that when someone talks to us, we "should" have an answer and "should" respond specifically to whatever the other person says. The first practice of dialogues like this one is surprising to many novice learners. Many of them are unaware of how strong this habit is and how uncomfortable they will feel when they try not to respond automatically to someone's queries. Well over half of my students have difficulties with this first exercise in learning how to ignore the prompts and questions of other people while assertively taking charge of what they want to say, instead of what the other person wants them to say. Responding in this new way is just not in their repertoire and these learners need repeated instructions to encourage their breaking this manipulable behavior pattern. When this balking occurs, my "encouragement" is somewhat less than sympathetic for student learners (but not so for more anxious patients). Up to this point, I usually have been a "nice guy" who is only trying to teach them to be more assertive. To help them get the most meaningful learning experience with me, I have found that it is beneficial to have at least one "tough guy" they can successfully cope with. In many classes, I am the only one I can count on to reliably play that role. At this point in their training, I begin to set myself up as *the* resident bastard (whom they can later cope with easily) with "encouragements" to work harder, like: *"What in the hell are you people doing!!!!?* Where in the rule book of life does it say: (deliberately, caustically, mimicking a simple mind reading from an imaginary script I hold in my hands) 'When someone asks me a question, I will answer it?' Show me the contract you signed that says that! You mean you didn't sign anything like that? (silence from the class) Then why in the hell do you act like you had? Do it again and this time do it the way I want you to do it. You don't answer any questions . . . You just BROKEN RECORD!"

A few of the students and patients learning to be assertive view, at least temporarily, their assertive rights and the systematic assertive skills as a means for "revenge," a means of getting back at their manipulators. At least one in every group or class asks a question like: "I understand what you are saying, but how can I use what you are teaching me to get my husband (wife, sister, teen-age child, parent, etc.) to do what I want him to do?" My answer is simple: "You can't!" and if you really examine this student's question in the light of your own experience with people, this answer makes a lot of sense. You can "con" someone into doing something, you can manipulate someone, and you can assertively say what you want someone to do, but you cannot control another adult's behavior consistently. If you lie to people and fool them into doing what you want, they can do the same to you; if you manipulate them into doing what you want, they can do the same to you; but if you assertively say what you want of them, all they can do is say "No" or tell you what they want in exchange, i.e., a workable compromise. Of these three options, the last assertive one is the most productive since it rapidly cuts through manipulation and enables you and the other person in conflict to communicate straightforwardly and work out a solution.

At least one student in each class will object to my analysis of systematic assertiveness as being the most straightforward way of coping with conflict, by saying: "Where's the safeguards? You might take advantage of the other person if he hasn't taken this class also. With these assertive skills, you could go over him like a steamroller!" While not sharing this student's fears at the helplessness of mankind in the face of systematic assertiveness, I could recognize his apprehension at giving people a set of verbal skills that would allow them to enforce their right to be their own judge, to place in their hands an effective means to do what they wanted to do. The best response I have heard to statements like the one from this student came from an old Peace Corps colleague, Mr. Fred Sherman, while visiting one of my classes: "These assertive verbal skills are like any other skills you learn; they are amoral. After you learn to drive a car, you can use that skill to take children to a Sunday school picnic, or you can use it to drive a get-away car for the Mafia." If you are your own judge, you are responsible for your assertive behavior also. What you do with it is up to you.

WORKABLE COMPROMISE

Many people learning to be assertive, often for the first time in their adult lives, do not understand why verbal skills like BROKEN RECORD are used. They ask: "What do I do when the other person doesn't give in or is assertive to me also?" The answer to this question is that our true sense of self-respect has a priority over everything else. Consequently, if you keep your self-respect through exercising your assertive rights with skills like BROKEN RECORD, you will feel good even if you do not achieve your goal immediately. Feeling good about yourself is a major goal of systematic assertive therapy. Once we feel good about ourselves, our ability to cope with conflict "snowballs." It is not just a wonderful little "extra." That you feel good about yourself, however, does not exclude the possibility of obtaining what you set out to get, in addition to maintaining your self-respect. The other person's being assertive back to you simply results in the conflict being settled on the real issues of the dispute, not on the relative personality strengths of the participants or who is the best manipulator. It is practical, *whenever you feel that your self-respect is not in question,* to offer a workable compromise to the other person. You could, for example, offer to wait a definite period of time for your merchandise to be replaced or repaired, agree to do what the other person wants next time, or simply flip a coin to see who does what and when. You can always bargain with other people for your material goals unless the compromise affects your personal feelings of self-respect. If the end goal involves a matter of self-worth, there can be no compromise.

With some exceptions, we cope better and in a healthier fashion through the use of systematic verbal assertion and the process of workable compromise. What are these exceptions—the situations where it is best not to be systematically assertive? There are several, so let's take a moment to look at them briefly.

It is not very realistic to be assertive in some situations. In situations where you have little control over what is going to happen, it is foolish and possibly dangerous (unless you are a trained professional) to assert yourself in the systematic manner outlined in this text. The situations where you have to limit your assertiveness are those that involve legal or physical factors.

Not all members of our federal, state, county, and municipal judiciary or law enforcement agencies are assertive themselves. Some members of these professions, unfortunately, cloak their own personal biases on how people "should" behave with their robes of office, and have the real, if not absolutely "legal" authority to act out on their personal feelings. It does little for you to persistently assert yourself in broken-record fashion to an angry judge. He may reward you with thirty days in the "slammer!" All you are likely to get from a policeman who jabs you with his nightstick is more of the same if you have any further dealings with him. On the other hand, by setting limits for your assertive behavior in such situations, I do not mean to imply that you have to shut up and say nothing. For example, if you are physically abused by a police officer it is foolish to protest on the spot. Get his badge number and report his behavior to his superior officer; if he does this often and a number of citizens complain, the police officer will change his hostile behavior.

This balance between restraint and assertiveness is pointed out in the case of Jerry. I first saw Jerry when he was seventeen. He had a history of three years of drug abuse, including the use of heroin, cocaine, and amphetamines. Jerry, like many drug-dependent patients, was extremely nonassertive and didn't know how to deal with the "straights": his parents, family, schoolteachers, the law, etc. Jerry stayed within his nonassertive drug culture for several reasons. His associates never criticized or harassed him, never got mad at him, never tried to make him do something he didn't want to do, and they let him do pretty much whatever he liked. Jerry did the same for them. He treated them in the same way—a nonassertive, acquiescent stand-off described in the glowing words, "Love," "Peace," and "Brother." Jerry stayed within his drug culture because he liked it; very few people bothered him, and he didn't know how to handle "straight" people outside his drug culture. With this background, Jerry was treated for drug dependency using assertive therapy as a means for getting him in contact and effectively dealing with non-drug people. After four months of assertive group therapy and two months of individual assertive therapy, Jerry dropped his job as drug pusher at his former high school, gained regular employment, and was enrolled in college within twelve months. After a twenty-four-month follow-up, Jerry had not relapsed into the use of any hard drugs but has occasionally used marijuana.

Prior to assertive therapy, Jerry was invariably stopped and frisked or had his car searched whenever he came in contact with the police. Even though he was "clean" whenever he was searched, and therefore not arrested, Jerry somehow was giving off cues to the police that were "suspect." Since therapy, Jerry has been stopped several times by police, *but his car has never been searched and he has not been frisked.* Jerry received traffic tickets on some of these police encounters after therapy, but felt strongly that he was not at fault on one particular occasion, that he didn't deserve a ticket then. Jerry reported to me after he appeared in court that he had asserted himself to the judge on this particular ticket. Fearing the worst, that Jerry was in for a stretch in jail for possible contempt of court, I was pleasantly surprised to hear that he simply told the judge in his own words what he thought had happened . . . and the judge agreed with him. For Jerry, being assertive in court meant simply to speak his piece, to tell his side of the story and be heard, whether anyone agreed with him or not. Jerry's court experience is a good example of balancing our assertive behavior with restraint in legal circumstances where someone else with the power to do so, can, if they wish, play tricks with our future.

The second situation where assertive behavior is inappropriate is also sensible and obvious: when you are at the physical mercy of other people. During a hit-and-run, a riot, robbery, or mugging, assertion is of little use to you. Walter, a graduate student in history at a local university, posed the question of what to do in the following situation. Walking home from class one evening, he encountered four large, tough-looking men on a dimly lighted street. Flicking out a switchblade knife, one of the men asked Walter for a "loan" of five dollars. Walter asked me what I would do in such a situation. My answer was: "Is that all you need? I can loan you twenty dollars!" When we have no other option, it is in our best interest to cooperate fully with someone who physically threatens us. Walter had confused, in his thinking—but not in his behavior (he "loaned" the mugger the five dollars)—the dividing line between being foolishly brave (stupid) and being assertive.) When someone points a gun or knife at you, it doesn't help much to say, BROKEN RECORD fashion, "You can't have my money," over and over again in the hope that the mugger will go away!

There are also situations where no matter how assertively persistent you are, you are going to lose; you are not going to achieve your material goal. No set of skills or procedures can guarantee 100 per cent success in getting what you want in every situation. To be more specific, failure is more likely in situations where you may try to use systematic assertive techniques (particularly in commercial and formal interactions) to renegotiate a priori structure. This, for instance, happened to one learner in a recent class who asked for coaching on returning a tire with a defect on its side. After that practice, he went back to the tire dealer, persistently used BROKEN RECORD to get his money back, and the dealer laughed at him. Reporting the failure of being verbally assertive to reach his goal, the class curiously asked him for the details of the interaction. Still puzzled after the postmortem inquiry, since they could find no lack in the student's assertive behavior, one of the class asked him why he thought the dealer refused a refund. The class was dumbfounded when the student reported that, "I guess it was because the tire had 24,-000 miles on it when I took it back." I found out later that he was trying to use assertiveness to regain his self-respect eighteen months after he silently accepted a defective tire. I give him credit for lots of *chutzpa,* but not much common sense. *Chutzpa,* incidentally, if you are not familiar with this Yiddish expression, is the prime personality trait of a man who murders both his parents and then pleads to the court for mercy because he is an orphan!

5

Assertive social conversation and communication

In both my general psychotherapeutic practice and in teaching people to be assertive, I have observed that to the degree that they *are* assertive, they are also socially adept. I have also observed that people who benefit from learning to be systematically assertive usually require some help in improving their social skills. The nonassertive person typically has some difficulty in communicating with others in social situations. He is shy. These adults, like many teen-agers, often find themselves tongue-tied, anxious, and at a loss for words even in a relaxed, nonthreatening social atmosphere. This observation makes me ask the question: Of what importance is social conversation in being healthy and happy and how is it related to our own assertiveness? The answer is a simple one but has implications for each of us in our important or even potentially important relationships with other people. Communication is the "glue" that keeps people together while a relationship grows and strengthens into a channel of mutual support, counsel, productivity, excitation, and satisfaction. In order for any social relationship to develop, both of the partners must have at least a minimal level of assertiveness in their dealings with one another. If they do not deal assertively with each other, even on their first meeting, the relationship may take months to develop, if it ever does. If a new relationship falters or fails, particularly those of a heterosexual nature between men and women, most likely one or the other of the pair did not assertively communicate to their social partner what type of person he or she is; their wants, likes, dislikes, interests, things they are doing or want to do, their ways of doing things, etc. The ability to talk about ourselves, who we are, how we live, and the ability to make other people comfortable in talking about themselves in the same way are assertive social skills. Assertive behavior, then, is much more than demanding your rights from other people or, as I have emphasized so far, keeping other people from manipulating you. In this social sense, being assertive is communicating to another person what you are, what you do, what you want, what you expect of life. Hopefully, the other person is assertive also and you can discover a basis for a mutually rewarding, self-sustaining relationship. Equally important, social assertiveness allows you to find out if there is little or no mutual interest and avoid a dead-end relationship that has no potential for either partner.

If you lack these social skills, the communication block may be due to a history of frustration in generally dealing with other people. Such a history of frustration could trigger an anxiety reaction within you in any new social setting. Your conditioned anxiety from past failures inhibits your spontaneity in talking about yourself as well as listening effectively to what the other person reveals about himself or herself.

In developing a training method for teaching non-assertive people to verbally cope with a potentially anxious social relationship, I have observed that, in a social setting, all of us tend to give out *free information* about ourselves that has not been asked for specifically. Much of this free information about ourselves is related to our interests, desires, prejudices, what makes us happy as well as what worries us, and our style of living. If you talk to someone else and use anything more than yesses, noes, or grunts, no matter what you say, you will give the other person a great many free clues and indications of what is important to you at that particular moment in your life.

FREE INFORMATION

In order to become an assertive communicator in a social setting, you must master two skills. First, you have to practice listening to the clues other people give you about themselves. Following up on the FREE IN-FORMATION people offer about themselves (which you have not asked about or commented upon) accomplishes two things in a social setting. The free information gives you something to talk about besides the weather and avoids those awkward silences in which you ask yourself: "What do I say now?" In addition, and even more important, when you follow up free information, you are both assertively prompting and making it easier for other people to talk about themselves by showing an interest in things important to them.

SELF-DISCLOSURE

The second skill that must be mastered in order to communicate effectively is SELF-DISCLOSURE. Assertively disclosing information about yourself—how you think, feel, and react to the other person's free information—allows the social communication to flow both ways. Without self-disclosure, the following up of free information would make a conversation very stilted, give the impression that you are playing the role of an interrogator or district attorney, or simply prying into the other person's life without sharing any of your own experience.

Prior to studying the social assertiveness dialogue that follows, let's first take a few moments and see how we can discriminate free information from other conversation and briefly discuss what self-disclosure is.

If you have just been introduced to someone new at a social function (better still, you have introduced yourself), you might ask that person, for example: "Do you live near here, Mary?" If Mary replies, "No," she has given you zero free information about herself. If, on the other hand, she replies: "No. I live in Santa Monica right near the beach," she has given you two bits of information that you did not ask for. First that she lives in Santa Monica, and second, in all likelihood, she likes the beach and goes there often. You also might get the free information that she is married, has three children, two dogs, and is simply waiting at the social function until her husband arrives. In any case, what do you do with the free information when you are given it? How do you follow it up both to get to know Mary better and let her know more about yourself? There are two ways to follow up free information someone gives to you. You might, in Mary's case, simply ask her what Santa Monica is like. This obvious course prompts Mary to tell you a lot about Santa Monica, but probably very little about Mary. In order to facilitate the social communication process, you have the option of asking Mary what she thinks of Santa Monica. For example, you might begin a question to her with self-disclosure: "I've never lived in Santa Monica, but friends have told me that it is a great place. How come you decided to live there?" This type of follow-up on free information is really directed more to the topic of Mary than the topic of Santa Monica. Other examples of free information might be that Mary makes ceramics, is taking a night course in typing, owns her own surfboard, is single, etc. Following up clues as to Mary's interests could emphasize getting more information about ceramics, typing, surfing, or being single. The follow-up of these clues, on the other hand, may emphasize how and why Mary liked or got into ceramics, typing, surfing, or still being single. In either case, whether we emphasize ceramics or how ceramics relates to Mary, we have the assertive option to choose either direction.

To complete our half of the social communication, it is necessary also to give information about ourselves to the person we are relating to. As in following up free information we are given, we have the option to talk about the subjects that interest others or about ourselves in relation to those subjects. Self-disclosure of the latter type may be as simple as saying, "I really don't know much about ceramics. Is it something you can explain or do you have to do it?" or "I've never talked to anyone before about ceramics. What's it all about?" or "I haven't been able to find time to do a lot of fun things like that. How do you manage it?" By disclosing information about yourself in responding to the other person's free information, you make it easier for him or her to prompt you for further information on your own interests, lifestyle, or even your problems.

In teaching people to recognize free information, follow up on it, and use self-disclosure, I use two practice exercises that I developed in the spring of 1970 at the Sepulveda V.A. Hospital. The first exercise is to pair off with an arbitrary partner and simply practice following up free information that the partner gives. The person learning to recognize free information does not offer any free information or self-disclosure. Instead he concentrates solely on recognizing and following up on the free information his partner gives him. After a sufficient amount of practice with both partners reversing the roles, the second exercise is used. In this one, the learner is instructed that for each bit of free information his partner gives him, he is to give one bit of self-disclosure back. After both partners have practiced the skill of returning information for information given while still prompting further information, they are allowed to engage in the process simultaneously. In this last step, if the conversation is observed, it appears as a very animated, engaging discussion with no hint of stereotyping or that both partners are employing learned skills.

In teaching people to assertively communicate with each other in social situations, someone invariably makes a statement like: "I think that the interchange between people isn't something you can artificially create. It's either there or it isn't. Practicing to talk to someone systematically is phony and mechanical!" I usually avoid a long, detailed discussion of the problems you can get into with such a preordained viewpoint. Instead, I point out its similarities to the observation of the little old lady, who upon watching Neil Armstrong make his giant step for mankind, was asked by a reporter if she, one day, would like to go to the moon herself. Her reply: "If God meant us to go to the moon, he wouldn't have given us TV sets so we could watch it from here!"

The following dialogue is a sample demonstration

exercise used in my assertive therapy groups. Although its style and content are set up for younger people in dating situations, the skills of recognizing free information and following it up with self-disclosure have been used just as successfully in social situations involving recently divorced men and women of all ages, social situations with no sexual roles involved, such as getting to know new neighbors, people meeting at parties, as well as new social relationships between men or between women.

Dialogue #3
Pete and Jean model the social conversation skills of FREE INFORMATION and SELF-DISCLOSURE

In this dialogue Pete and Jean are modeling the follow-up of free information for a group of Sacred Heart Academy and Cal. Tech. students on a weekend encounter series at the University of California at Santa Barbara. The dialogue centers around social conversation problems that young people have in dating.

Setting of the dialogue: Pete is just picking up Jean at her home for their first date.

PETE: Hi, Jean.

JEAN: Hi, Pete, how are you?

PETE: I'm fine, how are you?

JEAN: I feel like having a good time.

PETE: Great. So do I.

JEAN: Let's go, I'm all ready.

PETE: Okay, let's walk. It's only four or five blocks and we can talk as we go.

JEAN: Okay.

PETE: What did you do today? Anything spectacular?

JEAN: No, *I just studied all day*. [FREE INFORMATION] [Note # 1. Jean responded that nothing exciting happened today, i.e., "No." Then she gave free information that she was studying—a high probability behavior for a student, but not always to be assumed. Students do other things besides studying. Pete could then ask: (1) What does she usually do when not studying, (2) What sort of exciting things have happened to her lately, (3) What is she studying for, and (4) Why was she studying at this particular time.]

PETE: What are you studying for?

JEAN: I've got *two* tests coming up next week. [FREE INFORMATION about schedule]

PETE: What classes are you taking the tests in?

JEAN: Shakespearean literature and biology of reproduction. [Note #2. Pete could respond to Jean's statement in two ways: (1) Impersonal, or (2) Oriented toward her personal interests. The first would be a response such as "Tell me about Shakespearean drama." The second would be more personally oriented, i.e., "How did you become interested in Shakespeare?"]

PETE: *Gee, I like theater.* What a combination, Shakespeare and reproduction! I know why you're interested in reproduction. How come you're interested in Shakespearean drama? [SELF-DISCLOSURE]

JEAN: *My mother was a drama major in college before she met my father.* I guess I picked it up from her. [FREE INFORMATION about parents]

PETE: *My family never had any acting talent.* How do you feel about your mother giving up acting? *I think it would be neat to have someone close to you who knew all the Broadway and Hollywood people.* [SELF-DISCLOSURE]

JEAN: I think it would have been nice, *but I like her the way she is now, taking care of Dad and the family.* [FREE INFORMATION about mother]

PETE: Do you think that's your lifestyle—homemaker and all that? *Sometimes I think that must be a real bore for a woman.* [SELF-DISCLOSURE]

JEAN: I don't know. I know I don't want to get married yet. *I want to see what I can do on my own.* [FREE INFORMATION about personal goals]

PETE: *I feel the same way, I want to be independent for a while.* What would you like to do, be an actress? [SELF-DISCLOSURE]

JEAN: Maybe. *If I'm good enough to be successful at*

it. What are you studying for? [FREE INFORMATION about self-doubts]

PETE: I haven't decided yet whether to be a brain surgeon or a streetcar conductor.

JEAN: Funny! Funny! That's so old it died a natural death.

PETE: *I know it's bad, but it's my favorite joke.* Have you heard any good ones? [SELF-DISCLOSURE]

JEAN: No, *all I remember are elephant jokes.* [FREE INFORMATION on taste in humor]

PETE: *They're great too.* Maybe you know some I haven't heard? [SELF-DISCLOSURE]

JEAN: *I want to talk about you instead.* What are you going to do when you graduate? [SELF-DISCLOSURE]

PETE: Do you always interview all your dates this thoroughly?

JEAN: Come on. What are you studying?

PETE: I give up. I'll admit it. Aerospace engineering. *Just another one of the warmongers!* [FREE INFORMATION about political sensitivities]

JEAN: It's not that bad. *But you don't look like an aerospace engineer.* [FREE INFORMATION]

PETE: How should I look?

JEAN: (Giggling) You look more like a linebacker for the Rams.

PETE: *I thought so.* You're a jock lover. [SELF-DISCLOSURE]

JEAN: What are you complaining about?

PETE: You're right! What am I complaining about?

Disclosing private information about ourselves to other people is a very effective assertive skill, not only in social conversation but also when there is conflict between yourself and another person. Private feelings, worries, even lack of knowledge or indecisiveness cannot be dealt with by other people by their denying or disregarding the truth of your feelings. Someone else cannot make you feel good about doing something, for example, lending them a car, if you just plain worry about lending your car to anyone. You may balk at lending a car to someone and invent many reasons why you cannot lend the car at that particular time without ever admitting—even to yourself—that you feel worried and upset when you lend it out; the perfect "reason" not to do something you don't want to do. You may even worry when you know there is nothing to worry about. Whenever you have lent the car out in the past, nothing bad has happened. Such logic is beside the point. Your feelings may be irrational, but they are still your true feelings and must be respected. *Unfortunately, we seldom respect our own feelings of worry and uncertainty.* We might reason that we "should" not feel worried when someone wants to borrow our car. Instead of honestly saying either "No" with no explanation or "No, I get too worried when I lend my car to anyone," we invent reasons that sound more acceptable to ourselves. The type of voluntary self-disclosure I have been emphasizing is, of course, about things we assume we should hide: dislikes, worry, ignorance, fear, etc. Voluntary self-disclosure is not to be confused with the vomiting up of confessions of lack of self-worth having involuntary, automatic, almost conditioned characteristics. Your voluntary disclosure of negative factors about yourself and your own ready acceptance of them is probably the most potent and effective assertive skill in preventing manipulation and ensuring your own peace of mind. If other people react to your assertive disclosure of your inner self and worries by trying to convince you that you "shouldn't" or have no right to feel that way, your reply is simple and direct: "Perhaps so, but that's still the way I feel." Such an open and honest response is impossible to deal with manipulatively. When you make such a self-disclosure, the person you are interacting with must respond to you on the same level of honest personal wants or not deal with you at all. As we will see in many of the dialogues to follow, the appropriate use of voluntary self-disclosure is effective in dealing with manipulative used-car dealers, clerks, door-to-door salesmen, businessmen, mechanics, fellow employees, bosses, friends, neighbors, relatives, parents, and our children, as well as a means to improve our social communication and conversational skills.

So far, I have talked mostly about our verbal behavior with other people. The aim of systematic assertive practice is to present a person who is self-assured, adept in dealing with other people in conflict, and confident. Your assertive impact upon other people will likely be ineffective if at the same time you show observable anxiety cues. We all know people who say one thing but whose body says another. While others may not be able to put their finger on the cues that tell them we are anxious, they are still able to interpret them correctly. The most obvious cue that you are nervous in dealing with someone else is a lack of eye-to-eye contact. When you give a positive verbal message to someone but also appear anxious, that person will pay more attention to your nervousness than to what you tell him. Your chances of communicating what you want will be lessened since anxiety, in our Western civilization at least, is considered abnormal behavior and the model we use to deal with abnormal behavior is that used when we are confronted by an intoxicated person—a drunk. Most of the population will humor anyone displaying any signs of abnormality. Commitments made will usually not be honored but used only as an expediency to quickly deal with and dispose of the anxious person.

Lack of eye-to-eye contact, the most common anxiety cue, is a learned avoidance response. We learn to avoid eye contact without being aware of it. In the past, when we have made eye-to-eye contact in conflict and not coped well with that conflict, the other person made us nervous. Without realizing it, to reduce this anxiety, we develop a conditioned avoidance response; we shift our focus away from the person who makes us anxious and we feel better, at least temporarily. If we don't look at the other person, we don't get so anxious. After a while of successfully avoiding this anxiety, not looking someone in the eye becomes a habit.

Since it is an anxiety-produced response, the treatment of lack of eye contact is a simple one. In conjunction with the previous social conversation exercises I use the following phobic desensitization exercise to help people eliminate anxiety when making eye-to-eye contact. This exercise is always done in pairs with the learners seated approximately four to six feet from each other: "I want only one of you to keep looking at your partner's eyes and see if you can tell what he is looking at. If he's looking at your feet, you can probably tell it. If he's looking within an imaginary circle having a nine-inch radius around your nose, you can see his eyes change position but you can't tell what he's actually looking at. Now I want one of you from each pair to look at your partner's nose, chin, neck, Adam's apple, collar, upper chest, in that order, and let's see *when* your partner can tell you are *not* looking him in the eye. (Learners follow instructions.) Could any of you tell exactly when your partner was not looking you in the eye—not when he was moving his eyes—but when his eyes were still? What was your anxiety level when you looked him in the eye? Use a 'fear thermometer' scale of zero to 100. Zero means you are so relaxed you're going to fall asleep and 100 means you are about to hit the panic button. Remember your anxiety level and compare it to how you feel after we complete the whole exercise. Now I want both of you to focus your eyes wherever I tell you to. I'm going to have you gradually focus from your partner's toes to his nose and spend about ten to thirty seconds on different parts of the body. Ready: right foot—left foot—right knee— left ankle—right knee—bellybutton—left knee—right calf—left thigh—bellybutton—right elbow—chest— left shoulder—bellybutton—collar—left elbow—right shoulder—neck—left shoulder—top of head—left ear—chin—right ear—hairline—left ear—mouth— right ear—forehead—left cheek—right ear—nose—left ear—right cheek—left eyebrow—nose—right eyebrow—bridge of nose—left eye—nose—right eye—left eye—nose—forehead—right eye—left eye—right eye— both eyes—hold it there for one minute."

I have learners practice this exercise on their own

with friends, spouses, or whoever they can get to sit down with them for about three times a week for three weeks. In class, however, immediately after this exercise I have the same partners practice eye-to-eye contact while repeating the last part of the social conversation exercise. Most people find it difficult to look someone in the eye when they are answering a question or making a verbal statement. They find it difficult to concentrate. When this happens, I suggest that they still keep their focus within the nine-inch radius around their partner's nose, but stare at one ear, for example. Most learners find that looking at ears while answering a question produces less anxiety and disruption of their thoughts.

6

Assertively coping with the great manipulator: criticism

There are two major results when we systematically assert ourselves using the verbal skills I call FOGGING, NEGATIVE ASSERTION, and NEGATIVE INQUIRY. First, and most important—for the therapeutic goal of becoming whole, fully effective human beings—the practice of these skills can minimize our typical negative emotional response of anxiety to criticism, whether it's real or imagined, self-directed or from someone else. This internal change in our emotional reaction and attitude occurs with repeated practice of these skills; this is a clinically observed fact and not a theoretical assumption. Why the practice of these assertive skills causes this beneficial result could be the subject of another complete book on the theory of psychophysiology, behavioral or emotional change, and behavior therapy. Regardless of "why," the net effect of this internal process is that we feel less at war with ourselves and thus can feel more comfortable about the negative as well as the positive aspects of our personalities. Second, the practiced use of FOGGING, NEGATIVE ASSERTION, and NEGATIVE INQUIRY cuts our learned emotional puppet strings, those which make us automatically react, perhaps even panic, to criticism from other people; the learned anxiety triggered by criticism which allows us to be manipulated into defending what we want to do instead of doing it.

While at the Sepulveda V.A. Hospital in the spring of 1970, I was faced with the problem of teaching a skill that a husband or wife, for instance, could use to cope with manipulative criticism from a nonassertive, perhaps nagging spouse. I observed that almost without exception, the person being criticized becomes defensive and denies the criticism. This manipulative criticism occurs in the first place because the nagging wife, for example, has been taught that her wants have to be justified, have to be reasonable, must be able to "stand up in court" or even church. Like the rest of us who have been psychologically trained to keep in line, she has great trouble in giving logical, sound reasons to "justify" what she wants in life. She, like most of us, has been trained that she must have a reason to want the things she wants. If her husband does something that keeps her from doing something she wants to do, like just tinkering around the house instead of going out to visit friends, she has no assertive recourse to deal with his behavior but can only impose her own nonassertive, arbitrary, manipulative structure upon him *and criticize him for not behaving according to it.* If he wants to work on his car, for example, he must have a reason to "justify" it, otherwise he is in the wrong and is open to criticism. Manipulative criticism occurs so often in dealing with other people, since, as my grandmother used to say, you can always find something wrong with someone else if you really want to. We can easily find things to criticize by simply imposing our own arbitrary structure upon the relationship which outlines what the rules of right and wrong are; how things "should" really be. Each of us can and does impose our manipulative structure upon one another, and most of us have been well trained to automatically accept or even believe in the other person's imposed structure. A nonassertive wife might deal critically with behavior that displeases her by telling her husband: "You've just fooled around with the car all weekend!" The arbitrary structure she is trying to impose upon the marriage relationship and her husband's behavior is that it is somehow wrong to relax and tinker all weekend. This arbitrary right-and-wrong structure really has nothing to do with whether or not *she likes* her husband to relax all weekend instead of doing something else with her. That she would rather do something else is not manipulative. Coping with her wants by criticizing her husband's behavior is manipulative and it is

produced by her own nonassertiveness. She cannot justify her own wishes to visit their friends and get out of
the house. If the husband who tinkers and is criticized
for it automatically accepts his wife's arbitrary right-
and-wrong structure (it is somehow "wrong" for him to
relax and be casual), he must also automatically accept
as true any criticism of the deviation in his behavior
from his wife's right-and-wrong structure. Furthermore,
he must also accept that the criticism by his wife is relevant; he is in the wrong and "should" change whatever she criticizes. Since most of us have been taught to
feel anxious, nervous, or guilty when we make mistakes
(mistakes are "wrong"), the person being criticized, in
this case our nonassertive, relaxed husband more than
likely tries through logic, argument, or even countercriticism of his wife's daily behavior to deny the (totally
irrelevant) truth in the manipulative criticism. For example: "I did not work on the car all weekend! I didn't
even think of it when we had lunch yesterday! And I
took a nap this afternoon for at least an hour. Besides,
you should talk. All you do when I'm not here is watch
those silly soap operas on TV!" This "trained seal"
type of response to nonassertive criticism is invariably
followed by more criticism producing a cycle of criticism—denial of error—further criticism. As the cycle is
escalated, one or the other typically gets angry and
fights the partner, walks out, or both.

In such a situation of nonassertive criticism, some
other coping style besides defensiveness and denial of
real, imaginary, or suggested error is required for the
relationship to be less destructive to both partners. A
kind of behavior that would effectively, assertively, and
nonmanipulatively cope with criticism would contain
the following important elements:

1. The coping behavior would train you to distinguish
between (a) truths that other people tell you about your
behavior (that you always tinker with the car), and (b)
the arbitrary right and wrong that other people may
tack on to truths about your behavior by implying or

suggesting that you are in the "wrong" without openly saying so (that it is "wrong" to relax a lot).

2. The coping behavior would train you to feel comfortable when you are told a truth about your behavior in a critical fashion and the other person does not openly spell out the "right and wrong" involved in your behavior, but only implies through his or her critical tone that your behavior is "wrong" (all you do on the weekend is work on the car); not feeling so anxious about criticism you do not have to respond at all to implications or suggestions of wrongdoing and need only deal with the truths about your behavior that people tell you. (That's true, I do work on the car a lot.)

3. The coping behavior would train you to feel comfortable when a truth about your behavior is openly interpreted as wrongdoing within the other person's arbitrary structuring of his or her life (it is wrong for you to fool around with the car so much on weekends); not feeling so anxious about criticism you do not have to automatically accept the other person's arbitrary structure of "right and wrong," but you can instead inquire into the other person's structure and ask what is wrong about your behavior (I don't understand, what is it about me working on the car a lot that's wrong?); thus extinguishing use of manipulative structure and prompting the other person to state what he or she wants: "Well, I want us to visit our friends instead of staying home all weekend."

4. The coping behavior would train you to distinguish between (a) truths that other people tell you about your errors and mistakes (you forgot to put the cap on the toothpaste again), and (b) the arbitrary right and wrong that other people may tack onto the truths about your errors and mistakes (it is "wrong" to forget to cap the toothpaste tube).

5. The coping behavior would train you to feel comfortable about your errors, and while errors and mistakes are inefficient, wasteful, usually but not always unproductive, stupid, and usually in need of revision, nevertheless, in reality, they have nothing to do with

right and wrong—i.e., "That's true, it's stupid* of me to leave the cap off again."

The systematic verbal assertive coping skills—FOG-GING, NEGATIVE INQUIRY, and NEGATIVE ASSERTION—I have developed as a result of helping people to deal with manipulative criticism generated by our own or other people's arbitrary structuring of a relationship, contain, collectively, all the coping elements described in the above statements. Let us look at each of these verbal coping skills in turn, beginning with a detailed examination of FOGGING.

FOGGING

In teaching people to cope with manipulative criticism from other people, I instruct them *not* to deny any criticism (that's simply responding in kind), not to get defensive, and not to counterattack with criticism of their own. While at Sepulveda V.A. Hospital, in originally giving patients a starting point in learning to cope with criticism in this different way, I suggested that as a rule of thumb, they might learn faster by verbally replying to manipulative criticism as if they were a "fog bank." A fog bank is remarkable in some aspects. It is very persistent. We cannot clearly see through it. It offers no resistance to our penetration. It does not fight back. It has no hard striking surfaces from which a rock we throw at it can ricochet back at us, enabling us to pick it up and throw it at the fog once more. We can throw an object right through it, and it is unaffected. Inevitably, we give up trying to alter the persistent, independent, nonmanipulable fog and leave it alone. Similarly, when criticized, you can assertively cope by offering no resistance or hard psychological striking surfaces to critical statements thrown at you.

I have used other labels such as AGREEING WITH TRUTH, AGREEING IN PRINCIPLE, or AGREE-ING WITH THE ODDS to describe this assertive skill

---

*Alternatives: inefficient, wasteful, unproductive, etc.

when it is used in everyday situations to cope with manipulative logic, argument, guilt- and anxiety-inducing statements. My original clinical slang term of FOGGING seems to have made some permanent impression, however, since my colleagues and graduate students (and I myself) continue to use it even though it is an inadequate description of the many ways we can verbally assert ourselves using this skill in different situations.

Irrespective of the label used to describe this powerful assertive verbal skill, we can use it to cope in the following ways: (1) We can agree with *any truth* in statements people use to criticize us (AGREEING WITH TRUTH). For example, if an overprotective mother keeps checking up on her daughter even after the daughter no longer lives at home, the daughter might respond to her mother's criticism of implied or suggested wrongdoing with assertive FOGGING, as one of my patients, Sally, did:

MOTHER: You stayed out late again, Sally. I tried to call you until twelve thirty last night.

SALLY: That's true, Mom, I was out late again last night.

(2) We can agree with *any possible truth* in statements people use to criticize us (AGREEING WITH THE ODDS). In the case of Sally and her mom, if Mom criticized her with a statement of direct wrongdoing, Sally might still respond with assertive FOGGING.

MOTHER: Sally, if you stay out late so much you might get sick again.

SALLY: You could be right, Mom. (Or, That's probably true. Or, I agree with you, Mom, if I didn't go out so often I would probably get a lot more sleep.)

(3) We can agree with the *general truth* in *logical* statements that people use to manipulate us (AGREEING IN PRINCIPLE). In the case of Sally's mother, if she persisted in trying to impose her own rules of living

upon her daughter's lifestyle, Sally could continue to assert herself with verbal FOGGING.

MOTHER: Sally, you know how important looking good is to a young girl who wants to meet a nice man and get married. If you keep staying out late so often and don't get enough sleep, you won't look good. You don't want that to happen, do you?

SALLY: You're right, Mom. What you say makes sense, so when I feel the need, I'll get in early enough.

In the examples of assertive FOGGING just given, this obviously popular daughter added statements of her intention to be independent of her mother, such as: "... but I wouldn't stay up so late worrying about me if I were you." Or "... but I'm not worried about it." Or "... but I expect I'll be out late quite a bit now with all these guys wanting to date me."

As a first practice exercise in learning the assertive skill of FOGGING, I typically have students or patients pair off, with one practicing FOGGING and the other playing the role of a critical "resident bastard." The FOGGER is instructed to agree with anything he is criticized about by agreeing with truth, agreeing in principle, or agreeing with the odds. The FOGGEE, on the other hand, is instructed to begin his critique with negative comments about the learner's clothing and attitude, eventually working up to his moral character, probable sexual habits, and any other outrageous fantasy that comes to mind. After their roles are reversed and this practice is finished, I then make the rounds of the pairs individually and try to fade the distinction between classroom role-playing and realistic criticism. I do this so that any reduction in their anxiety response to criticism will not be limited to the practice situation. Without informing them of my intent, I have the learners run through a quick segment of their practice again and seriously interject threatening but unrealistic comments like: "You could do that better; that wasn't too good; you seem to be a slow learner; your partner seems to be much better at this than you; maybe you need in-depth analysis of your personality instead of a class like this," and so forth. At the point where the learner is able to routinely respond with, "You could be right," his reply is usually accompanied with a muzzled smile or at least a gleam of the eye. At this point, I have difficulty also in not bursting out in a belly laugh. Many times my control is less than that of the students', and consequently what starts out for them as an anxiety-ridden practice becomes a fun-filled experience. What a paradox! Having fun while someone criticizes you. Learning with this method is typically so rapid that occasionally I vary the format and have four learners work together—one FOGGER, one critic, and two coaches or observers. In the first part of the session, the observers coach the FOGGER. In the latter part of the session, they have to coach the critic to help him think up further outrageous and derogatory comments about the learner. Three critics vs. one assertive person is certainly not fair—for the critics!

Dialogue #4
A beginning practice
exercise using
FOGGING to
cope with
criticism

Setting of the dialogue: Two learners are practicing the use of FOGGING in a classroom. The criticism and FOGGING statements are chosen from the practice exercises of a number of students.

CRITIC: I see you are dressed in your usual sloppy manner.

LEARNER: *That's right.* I am dressed in my usual way. [FOGGING]

CRITIC: Those pants! They look like you stole them off the Goodwill rack without pressing them.

LEARNER: *They are a bit wrinkled, aren't they.* [FOGGING]

CRITIC: Wrinkled is the understatement of the week. They are positively dreadful.

LEARNER: *You're probably right. They do look a bit worse for wear.* [FOGGING]

CRITIC: And that shirt! Your taste must be all in your mouth.

LEARNER: *That's probably true. My taste in clothes isn't one of my strong points.* [FOGGING]

CRITIC: Anyone who dresses like that obviously hasn't got much going for them.

LEARNER: *You're right. I do have a lot of faults.* [FOGGING]

CRITIC: Faults! Is that what you call them? They are more like chasms. Your personality is one empty Grand Canyon.

LEARNER: *You could be right. There are a lot of things I could improve.* [FOGGING]

CRITIC: I doubt if you are able to do a job effectively if you can't even dress properly.

LEARNER: *That's true. I could improve my work on the job.* [FOGGING]

CRITIC: And you probably pick up your paycheck each week from the poor boss you are ripping off without feeling any guilt.

LEARNER: *You're right. I don't feel any guilt at all.* [FOGGING]

CRITIC: What a thing to say. You should feel guilty!

LEARNER: *You're probably right, I could feel a bit guiltier.* [FOGGING]

CRITIC: You probably don't budget the salary you cheat other people, hard-working people, not loafers like you, out of.

LEARNER: *You're probably right, I could budget my money better, and I do loaf a lot.* [FOGGING]

CRITIC: If you were smarter and had some moral sensibility you could ask someone how to buy better clothes so you don't look like a bum.

LEARNER: *That's true, I could ask someone how to buy better clothes, and I certainly could be smarter than I am.* [FOGGING]

CRITIC: You look nervous when I tell you things that you don't like.

LEARNER: *I'm sure I do look nervous.* [FOGGING]

CRITIC: You shouldn't be nervous, I'm your friend.

LEARNER: *That's true, I shouldn't be as nervous as I am.* [FOGGING]

CRITIC: I'm probably the only person who would tell you these things.

LEARNER: *I'm sure you're right about that!* [FOGGING with sarcastic emphasis]

CRITIC: You were being sarcastic.

LEARNER: *That's true, I was.* [FOGGING]

CRITIC: You are not here to learn to be sarcastic, you already know that! You are deliberately resisting how to FOG.

LEARNER: *You're right, I already know how to be sarcastic and I probably am fighting learning something new.* [FOGGING]

CRITIC: Only someone dumb does that.

LEARNER: *You're probably right, that may have been dumb of me.* [FOGGING]

CRITIC: You'll never learn to do this.

LEARNER: *You're probably right, I may never be any good at it.* [FOGGING]

CRITIC: You're scratching your ear again.

LEARNER: *That's true.* [FOGGING]

CRITIC: And you quickly pulled your hand away when I pointed it out.

LEARNER: *I did, didn't I?* [FOGGING]

CRITIC: And my pointing it out made you nervous again.

LEARNER: *I guess you're right.* [FOGGING]

CRITIC: You're hopeless.

LEARNER: *You may be right.* [FOGGING]

CRITIC: And what kind of hair style is that you have? It looks like one of those worn by those dirty hippies.

LEARNER: *It does, doesn't it.* [FOGGING]

CRITIC: And it looks just as dirty, too.

LEARNER: *That's true. It could be much cleaner, couldn't it?* [FOGGING]

CRITIC: You probably would like to live like them; never having to wash and rolling in sex.

LEARNER: *You could be right.* Maybe I should think about that! [FOGGING]

CRITIC: And you probably would enjoy all the sexual perversions they perform!

LEARNER: *That's a point. You may just be right there!* [FOGGING]

CRITIC: Now that I think of it, you seem like the type that wouldn't have to join a band of hippies to be taught sexual perversions. You probably know about them already.

LEARNER: *That's true.* I've made a lifelong study of sex. [FOGGING]

CRITIC: Yes, but I can see from your sneaky, beady eyes that you have already put some of them into practice.

LEARNER: (By this time grinning from ear to ear) *You may be right.* [FOGGING]

CRITIC: You shouldn't grin when you are told what's good for you.

LEARNER: *That's true, I shouldn't.* [FOGGING]

CRITIC: All you do is agree with me.

LEARNER: *You're right.* [FOGGING]

CRITIC: You sound like a yes-man with no spine or personality of his own.

LEARNER: *I do sound like that, don't I?* [FOGGING]

CRITIC: You don't *sound* like one, you *are* a yes-man!

LEARNER: *You may be right.* [FOGGING]

CRITIC: You're doing it again.

LEARNER: *That's true, I am.* [FOGGING]

CRITIC: I don't think you can say anything but "Yes" to someone!

LEARNER: *I can certainly see why you think that.* [FOGGING]

CRITIC: Well, can you say "No" and mean it?

LEARNER: *Perhaps.* [FOGGING]

CRITIC: Don't you know?

LEARNER: We'll have to see, won't we?

As you can see in this training dialogue, the practice of FOGGING does several things. First, it forces the learner to listen to exactly what the critic says. If the critic says, for example, "You sound like. . . ." the learner replies, "You're right, I do sound like . . ." If he says, "I think that you . . . ," the learner replies, "I can see that you do think that . . ." or "I can understand why you would think that . . ." The novice learns to respond only to what the critic actually says, not what is implied or what the novice thinks the criticism implies. It teaches the novice to be a good listener, to listen to what is actually said—not to read minds—by the critic instead of interpreting what is said to conform to the novice's own self-doubts and insecurities, what we all secretly feel or think. In addition, it forces the learner to think in terms of probabilities—what he would be willing to bet money on, not in absolutes, in yes or no, blacks or whites, 100 per cent or zero. Indeed, the learner may be a bit lazy on the job, but he still gets the job done. His hair probably does have some foreign matter on it, unless he just stepped into the classroom dripping wet from the shower stall. His sexual behavior (or lack of it) would likely be described as perverse by afficionados at both ends of the erotic spectrum. In short, any critical comment will have at least a grain of truth in it, depending upon the relative vantage point from which his behavior and personality are viewed.

At some time during or after the FOGGING drill, at least one sensitive student asks: "How can I agree with someone who tells me something that is not true. I'm not going to lie about myself!" Questions of this type, in my experience, are either prompted by deep feelings of insecurity about that very criticism that is "not true," i.e., the critique strikes a bit too close to home for comfort, or the learner has such a general lack of confidence in himself that he desperately needs to hang on to those positive things about himself; he is unable to suffer any slander about them. In working with these students, I usually say something like: "What would you do if someone told you that you were suspended three feet off the ground? Standing with your feet firmly on the ground and with this physical evidence before your eyes, you probably wouldn't say anything, but just burst out laughing. But how about those things for which you do not have absolute, guaranteed, incontrovertible evidence? For example, if someone says you are dumb, what do you say? You aren't dumb, are you? (Student always shakes head in negative.) Well, congratulations! You are very lucky, because speaking for myself, I'm very dumb. Sometimes I do very stupid things. Other times I'm brilliant, but a lot of times I'm dumb. Also dumb in comparison to what? In comparison to Einstein and Oppenheimer, I'm a village idiot. On the other hand, in comparison to a lot of people I know, I'm a positive genius. So when I'm told that I'm dumb, I can readily agree with it. You're probably right; compared to some people, I'm really dumb, and compared to myself, sometimes I'm a real clod. So I listen to what people tell me about myself in all things, and give them the benefit of the doubt. After all, they *may* be right, but then I still make my own judgment about it and do what *I* decide." One student pursued the matter and engaged me in the following short dialogue:

STUDENT: Do you know your IQ in specific numbers?

ME: Yes.

STUDENT: Is it above normal, above 100?

ME: Yes.

STUDENT: Then how can you FOG me if I say: "Your IQ is so far below normal that half a moron could replace you?"

ME: Simple. I'd say: "I'm not surprised you feel that way. Sometimes my brain works so poorly that I wonder if the IQ examiner didn't make a mistake."

STUDENT: Let's try something else. Are you queer?

ME: I don't think so.

STUDENT: Let me put it another way. Are you a practicing homosexual?

ME: No.

STUDENT: Then how can you agree with me if I say:

"You're the faggiest teacher I've ever seen. You swish all over the place!"

ME: Again simple. I can say: "Maybe you're right. I wonder if that's why I'm not as sexually potent as I used to be. At seventeen I used to think about sex all the time. Now I only think about it half the time!" I'm not perfect in anything. Want to try another one?

Another occasional comment I get from students, after I demonstrate FOGGING by having them criticize my teaching style is: "But were you *sincere* in agreeing with my criticism with FOGGING?" I answer this question with one of two (hopefully) thought-provoking questions in reply, either: "How sincere is a probability?" or as my colleague Fred Sherman often says in response to the same question in his classes in the San Diego area: "Does it really matter?" One interpretation of this type of question is that the student (or anyone else) who asks it is very wedded to logic and all the other external systems that can be used to manipulate you out of being your own judge. In thinking of one particular person who asked him this question, Fred remarked that in order for her to be happy with Fred as a teacher, he had to be "all sincere" or "all insincere." She wouldn't, or more charitably, couldn't allow him any middle ground between these extremes. Someone who is neither sincere nor insincere wasn't capable of being moved by her logic. As it turned out, the use of probabilities to describe what is reality and what is truth was not to her liking since it gave her a clear and unmistakable message of: "Hey. I'm not manipulable. I don't fit into your game plan. You don't like that? Okay. Find someone you're more comfortable with."

It is obvious, to me at least, from teaching hundreds of people to be more assertive, that FOGGING is the most popularly received of all verbal skills. Recently, after one class, I ran into a former student, a physicist at the Jet Propulsion Laboratories, set up and administered by the California Institute of Technology, and he told me an amusing story. The night before this incident happened, I had given an introductory demonstration of assertive verbal skills to a number of Cal. Tech. students on campus. The following day, the physicist noticed one of the student assistants in the laboratory going around all morning and indiscriminately using a FOGGING response in reply to anything said to him. He kept enthusiastically saying: "You may be right," to everything, including statements like: "You want some coffee?" Having heard me describe this typical phase of learning in class as "the impulse you get, after you are given a brand-new shiny set of tools, to go around looking for loose nuts to tighten up," and having gone through it himself, the physicist knew I would appreciate the humor inherent in the situation. I did, and the more he described this student's provocation of criticism from other staff members so he could practice FOGGING, the more an inane fantasy kept playing itself out in my mind. With all due apologies to JPL, Cal. Tech., their superb faculty and students, I couldn't help but picture this student saying to an irate professor: "You're right, I shouldn't have goosed you while you were leaning over the atom splitter."

With a Puckish glint in his eye, but also with some sympathy for the novice FOGGER, the physicist told me that he was tempted to go up to the unaware student and say something like: "Harry, I've noticed that you've been using a lot of FOGGING this morning. Don't you think you could save it for manipulative situations?" He restrained his impulse out of his own identification with the student's situation. He remembered how enthusiastic he himself felt in first being more assertive and learning to cope better with other people. In spite of his altruism, he still wished he could have heard the novice's probable response, "You mean you know this already?" and watch his jaw drop when he replied: "Of course. Everybody knows about FOGGING. Where have you been?" While appreciating the humor in his aborted prank, I asked him: "What makes you think he wouldn't have simply replied: 'You may be right. I probably am overdoing it'?" The physicist looked at me and said in kind: "I should have thought of that. He might have!" and we exchanged understanding grins.

The examination of all this somewhat serious, somewhat tongue-in-cheek discussion of FOGGING hopefully points out its therapeutic purpose—to enable the learner to look at his own personal qualities, the ones he has doubts about, without feeling insecure, and to say meaningfully, "So what? I can still cope quite well enough with what I have and be effective and happy." Just understanding this concept, however, is insufficient. The systematic practice of FOGGING provides what cognitive understanding—knowing you can agree with your critic—does not give, the reduction of conditioned, gut-twisting anxiety in response to the stimulus of personal criticism.

NEGATIVE ASSERTION

At the same time that I was working on the problem of teaching patients how to cope with manipulative criticism of their behavior through FOGGING, it became apparent to me that these people also made errors because of their reduced ability to cope with things in general. In order for them to be able to be more assertive, to begin again to live with other people, they also had to learn to cope with their errors without falling apart in the face of hostile criticism of these errors. As I began to teach nonassertive people in nonclinical settings how to cope, it became glaringly apparent that *many of us have the same difficulty* in coping with our errors in everyday life. As one novice learner asked: "How can I cope differently and keep my dignity and self-respect when someone criticizes me for making a mistake that, without a doubt, is a bonafide, 100 per cent error, not a probable one, and I am guilty of it?" If you are like him, like most of the rest of us, in order to cope more realistically with your errors in life, you must learn to change your verbal behavior when confronted with your error and modify your trained belief that *guilt* automatically is associated with making a mistake.

If you are nonassertive in coping with your mistakes, you can be manipulated by other nonassertive people through your feelings of guilt and anxiety into (1) seeking forgiveness for making the error and somehow making up for it, or (2) denying the error through defensiveness and countercriticism which provides your hostile critic with a verbal punching bag to aggressively work out his own feelings of frustration. In either case, you cope poorly and feel worse.

Again, as with most of the beliefs we learned in childhood, few of us can change our belief that errors are wrong *(we are guilty)* simply by thinking about it. Most of us must first change our verbal coping behavior when confronted with an error so that we can emotionally desensitize ourselves to possible criticism from other people (or from ourselves). Once this emotional change is accomplished through behavior change, the childish belief of guilt through error will automatically change. It is difficult to maintain a negative belief about yourself when it is no longer supported by feeling rotten about yourself as a result.

How, then, do you cope assertively with your errors? In the simplest manner, you verbally cope with your errors as if they are exactly that, no more or no less— errors are just errors. In the terminology of systematic assertion, *you assertively accept* those things that are negative about yourself. In the spring of 1970, during my appointment at the Veterans Hospital, I used the verbal skill that I call NEGATIVE ASSERTION to help people to learn more quickly in coping with errors or negative points about themselves. For example, when you are confronted in a critical, possibly hostile manner with an error you have made, you can assertively accept the fact of the error in the following way. Assume you have agreed to leave an information file on your desk at work so a fellow employee could use it over the weekend. On Monday morning, the friend approaches you and asks where the file was on Saturday. You remember that the file was locked up on Friday night and not left on your desk. What can you say? In negatively asserting yourself, you would probably say something like: "Oh, my God! I forgot to leave it on my desk! What an incredibly stupid thing to do! I must be brain-damaged! What are you going to do now?" Depending upon how your fellow employee receives this information, it would be repeated until he or she realizes that it serves little or no purpose to criticize your error since such behavior will not turn back the clock and produce the file when he needed it.

In other areas, NEGATIVE ASSERTION can be used to cope differently when receiving valid criticism of your performance in learning a concept, a new skill, a new language, a new trade on the job or in a social situation. In any of these situations, when substandard performance is pointed out, you can cope assertively as follows:

"You didn't do too well in . . . (criticism)*

"You're right. *I wasn't too smart in the way I handled that, was I?"* [NEGATIVE ASSERTION]

We can negatively assert ourselves even when our personal competence, habits, or appearance is critically appraised: "Sis, for a young girl with a good figure, you sure walk like a fullback." *"I've noticed that myself. I do walk funny, don't I?"* [NEGATIVE ASSERTION] or

"Sue, you shouldn't have cut your hair. It just doesn't suit you now." *"That was a dumb thing for me to do, Mom. I don't like it this way myself."* [NEGATIVE ASSERTION] or

"My God, Connie! That new outfit makes you look like mutton dressed up like lamb."
"I was worried about that. These new styles just don't suit me at all, do they?" [NEGATIVE ASSERTION]

One important point to remember, these assertive verbal skills were developed to help you cope with social conflicts, not physical or legal ones! If someone says to you critically: "You just ran over my foot when

---

*Examples: . . . figuring that out; . . . mastering that; . . . translating that sentence; . . . using that tool; . . . doing that work; . . . making an impression on Nancy.

you backed up your car," the appropriate response is *not:* "How stupid of me!" but instead, "Here is the number of my insurance company (or my lawyer)."

In using NEGATIVE ASSERTION to cope with criticism of your errors, the persistence of your critic will determine if you need assert yourself in other ways also, such as by using FOGGING and NEGATIVE INQUIRY. This type of mixed dialogue in response to criticism of error is given in Chapters 9, 10, and 11.

Although it may seem paradoxical at first glance, those of us who cannot cope assertively with criticism also seem incapable of coping with compliments. If we are hard-pressed to cope with criticism, it certainly seems as if we would take all the compliments we get as a relief from the negative marks chalked up against us. Unfortunately, for most of us, this isn't the case. When we are praised or complimented, we stammer, mumble something, look and act sheepish, feel like twisting our hat in our hands, and change the subject as quickly as possible. This coping inadequacy is not due to modesty. It has roots in our childish belief that other people are the real judges of our actions. If, on the other hand, we are independently assertive in our thoughts, feelings, and behavior, we reserve the final judgment of actions, even the positive ones, to ourselves. Such an assertive attitude does not make you loath to accept compliments and praise, but only to be the ultimate judge of the accuracy of such praise. For example, when you are genuinely complimented on your choice of clothes and you feel they suit you well, you might reply: "Thank you. *I think it looks nice on me too.*" (AGREEING WITH TRUTH). On the other hand, when you suspect manipulative flattery, you might respond: "Really, I don't understand. What is it about my clothes that makes me look so good?" (POSITIVE INQUIRY; see Chapter 7.) If you have mixed feelings about the thing, behavior, accomplishment, etc., for which you are complimented, you might disclose your true feelings; "I appreciate your compliment, but I haven't yet decided myself how good it is." When assertively coping with positive comments you may use different words from those in coping with negative comments, but the basic assertive coping behavior and attitude are the same; you are your own ultimate judge of all you are.

7

Prompting people you care about to be more assertive and less manipulative toward you

FOGGING works very well in dealing with the manipulative criticism of people you relate to formally or commercially, people who are not very close to you. FOGGING is a very effective skill for desensitizing you to criticism and actually reducing the frequency of criticism from others. It rapidly sets up a psychological distance, boundary lines between you and the person you FOG. It is a passive skill, however, and does not prompt the person you are coping with to be assertive himself—which is what you really want—instead of manipulative toward you, a condition much to be desired if you are in frequent close contact with this person, such as a husband, wife, parent, family member, or close friend. The probability of achieving assertiveness in the other person too is much more likely with the use of the verbal skill I call NEGATIVE INQUIRY. As in learning FOGGING, when you use NEGATIVE INQUIRY, you do not respond to your critic's statements of wrongdoing with denial, defensiveness, or countermanipulation with criticisms of your own. Instead, you break the manipulative cycle by *actively* prompting further criticism about yourself or by prompting more information about statements of "wrongdoing" from the critical person in an unemotional, low-key manner. As the label of the skill describes, you ask for more things about yourself or your behavior that may be negative.

NEGATIVE INQUIRY

To understand the concept of NEGATIVE INQUIRY, look at the difference between two similar statements in response to criticism. Let's assume for instance that they are in response to criticism from your wife (or husband as the case may be): (1) "I don't understand. What is it about my going fishing that is bad?" (2) "What makes you think going fishing is bad?" The first statement is an assertive, nondefensive NEGATIVE INQUIRY response that is noncritical of your spouse and prompts her to make further critical statements and to examine her own structure of right and wrong which she is using to cope in this particular conflict situation. The second statement is quite defensive, directing attention away from yourself and toward your wife. The second statement can easily be interpreted, and in most cases correctly so, as sarcastic and belittling toward her. The difference between these two statements, which seem to say the same thing, is enormous. With the first statement in response to criticism, you are pointing a finger at yourself and, in effect, saying: "Let's look at what I am doing that may be wrong or that you don't like." *You are also behaving as if criticism is not something to get upset over*. With the second statement, you point a finger at your wife (or whoever is criticizing you) and, in effect, say: "Who the hell are you to tell me anything?"

If in response to your statement of: "What is it about my fishing that is bad?" your wife comes up with "logical" or "good" reasons why fishing is bad, such as: "It gives you a headache . . ." or "It makes you smell . . ." or "It will tire you out . . ." you can still inquire (negatively): "I don't understand. What is it about going fishing and getting a headache (or getting tired or smelly) that is wrong?" By persistently using NEGATIVE INQUIRY to ask for more information about critical statements such as: "It will tire you out . . ." you will extinguish the use of such manipulative structure statements and your wife is more likely to assert herself about the subject that bothers her most about your fishing: i.e., "When you are so tired, we don't go out in the evening (or make love, or have any fun, or whatever)." The critical issue of the conflict in behavior is then out in the open and can be dealt with assertively by both of you, working out some compromise whereby you can go fishing and she can still get what she wants (if you do not get frightened and resort to your old responses of denial, defensiveness, and countercriticism to avoid assertively dealing with your wife's wishes).

The end result of the first NEGATIVE INQUIRY interaction will, in the best case, be an examination by your wife of her own arbitrary right-and-wrong structure, i.e., headaches are wrong, being tired is wrong, being smelly is wrong—the structure she is trying to impose to manipulate you in lieu of asserting her own wishes to do something else besides fishing or staying around the house in the evening. The optimal end result is your wife's discarding her coping through imposed right-and-wrong structure in the relationship and the initiation of asserting her own wishes to you. If she does not respond assertively by saying what she wants, the end result of the first NEGATIVE INQUIRY verbal interaction will, in the worst case, be a standoff, with her manipulative criticism temporarily extinguished. If the optimal end result of NEGATIVE INQUIRY assertion does not come about, and the interaction results only in a stalemate with the extinction of critical statements, you can attempt to break the stalemate by NEGATIVE INQUIRY prompting of your spouse to assert herself. For example, you might inquire (negatively): "I really don't understand. There must be some other reasons for me not to go fishing besides getting tired, smelling up the house, or having headaches. What else is wrong or what don't you like about my going fishing?" With such noncritical encouragement, your wife is more likely to respond assertively in telling you what *she wants* to do on the weekend, and some compromise that pays off for both of you can be worked out.

Unfortunately, much behavior in dispute results from this very common dealing in right-and-wrong structure. Examples of other behavior that husbands and wives in therapy get into conflict over through manipulation of each other's styles are dressing habits, neatness, not being on time, balancing the checkbook without any error, paying the bills promptly, social flirting, division of household labor, responsibility for the children, etc., etc., etc. Right-and-wrong manipulation in these behavioral areas can be extinguished by NEGATIVE INQUIRY to facilitate real negotiation of personal likes and dislikes, leading to a workable compromise.

In training people to grasp the nondefensive concept behind NEGATIVE INQUIRY, I have used the following general training dialogue as a first exercise. In this exercise, nonsituational criticism is directed to the learner by myself or another learner, and the learner is coached on appropriate NEGATIVE INQUIRY responses to this criticism. As in the FOGGING exercise, the critic first makes derogatory comments about the learner's dressing habits, a subject which most of us can tolerate with a minimum of distress. After the learner is able to cope with such criticism through NEGATIVE INQUIRY without denial, defensiveness, or aggressive countercriticism, the critic gradually moves his criticism into the more personal area of physical appearance and then into the personality traits and "moral" character of the learner. This standard training dialogue takes from ten to fifteen minutes and is repeated weekly in class, group therapy, and in homework exercises with a friend until the learner does not automatically respond defensively during the dialogue. The learner is instructed, as in the use of FOGGING, not to overlay the NEGATIVE INQUIRY verbal skill with sarcasm as novices are apt to do. Sarcasm—thinly veiled verbal aggression—in executing NEGATIVE INQUIRY will trigger alternative aggressive responses instead of repetitive criticisms from the critical person and in all likelihood will terminate the interaction and possibly the relationship. One of my patients, Sharon, showing up in group therapy with a brand-new black eye, commented: "I should have listened to you. Instead, I found out the hard way, you don't *sarcastically* fog or negatively inquire with your boy friend!"

Dialogue #5
A beginning practice exercise
using NEGATIVE
INQUIRY to
cope with
criticism.

PAUL: Beth, you don't look good today.

BETH: What do you mean, Paul?

PAUL: Well, I noticed the way you appear today. It doesn't look too good.

BETH: *Is it the way I look or is it the way I'm dressed?* [NEGATIVE INQUIRY]

PAUL: Well, that blouse doesn't look too good.

BETH: *What is it about the blouse that makes me look bad?* [NEGATIVE INQUIRY response]

PAUL: Well, it just doesn't seem to fit.

BETH: *Do you think it's too loose?* [NEGATIVE INQUIRY prompt]

PAUL: Well, maybe that's it.

BETH: How about the color of it, *does that make me look funny?* [NEGATIVE INQUIRY prompt]

PAUL: The color doesn't look too good.

BETH: *Anything else besides the color that's bad?* [NEGATIVE INQUIRY prompt]

PAUL: No, that's it.

BETH: How about my pants? *How do they look?* [NEGATIVE INQUIRY prompt]

PAUL: Not too good.

BETH: *What is it about them that makes me look bad?* [NEGATIVE INQUIRY response]

PAUL: They just don't look right.

BETH: *How about the color?* [NEGATIVE INQUIRY prompt]

PAUL: No, it's not the color.

BETH: *How about the cut of them?* [NEGATIVE INQUIRY prompt]

PAUL: They look sloppy.

BETH: *Is there anything else about me that doesn't come off right?* [NEGATIVE INQUIRY prompt]

PAUL: Well, you tend to talk a lot.

BETH: Let me understand this. I talk too much? [NEGATIVE INQUIRY prompt]

PAUL: You tend to drag things down and just keep going on and on and on.

BETH: *You mean I just won't give up?* [NEGATIVE INQUIRY prompt]

PAUL: Yeah, that's it, you just keep talking and won't accept what I tell you.

BETH: Well, let me get this straight now. *You're saying that I won't listen to you?* [NEGATIVE INQUIRY prompt]

PAUL: It's just that you don't seem to care if I tell you anything or not.

BETH: *It sounds like you're saying I'm insensitive, is that right?* [NEGATIVE INQUIRY prompt]

PAUL: That's it. You're insensitive.

BETH: *Is there anything else that I'm doing besides being insensitive?* [NEGATIVE INQUIRY prompt]

PAUL: Yes, you just seem different somehow.

BETH: *What is it about what I'm doing that's different?* [NEGATIVE INQUIRY response]

PAUL: What you're doing now, you're just doing something entirely different.

BETH: *Will you tell me some more about it?* [NEGATIVE INQUIRY prompt]

PAUL: No, I don't think so.

BETH: Well, next time we get together perhaps you'll feel like talking about it some more, okay?

PAUL: Okay.

Although NEGATIVE INQUIRY occasionally is useful in dealing with conflict in formal or partially structured relationships (especially in conjunction with the other assertive verbal skills), it helps most in assertively dealing with people you are close to, in unstructured equal relationships by: (1) desensitizing you to criticism from people you care about so you can listen to what they tell you; (2) extinguishing repetitive manipulative criticism from these people so it doesn't drive you up the wall; and (3) reducing the use of right-and-wrong structure by these persons in dealing with you, prompting them to *assertively* say what they want so that compromises giving both of you a piece of the action can be worked out.

Dialogue #6
Bobbie uses NEGATIVE INQUIRY to cope with a neighbor's manipulation.

An excellent example of using only NEGATIVE INQUIRY to deal with conflict between neighbors was reported by Bobbie, a suburban housewife learning to be assertive. Bobbie, through her lack of assertiveness, and because she had no children, and partially to keep from being bored out of her mind, had assumed the complete responsibility of maintaining her home and grounds while her husband engaged in his successful accounting practice. After learning BROKEN RECORD, FOGGING, and NEGATIVE ASSERTION, Bobbie was particularly fascinated with her introduction to NEGATIVE INQUIRY. The week after her first practice in this verbal skill, she reported the following short dialogue with her next-door neighbor, George. For several months, George has been talking of putting in a backyard swimming pool where he could sunbathe in the nude. Each time he spoke to Bobbie about it, she told him: "Great. You can get a super healthy tan that way." Bobbie felt, from George's reaction that, for some reason, this wasn't what he wanted her to say.

Setting of the dialogue: Bobbie is pruning some rose bushes along the common chain-link fence between their houses (which they shared the cost on) and her neighbor, George, approaches her from his side of the fence.

GEORGE: I'm going to have to start digging all these bushes out soon. This fence we put up five years ago is shot. I'll have to put a hollow brick wall in here.

BOBBIE: I don't understand. What is it about the fence that is shot?

GEORGE: It's just going to fall over one of these days.

BOBBIE: What is it about it that's going to make it fall over one of these days?

GEORGE: It's those trees you got behind it.

(Bobbie has several eight-foot Japanese maples planted alongside the fence with some branches poking through it.)

BOBBIE: What is it about the trees that will make it fall over?

GEORGE: It's those branches poking through. They are going to push it right over.

BOBBIE: I don't understand. What is it about the branches that will knock it over?

GEORGE: (Silent for a moment and then changing the subject) Do you know anything about pruning apricot trees? How about that one there? Do you think I pruned that one right?

Bobbie became aware during this interaction that George was trying to manipulate her into subsidizing half the cost of a voyeur-proof hollow brick wall between their homes. In her relationship with him, Bobbie really didn't give a damn if George was more assertive with her or not. She was satisfied that she could cope with his manipulative reasons on why she "should" pay for a new wall and let it go at that. She did not feel compelled to therapeutically prompt George to come right out and say what he wanted: a half-price screen so he could romp around in the nude. After all, she would only say "No" to his request even if she spent all that effort on prompting someone she really didn't care about to be more assertive. George, incidentally, on last report, never brought the subject up again.

Up to this point, I have stressed learning to be assertive by practicing the verbal skills of BROKEN RECORD, FOGGING, NEGATIVE ASSERTION, and NEGATIVE INQUIRY in response to manipulative attempts, however benign, to control your behavior.

The practice of these skills has a second purpose which it would be quite foolish to forget or even to underemphasize: *the breaking of our own habits of being defensive and anxious when someone tells us something that we don't like.* The truth is that our critics are not always manipulative or acting out of their own personal sense of insecurity. There are some of us in this frantic world who give others feedback on their behavior and performance without any other motivation than the noblest one, to help. A supervisor, however manipulative he may be with his wife, often refuses a merit raise in pay simply because performance on the job is not meritorious. In assertively dealing with this situation, for example, you can prompt further criticism from your supervisor using all the assertive skills, and empathic NEGATIVE INQUIRY in particular, to improve communication between the two of you. With these skills you give him several unmistakable messages: first, you are interested in improving your performance to the meritorious level; second, you do not crumple when criticized, but you seek criticism and use it; and third, by giving you more regular critical feedback in the future, he can help you achieve your goal of excellent performance on the job. An added side benefit from coping with such difficult situations in this nondefensive, assertive, and confident way is the improvement of relations, working and personal, between your critic and yourself. In my personal (and clinical) experiences in these situations I have found that when you respond nondefensively to your critic, you help make his sometimes very difficult job of giving negative feedback much easier by showing interest in his point of view.

Dialogue #7
Prompting criticism
of your work
to get a
raise

The following short dialogue between me and a student who wanted to know how to ask for a raise illus-

trates the point of using empathic NEGATIVE IN-
QUIRY to deal with nonmanipulative criticism without
becoming anxious and defensive of yourself.

ME: Harry, I've been meaning to ask you why you
don't recommend me for a meritorious raise.

STUDENT: Sure, Pete. It's simple, you didn't deserve
it.

ME: I don't understand, Harry. *What did I do that
was unmeritorious?* [NEGATIVE INQUIRY re-
sponse]

STUDENT: Well, for one thing, you're new on the
job. Less than six months, right?

ME: Right!

STUDENT: You haven't had the time to learn all the
ropes yet. You're not doing bad. You're just average.

ME: *What is it I'm doing that makes me just average?*
[NEGATIVE INQUIRY response]

STUDENT: You're making all the typical mistakes
that the new guy usually makes.

ME: *What am I doing specifically that I'm screwing up?* [NEGATIVE INQUIRY response]

STUDENT: A couple of things. Like, for instance,
that estimating job on the cost of the air ducts in the El
Rincon apartment building.

ME: Okay. *How did I screw up on that one?* [NEG-
ATIVE INQUIRY response]

STUDENT: You underestimated costs by three hundred bucks. We lost that because of your errors.

ME: *I guess that was dumb of me not to check my
figures out with one of the older guys or maybe even
you.* [NEGATIVE ASSERTION]

STUDENT: Don't worry about it. We all make mistakes and you are going to have your share of them.

ME: *Anything else I'm doing that's just average and
I could improve?* [NEGATIVE INQUIRY prompt]

STUDENT: A couple of other things.

ME: Let's hear them.

STUDENT: You're still a bit slow in getting the work
in.

ME: *I'm taking too much time?* [NEGATIVE IN-QUIRY response]

STUDENT: No. Not too much time. Just average for your experience.

ME: *Anything else?* [NEGATIVE INQUIRY prompt]

STUDENT: One more that I can think of. When you turn in your drawings, make the small print a bit clearer. After it's blueprinted, it gets hard to read.

ME: *Is that all you can think of now that makes me just average?* [NEGATIVE INQUIRY prompt]

STUDENT: That's about it.

ME: Okay, let me see, *it sounds like I'm not checking my work carefully enough, right?* [NEGATIVE IN-QUIRY prompt]

STUDENT: Yeah, that sounds like it.

ME. And *I could speed things up without making more dumb mistakes that cost money?* [NEGATIVE INQUIRY prompt]

STUDENT: Yup.

ME: And *I could be more careful of the neatness of the work I turn in?* [NEGATIVE INQUIRY prompt]

STUDENT: That sounds about it.

ME: Well, I want a crack at the meritorious list next time. I'd like to go over some of the things I may have an occasional doubt about with you. *Since I have to improve, I want to do it as fast as possible.* [NEGA-TIVE ASSERTION]

STUDENT: Sure.

In another example illustrating this point, I draw from my own experiences as a clinical intern. When I was a novice therapist, like all the others I had a weekly conference with an expert clinician on how well (or poorly) I had performed in working with patients. This was before I began my own work in developing assertive verbal skills for my patients to use to cope with conflict. As I had had most of my graduate train-ing in experimental learning theory and psychophysiol-ogy, my clinical supervisors strongly felt that I could benefit by being "coached" by an analytic (Neo-Freudian) supervisor. Feeling terrible in having to learn something I knew nothing about (except "Cocktail Party Freud"), I was quite nervous and defensive during that first feedback session on my performance in approaching the patient's problem using the analytical method. But about halfway through that first session, as I remember it, some of what my coach was criticizing me about began to make sense: when I began to translate what he was telling me, in Freudian terms, into what I was more familiar with—learning theory and behavior therapy. At that point I became fascinated with his analysis of the patient's problem and my performance. I began to prompt him to tell me more of the "why" of what I was doing that was poor and could he think of any other things I did that made the session more difficult for the patient. This I did to see if his clinical predictions would match my own, drawn from learning theory. In a crude way, I was making a NEGATIVE INQUIRY of my own performance to see how I could improve it and try to connect what he was teaching me to what I understood about behavior already. Needless to say, during that internship year I learned more about Neo-Freudian clinical technique than any other student of that professor! During our feedback sessions, I exhausted him! But he also liked it and once said: "Pete, you are one of the easiest students to work with that I know. You don't get defensive about learning and how you can improve your down-home, folksy, low-key, cornball, seductive style of therapy. You have even taught me something about psychophysiology." The lesson I learned from being nondefensive in an authoritarian situation? *If you are not dealing with manipulation, then prompting criticism may eventually result in praise,* and as it turned out for me, a lifelong friendship.

The idea of prompting criticism about yourself from others can also help improve communications in equal relationships as well as authoritarian ones. Someone you are close to—or would prefer to be closer to—may not be primarily manipulative in his or her style of interacting with you; instead this person may simply have a passive style of coping which makes it very difficult for him or her to assertively complain or state what changes are wanted from you in the relationship. *And without an outlet for resolving differences, an equal relationship is destined for failure.* You may also consider the possibility that your own past behavior, be it manipulative, or perhaps showing you as quick to anger when criticized, or perhaps at times even in fearful flight, may have been one of the factors causing this passivity in your friend or mate; or at least it has not helped him to change his equally destructive way of coping with you. The practiced use of such verbal skills as FOGGING, NEGATIVE ASSERTION, and NEGATIVE INQUIRY can be helpful in opening up close communication by giving you, the learner, an alternate way of prompting your mate to express him- or herself. These verbal skills, after much practice, also can give you the ability to cope with and look at any grievances you prompt from your mate that are attributed to you personally. Their use *first* in other situations reduces your automatic, conditioned response of feeling anxious and defensive when criticized and helps break your old habit of responding to your mate's criticism with such classics as: "What do you mean I'm always down on you? If you would change and shape up (do what I want you to do), you wouldn't upset me so much!" With such a manipulative and guilt-inducing response to your mate's criticism and request for change, is it surprising that he or she decides to take the passive route and withdraws from close ways of interrelating with you? As you will see, in some of the last dialogues in this manuscript, this empathic new way of coping with a passive partner by a formerly defensive and/or manipulative mate is discussed in detail.

Let us turn now to what the first half of this book has been leading up to: assertively coping with the common problems that other people are apt to give us in such generous amounts as we live our everyday lives.

8

Everyday commercial situations—
assertively coping where
money is involved

In previous chapters I talked about the systematic practice of each verbal assertive skill in turn. Although other verbal skills were also used in the dialogues given to explain each skill, each dialogue emphasized the use of one of the assertive skills over all the others. In everyday situations that require you to be assertive, you will be more adept in coping with manipulation if you remember that the verbal skills interlock very well in an assertive verbal sequence. In a particular situation, you might find it efficient to employ one or all of the skills to keep other people from manipulating you and to achieve your goal or a workable compromise.

Except for the specified training dialogues, all the assertive interactions offered in the following chapters are reports of real situations from learners using the systematic assertive skills out in the field. They were transcribed from notes, memory, tape recordings, and verbatim reports of students, patients, colleagues, acquaintances, and friends and were edited for purposes of confidentiality, brevity, clarity, and instruction. Some of the dialogues are quite short and, as you can see, are examples of how some manipulation is rapidly extinguished. Others are quite long, and are left in their lengthy state to emphasize how persistent you need to be in some situations. These dialogues are offered as examples of using all of the systematic verbal skills in a variety of situations. Although the situations given do not cover every possible instance where you might find assertive coping helpful, they do indicate how you can cope in similar situations, even though specific dialogues covering each instance are not given. Manipulation through guilt, anxiety, or ignorance induction is still manipulation, whether it comes from your used-car dealer, your physician, your lawyer, your friends, or your mother-in-law. The basic skills to cope with manipulation from any source are the same, even if different words are used. Although you may emphasize the use of one skill over another, depending upon the conflict you find yourself in, the systematic assertive skills of BROKEN RECORD, FOGGING, NEGATIVE INQUIRY, and NEGATIVE ASSERTION are general coping skills and are not limited in use only to certain situations or with certain people.

Dialogue #8
Coping with a
door-to-door
salesman

This first mixed dialogue is a training exercise that I use in class or therapy and, hopefully, the learners have the good fortune to encounter the situation on their doorstep. In this exercise, a stranger comes to your front door and introduces him or herself as either: (1) a disabled veteran of the Spanish-American War, World War I, World War II, Korean, or Vietnam conflict, depending upon his apparent age; (2) a representative of the society for all the world's crippled children; (3) a representative of a minority group in plight; (4) a college student working his way toward a scholarship; or (5) just a neighbor from down the way (who has never met you during the brief, fourteen-year period you have lived in your house or apartment) and is working on a project to send children from the neighborhood to summer camp in the mountains away from all the urban, suburban (or even rural) congestion, smog, and unhealthy influences. After introducing himself, the stranger then explains that he is selling subscriptions to a variety of interesting magazines and a certain percentage of the profit from your purchases will be donated by his company to the worthy cause he represents (see 1 through 5 above).

Setting of the dialogue: the door-to-door salesman has just introduced himself and his wares and starts out with a statement:

SALESMAN: I'm sure you would want to have these magazines in your home for your education and enjoyment.

LEARNER: I can understand how you would feel that way, but they don't interest me.

SALESMAN: You should think of the benefits that these crippled children will get if you buy these magazines.

LEARNER: *That's true, I should,* but *I'm not interested.* [FOGGING and BROKEN RECORD]

SALESMAN: If we get enough people to sign up, this could mean a real breakthrough in science and medical treatment for them.

LEARNER: *You're probably right,* but *I'm not interested.* [FOGGING and BROKEN RECORD]

SALESMAN: I can't believe that you would let these children go off suffering and unhelped.

LEARNER: *I can see that you don't believe that,* but *I'm not interested.* [FOGGING and BROKEN RECORD]

SALESMAN: All your neighbors have signed up.

LEARNER: *I don't doubt it,* but *I'm not interested.* [FOGGING and BROKEN RECORD]

SALESMAN: What kind of person doesn't care for little children, crippled children?

LEARNER: *I don't know.* [SELF-DISCLOSURE]

SALESMAN: (Taking new approach) Do you subscribe to any other magazines?

LEARNER: *I'm really not interested in buying any.* [BROKEN RECORD]

SALESMAN: Well, you see these are not the only magazines we have in this program. If you are already subscribing to some, I can probably renew your subscription to them and these poor children can benefit from you.

LEARNER: Thank you, but *I'm not interested.* [BROKEN RECORD]

SALESMAN: Is your husband (or wife) at home; I'm

sure he would be interested in this magazine on home tools.

LEARNER: *He probably would be,* but *I'm not going to buy it.* [FOGGING and BROKEN RECORD]

SALESMAN: Can I speak to him?

LEARNER: *I'm not interested.* [BROKEN RECORD]

SALESMAN: How about your children, we have a good set of educational magazines for them. You do want them to learn quicker and get good grades, don't you?

LEARNER: *That's true, I do,* but *I don't want to buy any magazines.* [FOGGING and BROKEN RECORD]

SALESMAN: You won't give an inch, will you, even for your own children?

LEARNER: *You're right.* I won't. [FOGGING]

SALESMAN: Well, I'm glad the rest of your neighbors are not like you.

LEARNER: *I'm sure you are.* [FOGGING]

In training learners to deal with commercial situations, many of them say that they just shut the door in the salesman's face because they don't want to even bother with him and his nonsense. I advise these students that assertively coping with situations like these that are not important is a safe, low-risk, real-life method of practicing to be systematically assertive in preparation for the more meaningful conflicts they have with other people. It's like running around the track to get in shape before you run in the real race. I urge them not to avoid such confrontations when learning, and after they become proficient and feel comfortable asserting themselves through such practices, then they can shut the door in the salesman's face if they want to.

Let's now look at a real-life dialogue in which a customer asserts herself to a department store manager in order to get a refund on defective merchandise.

Dialogue #9
Anne returns a pair of
defective boots to a
large department
store.

Anne, a young, attractive woman, purchased her first pair of calf-length boots specifically to wear to several parties during the holiday season. Midway through the first dinner party, the heel on the left boot fell off. This defect infuriated her at the time and prompted her to vow that she was going to get back the money that she had paid for this shoddy merchandise.

Setting of the dialogue: Two days later, she walks up to a clerk of the shoe department.

CLERK: Can I help you?

ANNE: *Perhaps,* but I'd prefer to speak to the manager of the shoe department. [FOGGING]

CLERK: He's busy right at the moment. Do you have a complaint?

ANNE: *I'm sure he is busy,* but *I'd still like to speak to him.* [FOGGING and BROKEN RECORD]

CLERK: (Silent for a moment) Let me see if I can get him for you.

ANNE: Good, *I'd like to see him.* [BROKEN RECORD] (Clerk disappears into doorway behind counter for a few minutes and then reappears and speaks to Anne)

CLERK: He will be with you in just a minute.

ANNE: (Looking at her watch) Thank you. (Five minutes pass. Anne approaches the clerk again and speaks to her.)

ANNE: What is the manager's name?

CLERK: (Looking distressed) Oh! He's Mr. Simon.

ANNE: I would like you to tell Mr. Simon that *I still want to speak to him. If he will not see me now, I want to know when he will see me or when I can see his supervisor.* (BROKEN RECORD and WORKABLE COMPROMISE]

CLERK: (Quickly disappears into room behind counter. She reappears a few moments later followed by Mr. Simon. Mr. Simon walks up to Anne and speaks.)

MANAGER: (Smiling) What can I do for you?

ANNE: (Showing manager defective boots) I want a refund on these boots I bought from you last week. They are defective. The heel fell off the first time I wore them.

MANAGER: (Examining boots) Umm ... This has never happened before to any of this line of boots. (Possibly implying: "What did you do to them?")

ANNE: *I'm sure that this has never happened before,* but it has happened now so *I'm really not interested in the other boots you sold.* I am only concerned about this pair and *I want my money refunded.* [FOGGING, SELF-DISCLOSURE, and BROKEN RECORD]

MANAGER: (Putting boots back in bag) Well, we like to see if we can fix anything defective before we make a refund. Let me send these to our repairman and we'll see what he can do.

ANNE: *I'm sure that you would like to see if you can fix them before refunding my money,* but *I'm not interested in getting them fixed. I want my money back.* [FOGGING, SELF-DISCLOSURE, and BROKEN RECORD]

MANAGER: It's not our policy to accept damaged merchandise for a refund.

ANNE: *I'm sure that is your policy,* but these boots are unacceptable and *I want a refund on my account.* [FOGGING and BROKEN RECORD]

MANAGER: (Looking curiously at Anne) You say you just wore them once?

ANNE: Yes, and *I want a refund.* [BROKEN RECORD]

MANAGER: Were you dancing in them?

ANNE: I don't understand. *What is it about dancing that is bad for these boots?* [NEGATIVE INQUIRY]

MANAGER: Well, some people mistreat boots when they are dancing.

ANNE: *I'm sure that's true,* but *are these boots*

constructed so poorly that they shouldn't be danced in?
[FOGGING and NEGATIVE INQUIRY]

MANAGER: No ... You should be able to dance in them.

ANNE: *I'm very glad you told me that. It convinces me that this is shoddy merchandise. I want a refund.* [SELF-DISCLOSURE and BROKEN RECORD]

MANAGER: I'm sure we can get them fixed perfectly for you.

ANNE: *I'm sure you feel that way,* but when I pay this much money for merchandise and it is defective, *it is totally unacceptable to me. I want a full refund to my account.* [FOGGING, SELF-DISCLOSURE, and BROKEN RECORD]

MANAGER: But we can't do that.

ANNE: *I'm sure you really feel that way,* but *I want a refund* and not repaired boots for my money. [FOGGING and BROKEN RECORD]

MANAGER: Well, let me see what I can do. (He walks away. Anne looks at her watch, and then looks around her. Behind her is another woman holding a pair of boots with one seam torn and an elderly woman in a sable coat sitting a few feet to one side. Noting that both women are paying attention to her confrontation with the manager, Anne begins to feel a little sheepish and embarrassed. This feeling is quickly dispelled when the older woman in the fur coat leans forward and says softly to her: "Stick to your guns, dear. Don't let him get away with it." After a few minutes, the manager reappears and walks up to Anne and speaks to her.)

MANAGER: I realize this is inconvenient to you, but I just spoke to our repairman. His shop is in the Wilshire district. If you take them to him now he can repair them immediately. That would save you a wait of a week if we sent them down.

ANNE: *I can see that,* but *I am totally uninterested in having these boots repaired. I will only accept a full refund on my account.* [FOGGING, SELF-DIS-CLOSURE, and BROKEN RECORD]

MANAGER: But we can't make a refund. The manufacturer won't allow us to make a refund that way.

ANNE: *I'm sure the manufacturer won't allow a refund.* But *I'm not interested in whether or not the manufacturer makes a refund. I want you to make the refund.* [FOGGING, SELF-DISCLOSURE, and BROKEN RECORD]

MANAGER: But that's the problem. If the manufacturer won't reimburse us I can't give you a refund.

ANNE: *I'm sure you do have a problem with the manufacturer.* But that's your problem, not mine. *I am not interested in your problems with the factory. I am only interested in you making a total refund.* [FOGGING, SELF-DISCLOSURE, and BROKEN RECORD]

MANAGER: But if we make a refund we will lose money.

ANNE: *I'm sure you will lose money,* but *that doesn't interest me at all. I only care about getting a full refund to my account.* [FOGGING, SELF-DISCLOSURE, and BROKEN RECORD]

MANAGER: I cannot make a refund. I don't have the authority.

ANNE: *I believe you, so I would like the name of your superior who can make a refund.* [FOGGING and WORKABLE COMPROMISE]

MANAGER: (Silent)

ANNE: Will you give me his name or shall I get it from somebody else? [WORKABLE COMPROMISE]

MANAGER: Let me see what I can do. (The manager disappears into the stockroom behind the counter for a minute, reappears, and speaks to Anne.)

MANAGER: We don't do this as a regular procedure, but if you will give me your sales slip, I will send a refund voucher for the boots up to Accounting.

ANNE: Thank you. (Turns and smiles to the young woman behind her holding another pair of defective boots.)

Anne was not a regularly enrolled student in an assertion class or a patient in therapy when she learned to be assertive. She was a nonassertive colleague who learned these skills and attitudes in bits and pieces from me during discussions over lunch or at social functions, and she put them into practice over a period of months. Curiously enough, Anne became very proficient in all the verbal skills on her own without benefit of the coached practice sessions that seem to better suit most novice learners. This particular interaction with the sales manager was the first of many successful experiences Anne has reported as she has gradually learned to be more assertive with other people. Like many other learners, Anne has undergone a major personality change; she has become more persistent, much less sensitive to criticism, acquired an ability to better cope with her errors, been less anxious about problems and conflicts with other people (less flight coping), and showed much less anger and aggressiveness (less fight coping) to people close to her. When I recently asked her to tell me about the one thing she valued most from her assertive learning experiences, she skimmed over these positive emotional changes within herself and emphasized her changed attitude toward herself and other people and the gain in general self-confidence that was produced from an ability to recognize and cope with manipulation by others.

Let's now look at the other side of the coin, an employee who assertively copes with a customer with a legitimate grievance.

Dialogue #10
Andy copes with an angry customer complaining about the delivery of defective merchandise.

Andy works in the service office of a large department store. He often works alone in the office in the late afternoon when the servicemen are out in the field and his boss is elsewhere on business. Like so many other people, Andy found it difficult to cope with the complaints of angry customers, becoming nervous enough sometimes to ignore phone messages, or even the ringing of his desk phone. The following dialogue is one he reported while practicing being systematically assertive on the phone at work.

Setting of the dialogue: Andy is at his desk, the phone rings, and he picks it up to speak to a customer complaining about an appliance delivery.

ANDY: Service department.

CUSTOMER: This is Mrs. Grandiose. You delivered my new refrigerator this afternoon and it doesn't work. I want someone to come out right now and fix it, or bring me another one.

ANDY: *I'd really like to help you,* but all the servicemen are out in the field right now on assignments and we probably won't be able to service your refrigerator until tomorrow. [SELF-DISCLOSURE]

CUSTOMER: That makes me really mad. When I ordered the refrigerator from you people, the salesman promised that he would deliver it on time this morning for my buffet dinner party tonight. First you deliver it at 3:00 P.M. and now it doesn't work.

ANDY: *Something like that would make you mad. If I were in your shoes, I'd be mad too.* [FOGGING and SELF-DISCLOSURE]

CUSTOMER: You have to get someone out here. I was promised it would be delivered on time and you would have it working in time for my dinner party.

ANDY: After promising you to deliver it on time and then falling down on the job, *we obviously fouled up. That was dumb of us.* [NEGATIVE ASSERTION]

CUSTOMER: Well, you have to get someone out here to fix it.

ANDY: *I'd really like to help you* out, ma'am, but *there is no one here but me at this time of the day.* [SELF-DISCLOSURE and BROKEN RECORD]

CUSTOMER: Can you come out?

ANDY: I'm not a service man, *I wouldn't know what to do to fix it.* Are you sure it's plugged into the wall? [SELF-DISCLOSURE]

CUSTOMER: Yes, I checked that already.

ANDY: It doesn't run at all? Doesn't even make a sound?

CUSTOMER: Not a thing.

ANDY: *Then I don't know what to tell you.* Didn't the delivery man get it running for you? [SELF-DIS-CLOSURE]

CUSTOMER: They fiddled with it when they moved it against the wall. I just checked it now to put food in and it's dead.

ANDY: *I'd like to help you out,* but *there isn't much I can do until tomorrow morning.* [SELF-DISCLOSURE and BROKEN RECORD]

CUSTOMER: That's no way to run a business. How can people count on you?

ANDY: *It sure isn't! We really goofed this time.* Tell you what I can do. *I will personally see to it that the serviceman calls you first thing in the morning.* [FOGGING, NEGATIVE ASSERTION, and WORK-ABLE COMPROMISE]

CUSTOMER: Can't you get one out tonight?

ANDY: *I'd really like to help you out,* but *there is nothing I can do about it this late in the afternoon. I'll take care of it first thing tomorrow morning myself.* [SELF-DISCLOSURE, BROKEN RECORD, and WORKABLE COMPROMISE]

CUSTOMER: I think I shall speak to your superior.

ANDY: *That's a good idea,* but he's not here now. [FOGGING]

CUSTOMER: Where can I reach him?

ANDY: *I don't know.* [SELF-DISCLOSURE]

CUSTOMER: Will you call and let me know when the serviceman is due tomorrow?

ANDY: *I'll do that personally, or you can call me in the morning before 9:00 A.M.* [WORKABLE COM-PROMISE]

CUSTOMER: Who shall I ask for?

ANDY: Just ask for Andy in the service office.

After successfully handling an angry customer with-out coming unglued as he had in the past, Andy felt he needed very little more assertive therapy, and I agreed with him. At the time of the interaction with this customer, Andy reported that he felt a little bit nervous during the entire dialogue and wondered if eventually he would be able to cope with situations like this one and also feel comfortable at the same time. I assured him that most learners still feel a bit nervous on their first assertive success because, up until then, they have a history of failure and still anticipate some trouble, no matter how much they practice outside of the real situation. With repeated successful exposures to conflict between people, there is no anticipation of a disaster, and consequently no anxiety. As predicted, Andy reported no nervousness in coping with customers thereafter.

Let's look now at another situation where the customer has to cope assertively on the phone with store employees and then the owner of the store to get what he wants.

Dialogue #11
Mr. and Mrs. Heath assertively
cope with an evasive
furniture store
owner.

Mark Heath's wife, Edith, recently purchased a couch after exhaustively looking for one she liked for more than six months. Originally delighted with her selection, she was dismayed to find that the seams of the cushions were separating after only eight months of light use. She promptly complained about this defect to the store where she purchased the couch. They picked up the cushions, repaired them, and returned them to her. Six months after the repair job, the same seams began to unravel again. Edith again phoned the furniture store and told the secretary of the owner that she wanted the cushions reupholstered and that a patch-up sewing job was unacceptable. Edith was told that while the owner was out of town on a buying trip, the man at the factory would be happy to pick up the cushions and do what was necessary. After speaking to the factory representative and specifically stating that nothing but reupholstery was acceptable, she was amazed to have the secretary from the furniture store call two weeks later and tell her that the cushions had been repaired. After she told the secretary again that nothing less then reupholstered cushions would satisfy her, the secretary responded that she could do nothing about it. The factory would only repair the cushions since the manufacturer would not guarantee the original fabric. Edith responded that she did not care about the factory's problems, she was only interested in what the furniture store was going to do; the store could keep the repaired cushions, and she wanted the owner to call her or her husband when he got back in town.

Setting of the first dialogue: the owner Mr. Grimson calls up Mark at work.

MARK: Mr. Grimson. Have you been informed of the situation about my couch?

OWNER: Yes. I'm just calling to let you know that the cushions are sitting right here in my office ready for you to pick up.

MARK: You've had them reupholstered then?

OWNER: No, that wasn't necessary. The factory technicians looked at the problem and decided that a nylon-latex reinforcement under the corners would do the trick. They are as good as new.

MARK: *I'm sure the factory techs feel that way, but I don't.* Your people assured us six months ago that the cushions were repaired properly and that was not true. *I wouldn't know what to do when they come apart six months from now.* There's hardly any fabric left on the corners right now. *I want those cushions reupholstered.* [FOGGING, SELF-DISCLOSURE, and BROKEN RECORD]

OWNER: Mr. Heath. You can take my word for it, these cushions will be okay.

MARK: *I'm sure you believe that, Mr. Grimson, but I don't.* [FOGGING and SELF-DISCLOSURE]

OWNER: But the problem is with the factory. They won't authorize reupholstering.

MARK: Mr. Grimson, *I don't feel I have a problem*

with the factory. I feel I have a problem with you. And I'm not concerned about your problem with the factory. I just want my cushions reupholstered. [SELF-DISCLOSURE and BROKEN RECORD]

OWNER: Let me think about how to work this out and I'll call you back.

MARK: When will you call back?

OWNER: I'm having lunch with the people from the factory Friday. I'll call that afternoon or Monday.

MARK: Okay, I'll be expecting your call.

Setting of the second dialogue: Wednesday of the following week, Mark calls the owner since he has received no word from him.

MARK: Mr. Grimson. *Have you arranged to have my cushions reupholstered yet?* [BROKEN RECORD]

OWNER: I couldn't get in contact with the factory people last Friday.

MARK: *I don't understand.* What has the factory got to do with this whole business? [SELF-DISCLOSURE]

OWNER: I'm trying to work out a deal for you with the factory and I'll do the best I can for you with them.

MARK: Mr. Grimson, *I'm really not interested in any deal you want to work out with the factory.* I purchased the couch from you, not the factory. You can make any arrangements you want to get the cushions reupholstered. *I just want them reupholstered, not repaired.* [SELF-DISCLOSURE and BROKEN RECORD]

OWNER: I've arranged a meeting with the factory manager again this Friday and I'll need some more time to work things out.

MARK: *Will you get the cushions reupholstered?* [BROKEN RECORD]

OWNER: I'm trying to see if I can get you a brand-new couch.

MARK: *I think that's very nice of you, Mr. Grimson,* but a new couch really isn't necessary. *I just want my cushions reupholstered.* [SELF-DISCLOSURE and BROKEN RECORD]

OWNER: Let me try it my way first. I'm sure you will be satisfied. In the meantime, why don't you pick up your cushions so you can use your couch?

MARK: *I'm sure I will be satisfied,* but in the meantime I'll leave the cushions with you *until they are reupholstered.* [FOGGING and BROKEN RECORD]

OWNER: Give me another week or two to see what I can do.

MARK: Okay. *If I don't hear from you within two weeks, I'll call you back.* [WORKABLE COMPROMISE]

OWNER: I'm sure I'll call you before then.

MARK: *If you don't for any reason, I'll call you so we keep in touch to resolve this.* [WORKABLE COMPROMISE]

OWNER: Fine. I'll do my best.

MARK: *I'm sure you will.* [FOGGING]

Setting of the third dialogue: Mark calls Mr. Grimson two weeks later.

MARK: Mr. Grimson, I haven't heard from you for two weeks. *Have the cushions been reupholstered?* [BROKEN RECORD]

OWNER: I had a meeting with the factory manager and they won't do anything. I did my best for you with them.

MARK: Mr. Grimson, *I'm sure you did your best,* but *I'm really not interested in what the factory can do or can't do. I'm only concerned with what you are going to do. I want those cushions reupholstered.* [FOGGING, SELF-DISCLOSURE, and BROKEN RECORD]

OWNER: (Silent for a few minutes)

MARK: Mr. Grimson. Are you there? Have we been cut off?

OWNER: I was just thinking. There may be another way I can work this out. Give me another few days to see what I can do.

MARK: *I'm sure there may be another way to work this out,* but if you can't pull it off, *I still want my cushions reupholstered.* [FOGGING and BROKEN RECORD]

OWNER: (Showing some irritation in his voice) Mr. Heath, I'm going to do everything possible I can for you. Please be patient a little longer.

MARK: *When can I expect your call?* [WORKABLE COMPROMISE]

OWNER: I promise I'll contact you Friday.

MARK: Okay, I'll expect you to call me then.

Setting of the fourth dialogue: Mark has called Mr. Grimson's office at 3:00 P.M. on Friday and the secretary informed him that Mr. Grimson was out of the office. Mark told the secretary that he wanted to speak to Mr. Grimson that afternoon, or he could call Mark at home that evening. At 4:45 P.M., Mr. Grimson calls back.

OWNER: (In a jovial mood) Mr. Heath. Some days there aren't enough hours even with time and a half.

MARK: *I don't understand what you're saying,* Mr. Grimson. [SELF-DISCLOSURE]

OWNER: (Slightly embarrassed) I just meant that some times there aren't enough hours in the day for me to get everything done.

MARK: *That's true. If I had a spare day myself, Mr. Grimson, I'd give it to you, but I don't.* [FOGGING and SELF-DISCLOSURE]

OWNER: (Sobered) Yes, well, here's what I want to do about your couch. I've ordered another one that will be delivered next month on the first. I'll send a van out to your house then and swap the new couch for yours.

MARK: *I think that's very good of you, Mr. Grimson,* but it's really not necessary. *All I want is my cushions reupholstered.* [SELF-DISCLOSURE and BROKEN RECORD]

OWNER: No, I want to do it this way. You've had enough trouble with that couch and the factory admits it's defective. We will absorb the cost since customer satisfaction is what keeps us in business.

MARK: *Why don't we just swap cushions? That will be fine with me.* [WORKABLE COMPROMISE]

OWNER: That won't work. The dye lots won't match perfectly.

MARK: Okay. I'll expect a call a few days before the first, so someone will be home to receive the delivery.

OWNER: I'll have the manager call you personally to arrange a date. By the way, what condition is the couch in? The cushions look brand-new. Is the rest of the couch like that?

MARK: Yes. Except for the cushion seams, the couch looks brand-new.

OWNER: I'll just use your old couch as a demo floor model and things will work out fine.

MARK: Thank you, Mr. Grimson. I appreciate your working this matter out.

OWNER: Not at all, I'm sorry this happened. Please send your wife down again to look at our new furniture lines. I'm sure she'll like them.

MARK: I'll tell her about it.

Mark had the most emotional difficulty in dealing with the very slick ploy used by the owner which implied that not only was Mark's problem with the manufacturer and not with the owner, but Mr. Grimson was behind Mark's cause 100 per cent and was moving heaven and earth on Mark's behalf against a very difficult opponent, those hard-nosed SOBs down at the factory. It was difficult for Mark to simply say that he didn't care about the factory; he was only interested in what the store owner was going to do about the problem. It was difficult, that is, the first time Mark said it. After that, it didn't bother him at all.

After being successful in coping with the owner and resolving the problem to his satisfaction, Mark realized that he had nothing to rely on during that conflict beside his own assertiveness and simply being persistent in saying what he wanted over and over again to the store owner. Mark had no legal recourse. He had no social or business-linked threats he could use as leverage on Mr. Grimson to force him to make good on the merchandise he sold. If he tried to make the owner feel guilty over what had happened, Mark would probably not have accomplished much of anything with that master manipulator. Mark could only assertively demand that the owner correct a fault in the merchandise he was sold. If the owner persistently refused, Mark could do nothing more. Being persistently assertive does not guarantee success, but as Mark and other learners have found out, most people in the commercial world have only a few noes in their coping portfolio also. After these noes are assertively coped with, a compromise shortly follows.

Changing perspective again, in the next dialogue a clerk has to cope face-to-face with angry or manipulative people as part of her job.

Dialogue #12
Dorothy copes with
the public in
her civil
service
job.

Dorothy is a clerk-typist in a civil service office that handles various legal procedures for the public. In her job, Dorothy alternates with several other women in performing clerical duties and dealing with people when they come into the office with their problems. Until she became involved in assertive therapy, Dorothy avoided working with the public whenever she could. She reported: "I always felt nervous and didn't know what to say when I couldn't give people what they wanted." Over a period of several weeks, Dorothy practiced being systematically assertive in coping with requests she could do nothing about. The following dialogue is a short sequence in coping with several requests and complaints made to her during this period.

Setting of the dialogue: Dorothy is standing behind the reception counter when two couples walk up to her.

DOROTHY: (To the first couple, a man and woman in their thirties) Hello, what can I do for you?

FIRST MAN: I would like to have my fingerprints taken and have this statement notarized.

DOROTHY: The notary is on the fourth floor now. Room 407. And we don't do fingerprinting. You will have to go to the sheriff's office on Third Street or to the police department on the other side of the parking lot.

FIRST MAN: The directory in the lobby says to come to this room.

DOROTHY: *You're right. Isn't that dumb? The notary moved four months ago and they still haven't changed the directory. You'd think by now they'd get around to changing it.* [FOGGING and NEGATIVE ASSERTION]

FIRST WOMAN: Why don't you do something about it?

DOROTHY: *I wish we could.* We send memos but the sign is still the same. *I don't know what to do about it.* [SELF-DISCLOSURE]

FIRST WOMAN: That's ridiculous. There must be something that can be done about it.

DOROTHY: *There should be something that could be done,* but *I don't know what it is.* [FOGGING and SELF-DISCLOSURE]

FIRST WOMAN: With all the taxes we pay, the county should at least give us the right directions.

DOROTHY: *You're right. It looks like we just goofed.* [FOGGING and NEGATIVE ASSERTION]

FIRST MAN: I was told that I could get my fingerprints taken here.

DOROTHY: *I'm sure you were,* but we don't take care of fingerprinting; we never have. [FOGGING]

FIRST MAN: I talked to someone over the phone in this office and she told me that you could take fingerprints.

DOROTHY: Who did you speak to? I'll find her for you.

FIRST MAN: I don't know, but I talked to this office.

DOROTHY: Well, if you did, *we really goofed. I always feel irritated when something like that happens to me.* [NEGATIVE ASSERTION and SELF-DISCLOSURE]

FIRST WOMAN: The county offices are always screwing up.

DOROTHY: *I know exactly how you feel. It sure seems like that sometimes, doesn't it?* [SELF-DISCLOSURE and NEGATIVE ASSERTION]

(First couple departs and Dorothy turns to second couple, an elderly man and woman)

DOROTHY: Now what can I do for you?

SECOND WOMAN: We want the inheritance forms.

DOROTHY: Gee, *I don't know anything about them.* I've never had anyone ask about them before. Let me find out. (Picks up phone, dials, describes the situation to her boss, listens to his response, and then turns again to the second couple) We don't have anything to do with inheritance forms. You have to go to the state offices. They're in downtown Los Angeles. I'll write down the address and telephone number. [SELF-DISCLOSURE]

SECOND MAN: The guard down in the lobby told us we could get the inheritance forms from this room.

DOROTHY: *I'm sure he thought you could get them here.* [FOGGING]

SECOND MAN: I wish you people would get your signals straight.

DOROTHY: *You're right. I wish we could too.* [FOGGING and SELF-DISCLOSURE]

SECOND WOMAN: Somebody ought to tell him not to send people on wild-goose chases.

DOROTHY: *I'll be happy to tell him on my lunch hour that we don't have the inheritance forms.* [WORKABLE COMPROMISE]

SECOND WOMAN: Do you know how much money we will lose if we don't get those forms in?

DOROTHY: *No, I don't.* [SELF-DISCLOSURE]

SECOND WOMAN: Well, it's an awful lot, let me tell you.

DOROTHY: *I'm sure it is.* [FOGGING]

SECOND WOMAN: Why don't you people have the forms we need instead of sending us all the way downtown?

DOROTHY: *I don't know.* I guess because they're state forms and this is a county office. [SELF-DISCLOSURE]

SECOND WOMAN: I'd think you government people would get together on something important like this.

DOROTHY: *I can understand how you feel,* having to make that trip all the way downtown. [SELF-DISCLOSURE]

SECOND WOMAN: You're too young to understand all the troubles we have. Wait until you're our age and see how much fun it is.

DOROTHY: *Maybe you're right. I don't know for sure how I'll feel when I'm older.* Anything else I can help you with? [FOGGING and SELF-DISCLOSURE]

SECOND MAN: (Pulling second woman away from counter) No, thank you. That's all.

Dorothy's assertiveness in coping with demands that she cannot satisfy needs no comment from me. She speaks for herself!

Let's now look at one of the easiest situations in which to get your money's worth by being assertive; getting your auto fixed by a garage mechanic.

Dialogue #13
Arnold gets
his brakes
fixed.

Arnold purchased a small economy foreign car and, after a thousand miles' use, noticed that oily leaks were evident on all four wheel rims. Taking it back to the dealer, he spoke to the service representative and was told that the problem was the brake cylinders and that they would be fixed. After picking up the car and driving it for a few days, Arnold was annoyed that the brakes squealed loudly whenever he used them.

Setting of the dialogue: Arnold returns to the dealership and speaks to the service representative.

ARNOLD: I had my brakes fixed under warranty here a few days ago and the brakes squeal badly. I don't want them to squeal.

REP: Well, there is nothing we can do about that. Those are the standard brakes and they all squeal that way.

ARNOLD: *I'm sure all standard brakes squeal that way,* but when I bought this car the brakes didn't squeal then and *I don't want them to squeal now.* [FOGGING AND BROKEN RECORD]

REP: We can't do anything about that.

ARNOLD: What's the service manager's name and where can I find him?

REP: He's in that office over there.

ARNOLD: *What's his name?* [BROKEN RECORD]

REP: Gerhard Braun.

(Arnold walks into Mr. Braun's office, finds him dealing with another customer's complaint, and stands there silently until the other customer leaves.)

MANAGER: Sit down, sit down. What can I do for you?

ARNOLD: (Still standing, looks down at the manager and speaks in a calm voice) What's this crap your service rep is giving me that you can't fix my brakes. They didn't squeal when I brought them in to you and now they squeal.

MANAGER: Do you have the work sheet?

ARNOLD: (Handing it to him) Yes, and *I want brakes that don't squeal.* [BROKEN RECORD]

MANAGER: It says here that the brake cylinders of all four wheels were leaking. We fixed them. Here's what happened. The mechanic probably found a little brake fluid on the brake shoes and decided to replace them to give you better braking action. He didn't have to do that, but we like to make sure that each car we repair is completely safe for our customers. We didn't charge you anything for them. You got a whole new set of brakes for free.

ARNOLD: *I'm sure what you say is true,* but when I

bought this car, the brakes didn't squeal and after you repaired it, they do squeal. *I want brakes on my car that don't squeal.* [FOGGING and BROKEN RECORD]

MANAGER: Well, those are the replacement brakes that the factory provides us. They are much better brakes than the original ones. They are harder and last longer and consequently they will squeal a little.

ARNOLD: Frankly, *I don't care what problems you have with your factory replacements. Perhaps they are better brakes,* but *I want brakes on my car that don't squeal.* [SELF-DISCLOSURE, FOGGING, and BROKEN RECORD]

MANAGER: But these are brand-new brakes we installed for you for nothing. We didn't have to do that. We did that as a courtesy to you. We just like to take care of our customers' driving safety.

ARNOLD: *It was very courteous* but *I don't want brakes on my car that squeal.* [FOGGING and BROKEN RECORD]

MANAGER: But if we put the original-style brakes back on your car, they won't last half as long as these new ones will.

ARNOLD: *These probably will last longer,* but *frankly, I don't care what kind of new brake shoes you put on my car as long as they don't squeal when I use them.* [FOGGING and SELF-DISCLOSURE]

MANAGER: (Silent for a few moments, biting his lip with a thoughtful, worried look on his face) Can you leave the car with me for this afternoon and pick it up at five o'clock?

ARNOLD: *Are you going to fix the brakes so they don't squeal?* [BROKEN RECORD]

MANAGER: If you leave the car with me this afternoon, I'll get the brakes fixed.

ARNOLD: I'd appreciate it very much, thank you.

Arnold found out in this interaction that the much heralded obstinacy of repair mechanics and garage managers is a myth (probably artificially cultured and promoted by the nonassertiveness of many of their customers). He found that the service representative had only a few stock, manipulative answers as to why repairs are unacceptable and the manager had even fewer. This dialogue may strike you as too easy with not much to use for coping with repairmen. In training novices to be more assertive, I consider it a stroke of luck if the manufacturer or the mechanic screws up something on their car. Sending learners forth to cope assertively with that sort of difficulty is one of the most meaningful and easiest homework assignments I can give them. Not one student has reported a failure in this commercial area even though some have had to stick to their goal for several weeks. Perhaps I owe some thanks to the fumbling Detroit giants since they consistently provide easy grist for the assertive mill!

In the next dialogue, you will see an example of a commercial situation in which asserting yourself requires a bit more persistence and the ability to cope with gross manipulation of your behavior over a period of weeks or at least several days.

Dialogue #14
Jack gets a refund
of $1,800 from
a used-car
dealer.

Jack is a part-time student who also works as a physiotherapist to support himself. He is dissatisfied with his occupation and is taking classes to get his degree and learn other occupational skills. Jack's old car finally gave up and had to be towed to a junk yard. Jack had known that it was only a matter of time until his old car would fall apart and he had prepared to purchase a new one by saving a portion of his salary for two years. Consequently, he immediately purchased a used car from a dealer the day after his old one failed. Since he had the money in the bank, Jack paid the entire $1,800 cost by check. On the day after he purchased his "new" car, its automatic transmission started to leak heavily. Jack brought the car back to the dealer and the salesman promised to have it fixed. Two days after getting it back from the repair shop, the transmission started to leak again. He consulted with me and we talked in detail about his options on getting further repairs, another car, or his money back, and how he could assertively cope with this problem. On the way back to the dealer the next day, the car kept stalling and was restarted only with great difficulty, eventually needing a push. As he drove into the dealer's lot, Jack decided that he wanted his money back and no further business with this used-car dealer.

Day 1: Setting of the dialogue: Jack walks into the sales office and speaks to the salesman who sold him the car.

JACK: Mr. Kirtz. That car you sold me is a piece of junk and I want my money back.

SALESMAN: What's the matter, boy? I thought we got you all fixed up Friday.

JACK: *That's right. I thought so too,* but the transmission started leaking again yesterday and now the car runs worse than my old one. *I want my money back.* [FOGGING, SELF-DISCLOSURE, and BROKEN RECORD]

SALESMAN: Well, we don't have anything to do with the transmission shop. You'll have to go see them about that.

JACK: *I'm sure you feel that way,* but you are the one I paid my money to, not the transmission shop. I don't have anything to do with them and *I want my money back.* [FOGGING and BROKEN RECORD]

SALESMAN: That don't make sense. Course you got to deal with them. You took your car over to them, didn't you?

JACK: *I did, didn't I? That was dumb of me to take it over there personally instead of insisting that you take care of the whole business, wasn't it?* [NEGATIVE ASSERTION]

SALESMAN: No, that's the way to do it. Let me explain something to you on how these things work. You see, we did what we said we would do! You don't have a problem with us! We don't have anything to do with that shop! Your problem is with them. You go see them about your transmission. We can't do anything about it here. We just don't have the facilities. That's why we sent you over there.

JACK: *I understand perfectly that you want me to go over to the transmission shop,* but I'm not going to do that. I don't have a problem with them. I have a problem with you and *I want my money refunded.* [FOGGING and BROKEN RECORD]

SALESMAN: If you feel so strongly about it, I'll be glad to call them up right now and speak to them for you.

JACK: Mr. Kirtz, if you want to call up the shop, go right ahead, but you are calling them up for yourself, not me. *I agree that I dropped the car off and picked it up,* but *I don't have anything to do with them.* I don't care what you do with the car. *I just want my money refunded.* [FOGGING and BROKEN RECORD]

SALESMAN: (Coolly looking at Jack) If you're afraid that we won't stand behind a car we sell, forget it! We'll get your transmission fixed for you!

JACK: *Mr. Kirtz, I'm sure you feel that way,* but you told me that the first time and it didn't get fixed. Frankly, after this, *I don't believe you when you tell me that.* [FOGGING and SELF-DISCLOSURE]

SALESMAN: That's no way to be, boy. After all the trouble I went to to get your car fixed right away. It's not my fault that the shop didn't do the job right. You got no cause to say that to me. We'll get your car fixed.

JACK: *I'm sure you really feel that way, Mr. Kirtz,* but *I still don't believe what you say* and *I want my money back.* [FOGGING, SELF-DISCLOSURE, and BROKEN RECORD]

SALESMAN: Well, if you have that attitude, there is nothing I can do about it.

JACK: *That may be true,* but *I still want my money back.* [FOGGING and BROKEN RECORD]

SALESMAN: I can't give you your money back. The papers have been processed in Sacramento. We can't change the legal papers. That's your car. It's registered to you. Nothing we can do about that.

JACK: *I'm sure you really feel that way*, so here's what we are going to do. *Let's you and I go talk to the boss of this place who can give me my money back.* [FOGGING and WORKABLE COMPROMISE]

SALESMAN: Well, I don't know if Smitty is around today.

JACK: *That's possible*, but if you don't start the wheels rolling to get my money back, *I'll still want to see him.* [FOGGING and BROKEN RECORD]

SALESMAN: I'll call and see. (Picks up telephone, dials, speaks to someone, and then speaks to Jack) He won't be in until tomorrow.

JACK: Okay. When can we see him tomorrow?

SALESMAN: He usually gets in around nine in the morning.

JACK: Will you be here at nine thirty?

SALESMAN: Sure, I'm here all day.

JACK: Fine, then I want you to speak to Smitty when he comes in. Tell him that I want the three of us to get together at nine thirty. Okay?

SALESMAN: That's fine with me.

JACK: Good. And by the way, here's the keys for the car.

SALESMAN: We don't need the keys to your car.

JACK: *I understand how you feel*, but I'm leaving the car right out there blocking your driveway and you'll probably want to move it. [SELF-DISCLOSURE]

SALESMAN: Take the car with you. You need transportation. We'll straighten this out tomorrow.

JACK: *That's true*, but *I'm leaving the car here.* [FOGGING and BROKEN RECORD]

SALESMAN: Suit yourself, but park it in the street.

JACK: I'm returning the car to you. *I don't care where you park it.* [SELF-DISCLOSURE]

SALESMAN: (No response: silently, sternly looks up at Jack and then down at the keys on his desk, picking at them with one finger)

JACK: See you at nine thirty tomorrow. (Leaves)

That afternoon shortly after leaving the used-car lot, Jack called his bank and asked to place a stop order on his check. The bank informed him that it had already paid $1,800 out of his account and they could not honor his stop order. Nevertheless, Jack was determined to assert himself and get his money returned.

Day 2: Setting of the dialogue: Jack and Mr. Kirtz walk into the manager's office.

MANAGER: Sit down. I hear you had some trouble with your car.

JACK: Yes, and I want a refund of my money I paid you for that car.

MANAGER: Why don't you want the car?

JACK: Mr. Kirtz and I went into that yesterday. Have you discussed this with him?

MANAGER: Yes, but it seems that the car would be all right as soon as we fix the transmission.

JACK: *I'm sure you really feel that way,* but *I don't believe it,* and *I want my money back.* [FOGGING, SELF-DISCLOSURE, and BROKEN RECORD]

MANAGER: Are you telling me I'm a liar?

JACK: Mr. Smith, *I really feel you believe what you are saying.* The fact is that I don't believe it. I've been through this talk of repair guarantee before and *I don't buy it. I want my money back.* [FOGGING, SELF-DISCLOSURE and BROKEN RECORD]

MANAGER: (Silent for a moment) You don't like the car, that's okay. Lot of cars I don't like myself. Tell you what I'll do. You go out on the lot with Bob and pick out any car you want and we'll take your car back and just make a price adjustment. That's a reasonable offer.

JACK: *That seems like a reasonable offer,* but I don't want another of your cars. *I just want my money back.* [FOGGING and BROKEN RECORD]

MANAGER: You worried about the condition of the replacement? Drive it around a week and if you don't like it we'll give you another one. If you want, I'll help you pick one out. Matter of fact, we got a great little car you'll really like. We can swap this one even. Bob, go get that little red jobbie in the back lot and bring it out front.

JACK: *I'm sure it is a nice car,* Mr. Smith, but *I don't want another car from you people. I just want my money back.* [FOGGING and BROKEN RECORD]

MANAGER: Well, that's impossible. All the legal forms were sent to Sacramento already. You own that car and it's registered in your name.

JACK: *I don't understand. What is impossible about taking the car back and giving money for it if it is possible to take the car back and give another car for it?* [SELF-DISCLOSURE]

MANAGER: That's no problem. We just send in a correction to change an error in the car registration.

JACK: *I still don't understand. What's impossible about sending in a correction about refunding money instead of exchanging cars?* [SELF-DISCLOSURE]

MANAGER: We just can't do that!

JACK: *I'm sure you really feel that way,* Mr. Smith, but *I still want a refund on my car.* [FOGGING and BROKEN RECORD]

MANAGER: Why won't you take another car? That would solve this whole problem. They're good cars.

JACK: *That's possible,* but *I don't want to chance another run-around. I just want my money back.* [FOGGING, SELF-DISCLOSURE, and BROKEN RECORD]

MANAGER: (To Mr. Kirtz) Bob, let me handle this. You go back to the lot. (Mr. Kirtz leaves.) (To Jack) You pissed with him the way he handled your repairs? I don't blame you. I don't think much of that stupid son of a bitch myself. Let's just you and I talk this over. I'll personally see your car gets fixed or help you pick out another one. I'll personally guarantee it. Isn't that fair?

JACK: As I said before, *it sounds very fair,* except that I don't want the car repaired and I don't want another one. *I just want my money back.* [FOGGING and BROKEN RECORD]

MANAGER: You're asking for the impossible. I just can't do that.

JACK: *I'm sure you feel that way,* so *is there someone over you with the authority to do it?* [FOGGING and WORKABLE COMPROMISE]

MANAGER: You'd have to talk to the owner.

JACK: What time can we see him?

MANAGER: He gets in some time after lunch.

JACK: How about two in the afternoon?

MANAGER: That's okay with me.

JACK: (Rising and leaving) I'll count on you to set it up and meet you here at two tomorrow.

Day 3: Setting of the dialogue: Mr. Smith escorts Jack to the owner's office, introduces Jack, and leaves.

OWNER: Sit down and make yourself comfortable. What's all this fuss about your car?

JACK: Has Mr. Smith explained the situation to you?

OWNER: Yes, but why do you want your money back?

JACK: The car is unsatisfactory to me and I want my money back.

OWNER: What's wrong with the car?

JACK: If Mr. Smith has explained the situation to you, you know that already.

OWNER: It seems like we are bending over backwards to satisfy you. We'll fix your car or give you another one. What's wrong with that? That sounds like a good deal to me. We don't do that for everybody, you know.

JACK: *I'm sure you don't,* but *I am not interested in this car or a second one. I just want my money back.* [FOGGING, SELF-DISCLOSURE, and BROKEN RECORD]

OWNER: Well, that's impossible to do.

JACK: *I'm sure it is difficult to make a refund,* but *I want my money back.* [FOGGING and BROKEN RECORD]

OWNER: We only want to do what's fair. Why can't you be reasonable?

JACK: *I'm sure you want to be fair. I want my money back.* [FOGGING and BROKEN RECORD]

OWNER: What do you think would happen to the

business world if every Tom, Dick, and Harry could just come in and get their money back because they changed their mind? How long do you think we could stay in business if we operated that way?

JACK: *I don't know.* [SELF-DISCLOSURE]

OWNER: Well, we just can't do it.

JACK: *I'm sure you really feel strongly about that,* but that car is on your lot and its keys are on your desk. *I'm not taking it back and I want a refund.* [FOGGING and BROKEN RECORD]

OWNER: That's a very unreasonable attitude to take.

JACK: *That's possible,* but *I still want a refund.* [FOGGING and BROKEN RECORD]

OWNER: You go around through life like that, you're not going to get along at all.

JACK: *You may be right,* but *I still want a refund.* [FOGGING and BROKEN RECORD]

OWNER: (Showing his temper; stands up, picks up the car keys, throws them down on the desk and shouts) You goddamn young punks, you think you can get away with anything! Come in here and think you're a smart ass! Only a deadbeat like you wouldn't keep his word on a bargain! Son of a bitch!

JACK: (Calmly and coolly) *I'm sure this upsets you,* but *I want to get my money back as soon as possible. I'd like to do some other things today besides this.* [FOGGING, BROKEN RECORD, and SELF-DISCLOSURE]

OWNER: (Jaw dropping agape and staring at Jack. Silent for a few seconds, he recovers his composure, smiles at Jack, and crosses around to where Jack is sitting, and shows an unbelievable change in attitude.) I'm glad you came to see me so we could straighten this out. A customer's goodwill is the most important thing in this business. Let's go down to the cashier's office so she can write you a check. Now if you ever need another car, you come in and see me personally. I can make you a great deal. We have the best selection in town. (Opens door for Jack, walks down the hall with his arm over Jack's shoulder, smiling and talking to

Jack with his TV sales pitch personality automatically switched on and operating)

After each encounter with the car dealer's staff, Jack kept in touch with me for feedback on how he had handled the situation and further coaching. We discussed the possible manipulative or fight-and-flight behavior that the sales personnel might display and I coached Jack on how he might cope with it. Incredible as it may seem, the particular behaviors we prepared for were exactly the behaviors Jack encountered, even to the point of the owner picking up the car keys, slamming them down on his desk, and cursing at Jack just prior to refunding his money. Jack's reply to this anticipated temper tantrum was the cool, coached response of: "I'm sure this upsets you, but I want to get my money back (not: can I get my money back?) as soon as possible. I'd like to do some other things today beside this."

As you might suspect, Jack was very pleased with the results of our detailed preparation for this learning exercise and his actual performance in the real situation. We had even planned for the possibility of the first salesman getting frustrated and angry or nervous and leaving, with Jack to call him back or to follow him wherever he went—an unlikely possibility since (1) the salesman's job was to deal with dissatisfied customers and he probably had a lot of successful experience in putting customers off in the past, and (2) Jack was well practiced in not getting angry himself, agreeing with the viewpoint of the salesman and yet sticking to the point of what he wanted—repairs, another car, or a refund.

When Jack saw me next after his encounter with the owner, he didn't wait for me to ask him how things went, but handed over a check made out to him and commented with a smile: "It was like shooting fish in a barrel." Although Jack's encounter with the used-car dealer makes a good story for encouraging other learners to seriously practice systematic assertive therapy, two important points must be kept in mind to place Jack's success in clear perspective. First, the immediate question that needs an answer was asked me by one of my colleagues when Jack told him of his success: "How did you know what to tell Jack? How could you predict what the salesman and owner would do so accurately?" Simple. No mystery. I made, as it turned out, a shrewd guess based upon my own experience and success in a similar encounter with a used-car dealer some twenty years ago when I was a student. My guess was that fight-and-flight patterns hadn't changed much since then and, at least for this used-car dealer, my guess was right. However, the advice I gave to Jack on what might happen, assertively coaching and preparing him for it, was only the frosting on the basic assertive cake. Having some information on how and when other people might use fight-or-flight behavior to deal with him when he did not respond to their manipulation was relatively unimportant in comparison to Jack's own general ability to cope assertively; this is the second point we need to keep in mind to place Jack's success in clear perspective. Jack learned to be more assertive to regain his self-respect and to stop manipulation of his behavior by other people. He did not exert all his effort in learning to be assertive just to get a refund on a used car, even though that was one obvious side benefit. If Jack had not decided to get a refund, or if the owner had refused a refund, Jack still had achieved his primary goal—to be able to stand face to face with someone and say what he wanted, not to be intimidated or manipulated, to solve a problem in conflict and thereby feel better about himself. These things he accomplished.

In the next set of dialogues, you can see how two people assertively coped with conflicts that often arise in another commercial interaction—getting and delivering medical treatment.

Dialogue #15
**Mary and Abel assertively cope
with difficulties in the
physician-patient
relationship.**

In this set of short dialogues, a woman learning to be more assertive enters into a discussion with her physician over things that worry her, and the second person, a psychiatrist, copes with the unrealistic, demanding father of a patient. The first, Mary, is an older woman who has suffered a mild cerebral stroke that temporarily disabled her for six weeks. Mary spoke to me about her problem in communicating her wants to her doctor about several things; most important, she wanted to resume taking female hormones orally after recovering from her stroke, but the doctor always injected the hormones and her bottom was sore for days after. In Mary's own words, the problem was: "How can I tell someone like that who knows a lot more than I ever will how to practice medicine?" Like many people (including some physicians with grandiose ideas) Mary confused a supervisor-authority type of relationship with a commercial one. Her doctor is not, and never was, Mary's ultimate judge on what Mary "should" or "should not" do medically or in any other area. In order to receive the type of medical treatment she wants, Mary, like other nonassertive patients, has to face the hard reality that doctors are only technical consultants who will recommend specific medical procedures that, hopefully, will remedy a specific problem. Mary as a patient is still her own judge of what she will or will not do and is ultimately responsible for following or not following her doctor's advice. On the other side, as you will see in the second situation, the doctor is responsible for what treatment he will and will not provide. Assertively worked-out limits on what treatment he will offer are also required by hard reality. The basic relationship between patient and doctor, therefore, is one that requires the negotiation of the details of the treatment procedures. This is, realistically, a commercial relationship, not one wherein an authority tells you what to do and you have no choice in the matter. Mary, however, had a fear that if she asserted herself to her doctor, he might not give a damn about her well-being anymore, or might tell her to find another doctor. While both of her fears could be possible end results, they were not likely. Mary had seen her general practitioner for more than twenty years; she considered him a family doctor, and trusted him. He was not likely to choose such radical options to deal with the assertiveness of an old patient. If, on the other hand, he had told her to go to hell in professional jargon, she would be smart to get professional advice from some other source and drop him like a bad habit. If a health professional is so unsure of himself and his expertise that he resists reexamining specific procedures questioned by a patient, I personally wouldn't let him treat my dog's nervous skin condition, let alone myself. As the following dialogue shows, Mary's doctor was able to cope with her assertiveness and still satisfy her wants.

Setting of the dialogue: Mary enters Dr. Beck's office and sits down.

DOCTOR: Well, Mary, the nurse tells me that your blood pressure is only 140 over 80. That's a big improvement from three weeks ago.

MARY: I've been doing all the exercises you said to do and taking it easy and slowing down.

DOCTOR: Good! Good! Let's see your arm. Can you move the wrist yet?

MARY: It's a little better this week. I still have trouble with my fingers. They just won't pick up things.

DOCTOR: That's going to improve soon if you keep exercising them.

MARY: I can raise my arm all the way up now and swing it around. I couldn't do that last week. That's a relief.

DOCTOR: It's going to keep getting better. I want you to continue taking the medication and we will drop it gradually as your blood pressure gets back to normal. Remember, you are going to have to take it for the rest of your life. I don't want you to stop taking it just because you feel better.

MARY: I won't. I don't want to go through this hell again.

DOCTOR: Okay. You look very good. I want to see

you again in two weeks. I'll tell the nurse to set up the appointment for you.

MARY: Doctor, I want to speak to you about the hormones you gave me before. I want to get back on them. They make me feel so much better. I had a spring in my step when I was on them. [SELF-DISCLOSURE]

DOCTOR: Sure. I think they help too. I'll write an order to get you a shot right now.

MARY: *That's what I wanted to speak to you about. I want the hormones, but I don't want to take a shot.* When the nurse jabbed me with that horse needle, I couldn't sit down for days. *I want some pills instead.* [BROKEN RECORD and SELF-DISCLOSURE]

DOCTOR: (Looking at Mary thoughtfully) It's much better to take hormones by injection. One zap and it's over with until you come in again.

MARY: *That's true, but I prefer the pills.* [FOGGING and BROKEN RECORD]

DOCTOR: If I give you pills, you have to remember to take them daily.

MARY: *That's true, I will have to, but I prefer the pills.* [FOGGING and BROKEN RECORD]

DOCTOR: Mary, the problem with pills is that a lot of women like yourself abuse them. They think that if two make them feel good, four will make them feel twice as good and they eventually take far too many and get in trouble.

MARY: *I'm sure they do, but I still want to take the pills instead of those damn shots!* [FOGGING and BROKEN RECORD]

DOCTOR: Mary, you have enough problems with this stroke. Why not take an injection now and we will talk about the pills when you come back next time?

MARY: *Will you prescribe pills for me then?* [WORKABLE COMPROMISE]

DOCTOR: I'd like to talk with you about it some more.

MARY: *I can understand that, but I still want the pills and I'm not going to take any more of those damn shots.* [SELF-DISCLOSURE and BROKEN RECORD]

DOCTOR: (Looking at Mary for a moment) I tell you what we'll do. I'll prescribe enough for you to take from now to your next appointment and then we will see how things are going. Okay?

MARY: *Okay. That's fine with me.* [WORKABLE COMPROMISE]

Mary reported that she was delighted at her doctor's reaction to her strong wishes and felt that something had changed between them for the better as a result of her asserting herself. Even though she had known Dr. Beck for twenty years, she was always nervous in his presence and a bit afraid of what he might think of her. After coping with her doctor's reluctance to do things the way she wanted them done, Mary reported later with a giggle and her soft smile that she felt more in control of what was going to happen to her when she saw her physician; consequently she was less afraid of him and more able to talk to him about the real problems of overcoming her disability.

One cause for the deterioration of the helping relationship between patients and physicians is the doctor's inability to cope with patients' anxiety and demands for specific information he cannot provide. Some physicians have difficulty in coping with demands without ridiculing patients, getting irritated, or telling them to leave and not come back until they get their minds fixed by a psychotherapist. This method of coping with anxious patients, even hysterical ones, leaves something to be desired. It is in sharp contrast to that of a close colleague, Abel, a psychiatrist. Abel has found it much more efficient for himself and for the good of his patients to assertively set limits on what he will do by talking to the patient or relative and explaining that these limits (usually a denial of a patient's request) are set by Abel and are not a manifestation of some professional code to deal with "hysterical" or "stupid" patients. Without taking anything away from Abel's skill and competence in choosing to cope with patients in this more realistic way, he is the first to admit that unlike a general practitioner, he cannot pass the buck by manipulatively telling a patient he is hysterical, unreasonable, and should go see a psychiatrist! Abel's skill in coping with demands he cannot, in professional conscience, go along with, is an excellent model for assertively working out the practical balance between what the patient wants and what the professional can give. I consulted recently with him on the problems in dealing with the parents of psychiatric inpatients. Abel invited me, with the consent of the father of a sixteen-year-old schizophrenic, to sit in on a meeting between himself and the father.

Setting of the dialogue: The father, Mr. Genic, has seen a remarkable change in the behavior of his son since he was hospitalized five days ago and wants to take him home over the weekend.

MR. GENIC: I'm really glad we brought him to you, Doctor. Larry is almost normal again.

ABEL: *I can see that Larry's improvement must make you feel much better, Mr. Genic, but he still has a way to go before he can be considered normal.* [FOGGING and BROKEN RECORD]

MR. GENIC: He's talking to me again and not just hanging his head and keeping quiet. I know he's much better.

ABEL: *He is better,* but *I don't want you to get your hopes and expectations up too soon.* [FOGGING and SELF-DISCLOSURE]

MR. GENIC: After we visited him last night, my wife said she would like to have him home this weekend.

ABEL: *Although Larry has improved, I don't think it is wise for him to go home on a pass yet.* [FOGGING and SELF-DISCLOSURE]

MR. GENIC: His sister is coming home on vacation from college. My wife would like to have him home to see her. She hasn't seen him for five months.

ABEL: *I'm sure your daughter would like to see him,* but *Larry isn't in shape yet to go home, even on a weekend pass. How about you bringing her here over the weekend to see Larry?* [FOGGING, BROKEN RECORD, and WORKABLE COMPROMISE]

MR. GENIC: I don't want to upset her by seeing Larry in a mental hospital.

ABEL: *I'm sure you don't*, but *she's a big girl now and I think she has to face the fact that her brother had a psychotic break sometime.* [FOGGING and SELF-DISCLOSURE]

MR. GENIC: I just want Larry to see her at home. Can't you give him some medication for over the weekend to make him feel okay?

ABEL: *I can and do give medication when weekend passes are granted to patients,* but *I don't have any medication that is going to enable him to cope with the stress of being with family at this point in his recovery. I wish I did.* [FOGGING and NEGATIVE ASSERTION]

MR. GENIC: I guess that I'll take that chance. I want him home on the weekend.

ABEL: *I'm sure you do, Mr. Genic,* but *I won't approve a pass for Larry this weekend.* [FOGGING and BROKEN RECORD]

MR. GENIC: You can't stop me from taking my son home!

ABEL: *You're right, I can't stop you,* and *I wouldn't want to. But if you refuse to follow my treatment plan, I will discharge your son to your care. You can sign him out A.M.A.* [against medical advice]. *It's your decision.* [FOGGING, SELF-DISCLOSURE, and WORKABLE COMPROMISE]

MR. GENIC: Isn't that taking this whole thing to extremes? All I want to do is take Larry home for the weekend.

ABEL: *I'm sure it must seem a bit extreme to you, Mr. Genic,* but *I feel that Larry is not ready yet to cope with his family,* and *I have no other option consonant with my professional ethics. I wish I did, but . . .* [FOGGING, BROKEN RECORD, and NEGATIVE ASSERTION]

MR. GENIC: Are you in charge of this hospital? I want to speak to your boss!

ABEL: You can speak to the administration if you wish, but *frankly I think all you will get from them is the soft-soap treatment.* They don't tell me what to do medically and I don't tell them what to do administratively. *Still, I'll make an appointment with them for you if that will make you feel any better.* (Reaching for the phone) [SELF-DISCLOSURE and WORKABLE COMPROMISE]

MR. GENIC: No! Don't bother. I'll just pick my son up on Friday afternoon.

ABEL: I'll have the ward nurse fill out the discharge papers A.M.A. and have them ready. *I'll also talk to Larry and see if I can help him prepare for the discharge, and prescribe a thirty-day supply of tranquilizers.* Okay? [WORKABLE COMPROMISE]

Larry's father took him out Friday afternoon and was back in Abel's office at 9:00 A.M. Monday with a different opinion on the value of Abel's advice. Even with continued medication over the weekend, Larry's behavior and mood in the family situation changed drastically, as Abel predicted it might. Although Abel's confrontation with the patient's father might seem, at first, a disaster from the treatment point of view, it was of great benefit subsequently. Upon Abel's recommendation, both the father and mother were engaged in family therapy with their son while he was still an inpatient, and later on a continuing outpatient basis. Larry showed continued improvement as his parents changed their own behavior, through therapy, toward each other and toward him. One important part of this therapy was that when Abel said something to this family, they knew he meant it—he gave them no confusing double messages and did not put any blame on them for choosing not to follow his professional advice. He simply spelled out what he thought might be poor coping and let them make their own decision on what to do about it. They learned from him that they could do the same thing, and did it!

9

Everyday authority situations—
assertively coping with
supervision or
expertise

Learners generally express greater self-doubts in coping with situations that have fewer a priori rules on how things are done—relationships that have less structure than the formal, commerical transactions talked about in the previous chapter. In commercial situations, all the rules are spelled out, sometimes in the form of a legal contract or even by procedures of common law, and most learners rely heavily upon this structure for guidance on what they "can" or "cannot" do. They feel more at ease in asserting themselves when there are a lot of accepted ways of doing things that other people respond to also. When there are fewer rules, less already-agreed-upon structure that spells out how things "should" be done, the novice learner has more anxiety about asserting himself. You may have noticed this same emotional and behavioral pattern in yourself. You can "get yourself up" to deal with the sloppy repairs to your car by rehearsing your angry feelings the night before you see the mechanic, but can you do the same thing with your boss who has a different type of relationship with you? There is less defined structure in your relationship with your boss than with your garage mechanic, more potential loose ends. If your mechanic doesn't like what you say, what can he do? Nothing! But what can your boss do if he doesn't like what you say? Can he fire you? Can he demote you? Can he give you all the lousy jobs to do? Is this possible result spelled out in the job structure you hired into? One answer to those questions is probably "No," if you are working under a signed legal contract worked out by your attorney or that of a union. Another answer, and probably a more realistic one, is that these outcomes are dependent upon what compromises you assertively work out between your boss and yourself. The assertive working out of compromises with persons holding authority (including yourself) is the subject of this chapter.

I use the word "authority" to describe this partially structured way of interacting with someone in its broadest meaning. One common meaning of authority is that a person has the power to tell you what to do, or vice-versa; parent-child and supervisor-employee relationships are examples. Another meaning of authority is that of *expertise,* as in teacher-student or speaker-audience interactions. In these cases, the a priori structure set up beforehand is that the student learns from the teacher, and the teacher grades the student's progress in learning. The younger the student, the more the teacher assumes the authority of a supervisor, or as we say in the trade, *in loco parentis*—in place of the parent. You may be curious as to why I have emphasized the commercial aspects of the physician-patient relationship more than its other qualities. After all, the original meaning of the title Doctor is *teacher.* Why not simply classify physician-patient relationships as one type of authority interaction because of the doctor's expertise in medicine? Initially, I assume that any physician I go to will teach me as much about my health as my garage mechanic will teach me about my car. Unless a physician is recommended by another physician whose judgment I trust, I start out with the assumption that I am in a commercial relationship and assertively ask for everything to be spelled out about medication, treatment follow-up, complications, fees, etc. Think of it this way: would you trust a strange mechanic to overhaul the Mercedes-Benz you drive in the Monte Carlo Grand Prix?

Thankfully, most authority interactions that involve expertise do not have the potentially serious consequences of our well-being that is inherent in medical treatment. One expert-authority interaction that can even be fun is the relationship between a speaker and his audience. This situation is also partially structured beforehand. The speaker agrees to speak and the audience agrees to listen; definite initial roles are agreed upon. The expert presents new information to his audience—other professionals, students, the general public, fellow staff, other club members, etc.—and the audience responds with requests for more information or clarification and applause (hopefully!). The rest of the interaction between the parties is up for negotiation. How the speaker conducts his talk, the conditions under which he will speak, the material he will or will not cover, for instance, depend mainly upon how he asserts himself to his audience. Coping assertively as the leader or speaker to large groups of people, as in some of the following dialogues, can help you in this very difficult area where knowing what you want to say is not enough to demonstrate your expertise; knowing how to say what you know and how to assertively present your point of view in the face of criticism or even hecklers is equally as important to give your listeners some confidence in what you are saying.

Being assertive is particularly appropriate in some authority relationships where the a priori structure is quite scanty, such as in job interviews where the job applicant ofttimes is asked a number of idiotic questions and can rely only on himself to present a marketable picture of his skills and abilities to the interviewer.

In the following dialogues, the emphasis of being assertive is on working out mutual compromises that build upon the already existing structure in the relationship and at the same time to reduce any manipulative structure that may have been imposed unilaterally by one person in the conflict. This attempt at coping better within authority interactions is valid from both the viewpoint of the subordinate and from the viewpoint of the person in authority. The employee, for example, can assert himself to cope with manipulation from his boss, and the boss can assert himself to the employee both within the already established and agreed-upon rules of the job and in the gray area of behavior between them where no established procedures already exist.

With this brief introduction, let us look at the first dialogue in a series dealing with conflict in authority interactions: a dialogue where an employee assertively copes with excessive demands made upon his personal time by his employer.

Dialogue #16
Mike stops being the elastic
in a poor system of
overtime coverage
at work.

Mike is eighteen, recently out of high school, and working on his first job as a counterman in a franchised food sales operation. The shop where he works employs ten people on an irregular schedule to cover fourteen hours, seven days a week. With this kind of operation, absenteeism is a problem, and employee attrition is high. Mike worked in this job part-time when he was a senior in school and became a full-time employee when he was graduated. He is a conscientious worker and, in addition to maintaining his own schedule of work, has filled in for other employees when they were "sick," at the request of the manager. Mike's feelings about his job are mixed. He enjoys working in the food business and serving all types of people, yet the irregular schedule interferes with his social life and this aspect of the job bothers him. Even more bothersome is the manager's habit of calling on him to fill in for others. Although he resents being called for overtime, he does not know how to cope with the requests of Mr. Teague, the manager. He's afraid he'll alienate Mr. Teague and be fired if he asserts himself and says "No" to any of the overtime requests. After coaching in his assertive group, Mike reported the following dialogue between himself and the manager.

Setting of the dialogue: Mike is at home late Friday night when the manager telephones him.

MANAGER: Mike. Greg is sick and I need you to cover the morning tomorrow.

MIKE: That's rough, Mr. Teague. I have something on for tomorrow and won't be available.

MANAGER: Well, you'll have to call it off, I need you tomorrow.

MIKE: *I'm sure you do,* but *I'm just not available.* [FOGGING and BROKEN RECORD]

MANAGER: What is it? A doctor's appointment.

MIKE: No, nothing that serious, *I just won't be available tomorrow.* [BROKEN RECORD]

MANAGER: What are you going to do?

MIKE: *It's personal, Mr. Teague. Just something I've been trying to get up enough guts to do for a long while, so I won't be available tomorrow.* [SELF-DISCLOSURE and BROKEN RECORD]

MANAGER: Can't you put it off? You're leaving me in a bad situation.

MIKE: *I'm sure I am,* Mr. Teague, but *if I put it off this time, I'll probably never do it and I'd be disgusted with myself,* so *I won't be available tomorrow.* [FOGGING, NEGATIVE ASSERTION, and BROKEN RECORD]

MANAGER: I can fix it so you get Sunday off if you come in tomorrow.

MIKE: *I'm sure you would,* Mr. Teague, but *I won't be in tomorrow.* [FOGGING and BROKEN RECORD]

MANAGER: Well, that leaves me in a fix. I don't know who I can get to cover Greg.

MIKE: *That is a fix,* but I'm sure you'll work something out. [FOGGING]

MANAGER: That's all right, it'll be rough but I'll get someone to cover it.

MIKE: *I'm sure you will.* [FOGGING]

MANAGER: Greg will probably be off Tuesday too. I'd like you to cover his shift if he doesn't show up.

MIKE: *He probably will be out sick,* but *I won't be available Tuesday either.* [FOGGING and BROKEN RECORD]

MANAGER: Who am I going to get to replace him then?

MIKE: *I don't know.* [SELF-DISCLOSURE]

MANAGER: This is hard to take, Mike. You have always been so reliable before.

MIKE: *I'm sure it is,* Mr. Teague. *I don't know how it happened, but I've always been available whenever you asked me before, haven't I.* [FOGGING and NEGATIVE ASSERTION]

MANAGER: Well, I'll just have to find someone else I can count on.

MIKE: *That's true,* but *why don't you give me a call next time you need a replacement* and see if I'm free. Maybe I'll be available, maybe not. Doesn't cost anything to ask. [FOGGING and WORKABLE COMPROMISE]

MANAGER: Okay. We'll see.

MIKE: I hope you can get someone to cover for Greg.

MANAGER: I'll find someone, don't worry about it.

MIKE: Okay, see you.

Mike reported that after this dialogue with his boss, he felt much more confidence in his ability to cope with him on the job. An important part of Mike's feeling better about himself was, of course, the result of standing up to the pressure that his boss put on him to cover for other employees' absences. What struck Mike as amazing, however, was the degree to which Mr. Teague would go in trying to work out a compromise that was acceptable to Mike. Prior to this dialogue, Mike felt that he had no option but to do what was requested of him. After the dialogue with his boss, Mike felt that Mr. Teague had some respect for him and his wishes, that Mr. Teague would try and work with him in a difficulty instead of ordering him around.

Over a period of several months, Mike dealt with Mr. Teague on this new, straightforward basis of making his mind up as he went along and telling Mr. Teague what he wanted or didn't want. Mr. Teague adapted to this change in Mike's behavior and showed no apparent signs of upset with Mike. My guess, and it is only a guess, is that Mr. Teague previously thought of

Mike as a nice kid who had to be directed and controlled (and consequently used). I suspect that now he
neither thinks of Mike as a nice kid who needs direction nor as a young punk not to be trusted, but as an
adult man whom he works with.

Within the employer-employee context, in the next
dialogue, we see the other side of the coin: a supervisor
assertively dealing with a manipulative employee.

Dialogue #17
Sam tells his employee
of an increase in
workload.

Sam, thirty-seven, is a supervisor of fourteen employees in a small department of a large business firm.
Some of the fourteen employees he supervises are
friends of his and Sam worries about how to maintain
their friendship and still be an effective, fair supervisor
to everyone. While he believes in such slogans as:
"Business and friendship don't mix," and "Bosses are
not here to win popularity contests," Sam feels that to
be an effective supervisor he should not have to be
cold, unfriendly, standoffish, or uncaring about his employees. At the time of this dialogue, Sam was in a very
uncomfortable position. During the previous week, the
company executive decided in conference with all department heads that an economic cut-back policy was
to be implemented as soon as possible. At the time of
the meeting, Sam presented the problems of his department to the conference and expressed his doubt that
much money could be saved in his area. While listening
to his problems, the conference still decided on a blan-
ket cut-back of budget for all departments. These temporary workload increases had occurred twice in the
past during his employment in the firm and Sam felt
anxious when he had to explain to his employees that
they would have to increase their productivity. He also
felt that he had coped poorly with the situation in the
past by resorting to an uncaring, withdrawn, "tough"

image of a boss, and he felt both nervous and guilty in dealing with his friends afterwards.

The following training dialogue was set up to aid Sam in appropriately coping with his employees in a different way. Sam was instructed not to give any excuses for the increased workload, not to defend the policy made at the executive level, to simply agree with any possible truths about himself or the cut-back policy that his employees offered in opposition to the proposed increase in workload, to accept any statements of possible breakdown of the system, *and yet still require the cooperation of his employees in implementing the work increase.*

Setting of the dialogue: Sam approaches Harry, a friend, to tell him of the workload increase, over a coffee break.

SAM: (Seeing Harry in the coffee lounge and approaching him) Hi, Harry. You got a minute?

HARRY: Sure, Sam. Sit down. What's up?

SAM: You've heard about the department head meeting last week?

HARRY: I knew there was one, but that's all.

SAM: When the dust settled down, the economy cutback program was decided upon. The net result is that our department is required to show a 15 per cent increase in workload for the next three to six months without an increase in people or budget.

HARRY: That's a chuckleheaded idea. Christ! We're overloaded now and just making it by the skin of our teeth. Did you tell them that?

SAM: (Smiling) I didn't tell them that they were chuckleheads, but I did tell them that I thought it would be extremely difficult, if not impossible.

HARRY: What did they say?

SAM: Same thing I'm telling you. There will be an increase in workload.

HARRY: Sam, I don't know about the others, but I'm just about snowed under now. I can't take a 15 per cent increase in workload. I don't think I can take any, let alone 15 per cent.

SAM: *I agree with you, Harry. It probably won't work and you and the rest of the people with increases may have trouble,* but *nevertheless we still have an increase in workload.* [FOGGING and BROKEN RECORD]

HARRY: That's a hell of a note. Did you tell them that it won't work in our department?

SAM: *I agree. It is a hell of a note.* They didn't listen to my warnings. I told them pretty much what you're telling me. Only more diplomatically. [FOGGING]

HARRY: If you were less diplomatic and laid it right on the table, maybe they would have listened more to what you told them.

SAM: *Perhaps.* [FOGGING]

HARRY: Perhaps my ass. If you had laid it on strong they wouldn't be shoving 15 per cent down our throats. They don't know how overloaded we are already.

SAM: *You are probably right,* but *we are still going to have to increase the caseload.* [FOGGING and BROKEN RECORD]

HARRY: But I'm having a hell of a time getting everything done now. You know that!

SAM: *That's true, Harry, so I want you to let me know right away whenever things get out of hand.* After the first month I want you and everybody else to write a memo to me about their specific problems so I have some ammunition if I have to go back upstairs to let them know what is happening. [FOGGING and WORK-ABLE COMPROMISE]

HARRY: Well, I don't think I can take on a 15 per cent increase.

SAM: *You're probably right,* so we will start small at first and see how things go. You have sixty cases on your books now. *Pick up four more out of the new cases in the next two weeks.* [FOGGING and WORK-ABLE COMPROMISE]

HARRY: Sam! Four new cases will take at least eight hours to prepare and write up to start with. I can't do them without working overtime.

SAM: *You may be right.* If you find you can't spare

any time from the old cases to work up the new ones and have to work late, *just keep tab of your time and I'll set it up as comp time on our own schedule.* [FOGGING and WORKABLE COMPROMISE]

HARRY: Well, I sure as hell don't like it.

SAM: *I agree, Harry.* I don't blame you for getting upset. But the decision's out of our hands, so *let's see how things work out.* Okay? [FOGGING and WORKABLE COMPROMISE]

HARRY: We'll see.

SAM: Okay?

HARRY: Okay.

This critical dialogue of Sam's behavior and company policy was repeated several times with variations of manipulative threats running from union protests to social isolation of Sam from his friends. After sufficient practice, Sam reported that he felt quite comfortable and relaxed during the actual encounters with his employees, and they showed no anger toward him and accepted the increases with very little protest, criticism, or attempted manipulation.

Again looking at the "flip side" of things, in the next dialogue we see how an employee assertively copes with an employer who meddles in her personal life.

Dialogue #18
Betty copes with a
boss who meddles
in her personal
life.

Betty is an animated, very attractive young secretary, who was recently divorced. Betty's main problem immediately after her divorce was coping with unwanted interference from her boss. He was an older married man who assumed a fatherlike role toward Betty when she was undergoing the emotional and behavioral crisis of changing her lifestyle from that of a somewhat sedate married woman back to that of a more active single woman. Although Betty had doubts about shar-

ing her personal decisions and troubles with her boss,
she felt emotionally and intellectually inadequate to
simply tell him to keep his nose out of her business.
During the past several months, he inquired into the
status of her living arrangements since her separation.
She told him of the apartment she was planning on
moving into, and he promptly told her that she
shouldn't live in that apartment, that she should seek
another one having specifications that he outlined for
her. He inquired into her social life and when she told
him of the various men she was dating, he promptly
told her why they were not the type she should associate with. He even inquired into the activities that Betty
was engaged in. When she told him about her night
school and bike riding, he promptly told her what classes she should take and what kind of bike she should
ride. She identified him strongly with her father (with
whom she was to cope successfully later), and thought
that since she had been doing stupid things around the
office during the emotional crisis of her separation, she
had no recourse but to let her boss interfere as a way of
making up for her errors. Over a period of weeks, Betty
practiced being more assertive with her boss. Her aim,
of course, was not to be frightened of him but at the
same time not to lose her temper and tell him off, thus
destroying their working relationship, forcing her either
to quit or be fired. Her goals were (1) to *desensitize*
herself to her boss's critical or even well-meaning but
still interfering statements, and (2) to eliminate his ten-
dency to make such statements in the first place. She
wanted him to behave toward her as a responsible,
functioning adult woman who did not require instruction or approval on how she conducted her personal
life.

Setting of the dialogue: Betty is seated at her desk
and her boss walks out of his office and speaks to her.

BOSS: How're things today?
BETTY: Just fine.
BOSS: Working on this month's eligibility lists?
BETTY: Yes.

BOSS: Any problems?

BETTY: No.

BOSS: I hope you do this month's lists better than last month's.

BETTY: *That was a mess, wasn't it?* [NEGATIVE ASSERTION]

BOSS: It sure was.

BETTY: *You're telling me! God, did I screw that up!* [NEGATIVE ASSERTION]

BOSS: I hope you get settled soon so you're not so upset that it interferes with your work.

BETTY: *That makes sense. So do I.* [FOGGING and SELF-DISCLOSURE]

BOSS: Have you decided on your extension classes yet?

BETTY: Some of them.

BOSS: You're not going to take that medieval literature class, are you?

BETTY: *I haven't decided yet.* [SELF-DISCLOSURE]

BOSS: You shouldn't take that one. That's just a plain waste of time.

BETTY: Yeah, *it could be.* [FOGGING]

BOSS: Well, are you going to take it?

BETTY: *Maybe, I haven't decided yet.* [BROKEN RECORD]

BOSS: You should take something practical where you'll learn something worthwhile.

BETTY: *You're probably right.* We'll see soon when I decide. [FOGGING]

BOSS: Well, I hope you make a sensible decision.

BETTY: *So do I.* [SELF-DISCLOSURE]

Betty told me of this dialogue the next day. She was still then almost euphoric at times during our therapy session over how she could cope with her boss's interference with so little effort and no gut-wrenching anxiety. Like other novices, however, she found that one quick, assertive dialogue was insufficient to eliminate the manipulation of those she was in daily contact with. It was necessary to repeat similar dialogues on other subjects, such as her choice of living arrangements and of boyfriends, several times before her boss ceased telling her what to do in her personal life. Not surprisingly, after becoming more assertive toward her boss, Betty felt more at ease in her job, and the number of mistakes she made at work dropped sharply. As Betty put it, "I look forward to work now. I feel I'm productive and doing something worthwhile." Also, not surprisingly, Betty began to look around for a better job with more interest and responsibility than just clerking and found one within two months as an assistant office supervisor. Quite surprisingly, however, Betty reported that being more assertive to her boyfriends, especially with Stan whom she liked the most, produced a change in her sexual relations that to her was amazing. Betty began to have consistent orgasms in her sexual relations with Stan, something that in the past with other men, including her husband, was chancy at best.

If you are like many learners, you may have the same difficulties in dealing with a situation that plagues you with anxieties: an interview for a job or acceptance into a training program of some sort. In the next set of dialogues, you can see how two learners were trained to cope assertively with an interviewer and the questions he might ask them.

Dialogue #19
Milt and Dee practice to take graduate school and job interviews assertively.

In the first dialogue, Milt rehearses being interviewed for acceptance into graduate school. Milt is a bright young college student who popped into my assertive group one afternoon. He was referred to me by a colleague who had seen Milt for pre-med student counseling and thought he could present himself more assertively. A bit anxious and out of breath, Milt explained to the group that he had an appointment the following day to be interviewed by an alumnus of a medical school. His counselor talked with him about it, asked him a few likely questions about what the interviewer might want to know, listened to Milt's style of responding, and told him to hot-foot it over to the assertive group to see what could be done. Milt accepted the fact that we thought little of his chances for improving his confidence in so short a time (our estimates on how much time was needed were way off the mark), but he still wanted to see if he could feel a bit more relaxed and look less of a fool in the interview by working with us even for an hour or two. We ran a mock interview that afternoon with all of us rotating as the interviewer asking some of the pertinent as well as the inane questions we had once been asked ourselves. While one of us role-played the interviewer, the rest of us coached Milt on assertively talking about himself and why he wanted to go to medical school. We ran through several coached dialogues in the two hours we had available, the last, edited version of which is presented here.

Setting of the dialogue: The elderly Dr. Alumnus invites Milt into his office and they sit down across a desk from one another.

DOCTOR: (Looking at the papers in his hand) It seems that you prepared a well-written and comprehensive application.

MILT: Thank you. I spent a lot of time on it. [SELF-DISCLOSURE]

DOCTOR: (Looking now at Milt) Tell me, why do you want to be a doctor?

MILT: *I really don't know any one good answer to that. I'm sure I should, but I don't.* I have a lot of different reasons. I've always wanted to be one. I've had a lot of other interests, but I keep coming back to medicine as the thing that fascinates me most. I like people ... I like working with them and helping them. I like solving problems and figuring things out. I like working with my head as well as my hands. *Am I rambling on too much for you?* [SELF-DISCLOSURE, NEGATIVE ASSERTION, and NEGATIVE INQUIRY]

DOCTOR: No, go right ahead.

MILT: *Okay, I'll just talk about what's important to me.* I like working in a laboratory. Biology fascinates me and I like working with patients as a volunteer aide at the UCLA Med Center. I like the idea of being a professional. These are the things I think of when I think of the idea of being an MD. (Then smiling) I heard the pay is good too. [WORKABLE COMPROMISE]

DOCTOR: (Not smiling) Yes, well, why do you specifically want to go to the University of South Such-and-such Medical School?

MILT: *I have no first hand information,* but I've talked to a lot of MDs about different schools and they tell me USS is known for turning out graduates. I'd like to get my MD from a school with a reputation. [NEGATIVE ASSERTION]

DOCTOR: What do you want to be doing five years from now?

MILT: I hope to be practicing medicine in some capacity.

DOCTOR: What capacity?

MILT: (From Milt, with no coaching) *I don't know yet.* General practice fascinates me with the variety of problems patients bring to you. Psychiatry also interests me. [SELF-DISCLOSURE]

DOCTOR: Psychiatry and the other specializations take at least three years residency beyond your schooling and internship.

MILT: *Yes, that's true,* but *I've found that if you're doing what you want to do, time passes quickly.* [FOGGING and SELF-DISCLOSURE]

DOCTOR: What do you want to be doing five years after you graduate?

MILT: *I really don't know at this point for sure.* It depends a lot on what I experience in med school. I don't think that I would like to go right into private practice. I think I would like to work in an inpatient setting first until I really know what I'm doing. [SELF-DISCLOSURE]

DOCTOR: You seem unsure of yourself, like you may

not be confident enough to practice medicine on your own

MILT: *I'm sure it sounds that way,* but that's not what I mean. *I think I will make a damned fine MD.* I'm smart enough, it interests me, and I work hard. I'm not afraid of getting my hands dirty. [FOGGING and SELF-DISCLOSURE]

DOCTOR: (Somewhat sarcastically) Well, we'll try to teach you to keep them clean. I've been looking at your transcript and your grades look fine except for one area. You got a "C" in organic chemistry. (Looking up at Milt for an explanation)

MILT: *That's true. Organic was one of my weak areas.* I have been auditing the course again, and I have a friend tutoring me on it. Organic for me was like trigonometry. *It took me three weeks in trig to figure out what in hell they were talking about and how everything fit together. I don't think I'll have any problem with it now though.* I'm in the second course and I expect an "A" or at worst a "B." [FOGGING, NEGATIVE ASSERTION, and SELF-DISCLOSURE]

DOCTOR: Medicine is demanding. Especially if you are in general practice like I am. There have been times when I wished I'd never gotten into it. Patients bug you. Nurses bug you, relatives bug you, other doctors bug you. Everybody expects you to have the answer to their problem and you have to work long hours, sometimes for nothing. How do you know you can take the pressure?

MILT: *You're right, I can't give you an absolute guarantee that I can cope with all the pressures, but I think I can.* I've worked under a lot of pressure in college to get good grades. I've burned a lot of midnight oil, and so far I've made it. All my experience tells me that I can do it. *Sometimes I tell myself: "To hell with all this work; why are you always working so hard?"* But I keep at it though. *I don't know the answer. Maybe I'm a masochist.* [FOGGING, NEGATIVE ASSERTION, SELF-DISCLOSURE, and NEGATIVE ASSERTION]

DOCTOR: Sometimes I think I am too. I assume that you have applied to other schools.

MILT: Yes, *I thought it best.* Even though I want to go to USS, everybody tells me to make other applications in case I'm not accepted. Is that what you did when you were a student? [SELF-DISCLOSURE]

DOCTOR: Yes, it's a good idea. (Silence)

MILT: *Anything else you would like to ask me? My weaknesses or my strengths?* [NEGATIVE INQUIRY]

DOCTOR: You tell me. What do you consider your worst weakness?

MILT: *This is my own opinion. Other people might have a different viewpoint. I think my weakest area is lack of experience. I'm young. I'm naïve with other people. I'm not as assertive as I could be. I tend to get rattled in interviews.* When we first sat down, I thought my mind was going to be blank from nervousness. But I think that experiences like this one will help me overcome these feelings, or at least I hope so. [SELF-DISCLOSURE, FOGGING, and NEGATIVE ASSERTION]

DOCTOR: (Interrupting) You seem to be doing just fine now. You don't look nervous at all.

MILT: *I'm sure I don't, but inside I'm still not comfortable.* [FOGGING and SELF-DISCLOSURE]

DOCTOR: Maybe it's how you behave on the outside that really counts instead of how you feel on the inside.

MILT: *I'm sure you're right,* I'll see what happens. [FOGGING]

DOCTOR: What do you think is your greatest strength?

MILT: As I said before, this is just my impression. *I may be wrong, but I think it's good study habits, perseverance, a willingness to work hard, and some brains. And, maybe the most important thing, I like people, and I like medicine.* [FOGGING and SELF-DISCLOSURE]

DOCTOR: Anything you would like to ask me?

MILT: Yes, I'd like to ask you some questions about USS and med school. *Things that I know very little about. I'm sure they sound naïve and unsophisticated,* but I'd still like to get your opinion about these things. [SELF-DISCLOSURE and NEGATIVE ASSERTION]

DOCTOR: Sure, go ahead.

Milt then asked the following questions which we prompted from him concerning things he would like to know.

1. I am interested in research. How do you go about getting involved in it at USS?

2. Are there any areas during the first year of training that the faculty want you to be strong in and really know well aside from the general material that everyone should know?

3. Do you know any general references that I can study this summer to help me prepare for my first year in the fall?

4. What sort of summer jobs can a med student get at USS to help pay living expenses during the academic year? Are there any that allow you to learn as well as earn?

At the end of two hours of assertively practicing to take an interview, we saw an obvious difference in his ability to field questions we had not coached him on. We asked Milt to let us know how he fared in the interview but we never heard from him again. I learned from other sources that the interview went well for him as did others he took. He was accepted at several medical schools and enrolled in one we had not practiced for. Milt's success brings to mind the old motto of the navy's construction battalions of World War II; "The difficult we do right away, the impossible takes a little longer!" Milt's lack of assertiveness in taking interviews was obviously, in their terms, only a difficulty. Milt's rapid change even surprised me, and I'm not often surprised.

As you may have figured out for yourself, Milt's practice in preparation for a graduate school interview was really a role rehearsal for a job interview, an experience that most of us view with distaste or even some anxiety. Many learners in assertive training request coaching for job interviews and most of the learners who assertively practice for a job interview report afterwards that they felt more at ease in the stressful situation and they coped more realistically with it, *whether or not they got the particular job they were seeking.* The rehearsal of coached dialogues for job interviews is, except for specific details of the particular job, identical to Milt's rehearsal. In working with nonassertive people as well as with a population of psychiatric patients sufficiently recovered to go back to work and lead productive lives again, several points are consistently raised by these learners: things that they have the most difficulty dealing with in job interviews. Job interviews make them quite nervous and they typically try to hide their nervousness instead of prefacing the interview with a statement like: "I always get a bit nervous applying for a job. Will that interfere with the interview?" (NEGATIVE ASSERTION and NEGATIVE INQUIRY) Most don't know how to respond to specific negative comments about their work history and experience. Very often, they transmit their doubts about their ability to perform even minor job skills to the interviewer and consequently give the interviewer the impression that they are fragile and may have to be handled with kid gloves on the job, a possible future headache that the company can well afford to do without. My own clinical observations of these difficulties in job interviews were confirmed for me by counseling staff of the State of California Department of Rehabilitation. In a recent southern California meeting of these counselors, at which I was invited to speak on systematic assertive therapy, the main topic of discussion centered around preparing a client for a job. For many of their clients, these counselors agreed that the main problem was enabling them to get a foot in the door at the job interview—not preparing them to do their jobs competently. These clients (as well as many nonassertive people in the general population) seem to have what I can only describe as an unreal "sharing" attitude toward job interviewers. At times of decision, these unfortunate people seem to take no responsibility for their own circumstances. The classic response that I think best describes this "sharing" attitude was reported by a patient who "tried" to get a job prior to my working with him. When he was asked in a job interview, "Can you drive?" (since the firm often had to deliver paperwork in a rush), instead of simply saying "Yes" (he could drive) or even "Yes, but I will have to get my license renewed," he replied: "I used to before I was committed to the mental hospital for six months. When the Department of Motor Vehicles found out I was committed involuntarily, they took my driver's license away." As you might guess, the job interview terminated immediately. Although this instance of "confessing one's sins" is a very gross example of how to demonstrate your nonassertiveness and lack of confidence in yourself to a job interviewer, this behavior pattern and attitude are not limited to ex-psychiatric patients. Many of the learners that I teach to cope with job interviews have the same difficulty. When an interviewer delves into an area where the learner experiences self-doubts, they report that they become rattled and exaggerate their supposed shortcomings, confess their self-doubts, then try to overcome this beginning by justifying their limitations in the eyes of the interviewer.

You may ask yourself some of the same questions that novice learners in assertive training ask on how to cope in a job interview. What do I say when the interviewer diplomatically says: "You're a bit younger than the person we are looking for (or a bit older)," or "It seems that you don't have as much experience as we would like in this position (or too much experience)," or "You seem to change jobs frequently (or were stuck in one job a long time)," or any of a number of equally open-ended remarks made with the purpose of prompting the applicant to talk about himself. In the following dialogue, Dee, a young file clerk who is learning how to assert herself, is coached on how to respond to the anxiety-producing statements she may encounter in a job interview.

Dee said that on her last job interview before assertive training, when the interviewer asked her "Can you type?" she replied: "I can't type more than forty words a minute and I make a lot of errors." She then tried to explain this apparent lack of job skills by saying: "I never was very good at typing, I failed the typing course twice and had to take it a third time before I passed it." The job she was applying for was that of an office clerk and did not require typing as a prerequisite for the job. Dee and I discussed her problem in taking job interviews in the following dialogue.

ME: My guess is that the interviewer asked if you could type to find out if you would type an occasional letter when the typists and secretaries were busy.

DEE: I didn't think of that.

ME: Could you type an occasional letter?

DEE: Sure.

ME: Then why didn't you tell him that or just say "Yes" when he asked you, instead of spewing out all that garbage on how poor a typist you are?

DEE: Looking at it now, I don't really know. I guess that I didn't want to get caught in promising something I couldn't do.

ME: Did you ask him if typing was required for the job?

DEE: No. The notice didn't say anything about typing.

ME: Didn't you feel a bit curious about why he was talking about typing when the job description didn't mention it?

DEE: When he started to talk about typing, my mind went blank ...

ME: ... and you started to spew out garbage.

DEE: ... and I started to spew out garbage.

ME: Let's try it now. I'll interview you for a job and Kathy will coach you if you need help.

DEE: Okay. What job?

ME: You decide. Janitor, brain surgeon, CIA agent,

the same job; it doesn't matter. It's the same for all of them.

DEE: I'd like to go over the part I had trouble with in the last one.

ME: How about other things he could throw at you?

DEE: Okay, those too.

ME: (Role-playing) Can you type?

DEE: Yes.

ME: Good, we occasionally have busy periods in the office and we like to have everyone help everyone else.

DEE: *That's a great way to do things,* but *I don't understand, is typing a required skill for this job?* [FOGGING and SELF-DISCLOSURE]

ME: No, but as I said we would like someone who is flexible.

DEE: *I ask that because I don't want to give you the impression that I'm an expert typist. I'm not. If you really need someone super-fast, I don't fill the bill. But I can bang out a letter in a pinch or do some memos.* [NEGATIVE ASSERTION]

ME: No, your job would be mainly in the office keeping things up to date and in order.

DEE: That sounds fine to me.

ME: I see from your application that you don't have much experience in working in an office.

DEE: *That's true in terms of work time,* but at the places I worked before, I learned an awful lot about office procedures. You had to work hard and learn fast to keep your job. [FOGGING]

ME: I also see that you changed jobs frequently.

DEE: *Yes, I did.* When a better job came along, I took it. [FOGGING]

ME: Well, we like our employees to stick with us.

DEE: *I'm sure you do.* What incentives do you offer to keep your employees from going to other jobs? [FOGGING]

ME: I'll tell you about our employee benefit plans a little later. You are a bit younger than most of the employees we like to hire.

DEE: *I'm sure I am and I don't blame you for being cautious.* A lot of girls my age aren't very mature and don't seem to get along with other people, but that isn't a problem for me. [FOGGING]

ME: I see you only have experience as a file clerk.

DEE: *That's true,* I haven't had enough experience yet to even think of things like being a supervisor. [FOGGING]

ME: What do you expect to be doing in a few years?

DEE: Hopefully working for you, but that depends upon things like raises and advancement. *I don't know enough about this company yet to give a realistic answer.* [NEGATIVE ASSERTION]

ME: Is there anything you would like to ask me?

DEE: Yes, I'd like to know about salary, working conditions, benefits.

ME: (With great gusto to reinforce Dee's new approach to a job interview) Fantastic. You're hired!

DEE: (Grinning, and then thoughtful and serious) But what if I didn't type and he wanted me to?

ME: You mean he's changing his mind after placing the advertisement?

DEE: Yeah. What happens then?

ME: Why not role-play it and see what could happen?

DEE: Okay.

ME: Can you type?

DEE: No.

ME: Hmm. We had hoped to get someone who could type a little to help out the other girls in the office.

DEE: (Without coaching) Does that mean that you won't hire me?

ME: Yes. I'm afraid you don't meet our qualifications.

DEE: What do I say now? I lost the job. I'd just get up and leave.

KATHY: (Interrupting) Dee, there's more at stake here than just getting or not getting a job. How does it make you feel when the interviewer said you don't meet his specifications?

DEE: It makes me mad as hell for him to put out a crooked advertisement for a job and then waste my time going down there for an interview.

KATHY: Then why not tell him that?

DEE: Why not? Okay!

ME: (Repeating) Yes. I'm afraid you don't meet our qualifications.

DEE: That makes me mad as hell. You wasted a whole morning for me by saying one thing in the paper and then telling me something else when I get here. If you want someone who can type, then pay for it. (Breaking role-playing) What do I do now?

KATHY: Nothing. Just sit there and look him in the eye.

ME: Well, you should have known that general office skills means some typing.

DEE: (Picking up the interviewer's attempted manipulation) I can understand why you would say that, but your way of doing business makes me mad.

ME: Well, I'm very sorry that we have inconvenienced you.

DEE: I'm sure you are, but your way of doing business still makes me mad.

ME: What can I do? I apologize for your inconvenience.

DEE: You can be more specific in your job descriptions in the future so you don't waste my time again.

ME: (Breaking role-playing) What can I say, Dee? You've pinned me to the wall.

KATHY: How do you feel about what you just did?

DEE: I feel really good. It doesn't make sense. I lost a job, but I feel good.

KATHY: Maybe because you told the interviewer what you thought of his shenanigans? Think about it!

In training nonassertive people to cope adequately in a job interview, I stress three things. First, I train them to listen to what the interviewer asks or says, not what they think he means by the question or statement. Second, I train them not to deny any of their possible shortcomings that the interviewer may point out, and third, in spite of any supposed shortcomings, I train them to tell the interviewer that they think they still can do a damn good job for the company.

With no modesty at all, I use my own experience in job interviews as a model after which they can pattern their own behavior. For example, I tell my students and patients: "When I was interviewed for my present position one of the questions put to me was: 'Can you teach crisis intervention?' And my answer was an immediate 'Yes.' I was hired on the spot. It really didn't matter that I spent the next week brushing up on crisis intervention methods and then arranging for the whole staff to be trained in crisis intervention at the Los Angeles Psychiatric Services Clinic. I was asked only if I could teach crisis intervention and the truth was that I could. I listened only to what the interviewer asked, not what I thought he meant by the question. If I were asked by the job interviewer on the other hand, 'How much experience do you have in crisis intervention?' I would have answered, 'Very little beyond the exposure you get in general clinical training, but I am very much interested in it and I would hope to get a lot of field experience in crisis intervention here.' If then the interviewer stated: 'We would like to get someone who could teach crisis intervention to the rest of our staff,' I would have replied, 'That's no problem. I've been teaching psychology for ten years now and if I didn't feel adequate to teach crisis intervention, I would make arrangements for an expert to consult here at the clinic or arrange for the staff to attend a workshop where the experts are.' I gave a clear message to the interviewer—the way I responded to his questions didn't matter—I was confident that I could solve problems and get a job done that he wanted done. The ability to solve problems for his organization and get a job done is really what a job interviewer is looking for in an applicant, no matter what the job title—clerk, manager, bookkeeper, salesman, repairman, lathe operator, truck driver, janitor, or psychologist."

In the next dialogue, we see how a job applicant copes with a situation many of us would like to find ourselves in: assertively making no commitment to a possible employer while choosing the best of two offers of work.

Dialogue #20
Carl copes with a manipulative
movie producer.

Carl is a talented young actor with three movie roles that have earned him good reviews. Because of his success, he and his agent planned a campaign for his screen career that involves careful review and selection of any roles he is offered in the future to get the most financial and professional achievement out of them.

Carl knows that he is talented and has the potential to become a sought-after actor. Unfortunately, Carl also feels that he must do everything desired by the producers he deals with to maintain their goodwill or he might be passed by. Carl's belief that he must act like a "goody two shoes" toward producers is unsupported by reality. Carl's assumption that talent alone is not sufficient to be successful is quite correct. His assumption that the goodwill of these producers is essential to his success is not correct. Evidence to the contrary is available to Carl and all his peers, but is misinterpreted by them. The three actors in the movie industry who work whenever they want and pick and choose their jobs are George C. Scott, Marlon Brando, and Peter Falk. These gentlemen behave publicly as if they do not feel they require the goodwill of producers or indeed certain other segments of the movie industry, and they are reputed to be very assertive in their private dealings in negotiating movie roles and contracts as well. Although equally great acting talent is not common to all three of these gentlemen, a high degree of assertiveness is. To Carl and his fellow actors in his group, these three persons are viewed as eccentrics or "crazies" since they are not manipulable and find it easy to assertively demand what they require for themselves and typically get it. Carl himself is amazed at their finding work consistently but writes off their successes as something peculiar to their personalities and places himself in an infantile, or at best childlike, relationship to his possible employers.

At the time of this dialogue, I was consulting for a drama study group that included Carl, a former Broadway musical star, and other young actors and actresses whose faces were so familiar from their TV commercials but had no names to go with them. I was consulting on how to be systematically assertive to casting directors, reading committees, directors, production assistants, producers and the whole lot of fringe "backers," "experts," "critics," and "gofers" that the actor must cope with. Carl brought up a problem of being pressured and manipulated by the producer of a film soon to go into production. Carl's agent has two possible contracted roles in negotiation, one of them with this producer. His agent may recommend that he take one over the other, neither, or even both if scheduling commitments could be worked out. The producer, on the other hand, wanted Carl to sign a production contract with him immediately. Carl's agent meanwhile was negotiating on the second possible role. Carl did not want to tell the producer that he was considering another role in place of the one being offered for fear that he would lose the producer's goodwill on future negotiations or that the producer would use this information to foul up the negotiations on the other contract. In short, Carl had a problem in communicating his desire not to make a commitment immediately and to negotiate a commitment time limit sufficient to decide which role to contract for. Carl had had an encounter with the producer shortly before the consultation with me; he had begged off giving his decision but had promised to see him as soon as possible. The following coached dialogue was set up in the drama group to allow Carl to practice being systematically assertive in avoiding a premature commitment without being rude, short, apologetic, or making the producer angry or insulting him. Although the setting of this situation dialogue is the exotic cinematographic production business, systematically asserting oneself to one's present or future employer to avoid a manipulated commitment is equally applicable in almost all other life occupations.

Setting of the dialogue: Carl is seated in Mr. Mogul's office as the producer breezes through the waiting room, greets Carl, and whisks him into his inner office.

PRODUCER: Carl, this is the role for you. If this doesn't make it for you, nothing will. I've just come from upstairs and everybody is really enthusiastic over you playing the role of Marvin.

CARL: That's great. *I agree with them. I think I could do a good job on it too.* [FOGGING]

PRODUCER: Fabulous! All we need is the contract signed and we'll have a drink on it.

CARL: Great! I'll have the drink if I sign, but *I still want some time to decide.* [SELF-DISCLOSURE]

PRODUCER: What do you need time for? It's a great part and the money's good. Hal thinks so too. He's your agent and he negotiated the terms.

CARL: *I agree,* but *I don't want to make a commitment yet.* [FOGGING and BROKEN RECORD]

PRODUCER: Carl, we really want you on this production. I've worked hard upstairs to get the rest of the staff enthusiastic for you. We all want you now. Don't let me down after all the trouble I went to for you.

CARL: *I hope I don't disappoint you, Sol,* but *I still don't want to make a commitment right now.* [SELF-DISCLOSURE and BROKEN RECORD]

PRODUCER: We leave for location in two weeks. We need a commitment right now. Don't pass up this part, Carl.

CARL: *You're probably right, Sol, so how long can you give me to decide?* [FOGGING and WORKABLE COMPROMISE]

PRODUCER: I'll need your signature by tomorrow.

CARL: *I'm sure you do, Sol,* but that's not enough time for me. *How about if I let you know before you leave for location?* That's two weeks. That should be enough time for me to decide. [FOGGING and WORKABLE COMPROMISE]

PRODUCER: Carl! We can't do that. We'd have to break off production and come back here to get a replacement if you said no; screw up the whole schedule!

CARL: *I don't understand.* Don't you have a second choice picked out? [SELF-DISCLOSURE]

PRODUCER: Not yet. We haven't found anyone near you for this part. If you don't sign, Carl, you'll be missing a great role.

CARL: *You're probably right, Sol, but I still want some time to decide.* Let's look at the calendar. You leave on the twenty-eighth, right? *I'll give you my decision on the twenty-third.* That would give you five working days to find someone else, if I say no. How's that sound? [FOGGING, BROKEN RECORD, and WORKABLE COMPROMISE]

PRODUCER: That's cutting it very close for me, Carl.

CARL: *I'm sure it is, Sol,* but *I need time* and you need time. *This gives us both some leeway.* [FOGGING, BROKEN RECORD, and WORKABLE COMPROMISE]

PRODUCER: You give me no choice. What way is that to be after all I've done for you?

CARL: *You're right, Sol, it's a hell of a way to operate. I wish I could let you know that I would sign,* but *I'm not going to make a commitment right now.* [FOGGING, SELF-DISCLOSURE, and BROKEN RECORD]

PRODUCER: If you decide earlier, you will let me know right away?

CARL: Of course I will, Sol. *As soon as I decide.* [WORKABLE COMPROMISE]

PRODUCER: We're counting on you for this part.

CARL: *I know you are, Sol,* and *I want to take it,* but *I just need more time.* [SELF-DISCLOSURE and BROKEN RECORD]

I was amazed at the quickness Carl displayed in being able to pick up the elements of the assertive skills and use them after only a small amount of explanation and coaching (less than three hours and several bottles of California wine). Perhaps the quickness was due to his excellent skill as an actor; he was familiar with role-playing. All he needed to do was learn a new script. As things turned out, Carl learned his new, more assertive role very well. In his meeting with the producer, Carl got what he wanted, a delay in commitment that was to prove very important to him. After his agent finished negotiations with the second production company, they both decided the second offer was the better of the two deals, and took it. As a result, Carl spent six enviable months on a tropical island perfecting his craft while working with and learning from a major star and consummate actor but keeping his word to the first producer to let him know by a scheduled time.

While Carl's success story is interesting and a glamorous one to tell, you might ask, as did my New York editor (and Carl himself at the time of my consultation), what could Carl say if Sol the producer said something like: "Commitment, commitment! Whaddya really mean?" Carl, like Carlo in the chapter on BROKEN RECORD, was instructed that just because Sol says or asks him something does not mean that Carl has to give an answer or response in any way related to what the producer says. The following short dialogue illustrates this point:

SOL: Carl. What the hell is holding you up? Commitment, commitment! Whaddya really mean?

CARL: I understand you want an answer now, Sol, but I won't give a commitment until the twenty-third.

SOL: Your agent agrees to this. Don't you?

CARL: I understand how you feel, Sol. You want me to sign right now, but I won't have an answer until the twenty-third.

SOL: Are you into another part? Is that what this is all about?

CARL: I understand how that possibility would worry you, Sol, but I won't have an answer for you until the twenty-third.

As you can see from this short, hypothetical dialogue, all Carl really needed to field anything Sol the producer could throw at him was an emphatic but persistent and unflappable BROKEN RECORD response.

In the next set of dialogues, we see a problem area related to "show biz," i.e., assertively coping with large groups of people while speaking publicly, giving an invited talk, presenting a report, etc.

Dialogue #21
Susan demonstrates how to deal
with criticism of her
public-speaking
ability.

Recently, my good friend and colleague, Ms. Susan Levine, MSW, was invited to give a two-hour talk to a local meeting of the National Association of Social Workers. While Sue was specifically requested to talk on how to train clients to be more assertive, the subject of her talk—systematic assertive therapy—is not the point of this dialogue. Comfortably presenting your views in public is. A number of learners, like teachers, sales managers, etc., who spoke in public regularly on a variety of subjects have reported experiences identical to Sue's in using this method of overcoming anxiety in public speaking.

Sue had never before given an invited presentation to a group of her peers and, like most people, she was a bit nervous and apprehensive about how well she would carry it off. I could empathize with her feelings, remembering how nervous I was the first time I had to speak to a professional group. My assumption about Sue's predicament was that she was feeling the same about her first invited talk as I had about mine: knowing the material, yet feeling unsure of herself and her speaking abilities. In spite of all her experience and competence, Sue found that there is something about that first invited talk that strikes fear in the hearts of us all. Perhaps because of this irrational anxiety, she asked me if I would role-play the manipulative parts in her demonstration of the assertive verbal skills—to be her "second banana" on the speaker's dais and be manipulative upon her cue. I agreed, and as it turned out, Susan overcame her anxiety, gave a great talk to the association of social workers, I had a great prime rib dinner, and we both had a lot of fun. I could not help but notice, however, and my observation was later confirmed by Susan, that up to the point of demonstrating the skill of FOGGING, she was a bit tense. After that role-playing she was completely relaxed and at ease with her audience, no matter what comments or questions they posed ... even the hostile ones! Her more relaxed attitude was a result of what we did in the FOGGING demonstration. Sue asked me, in front of her audience, to criticize her presentation, even to invent criticism if I couldn't find specifics to fault her on. As you can see from the following dialogue, my critique of Sue was worse than anything she could have rationally expected from her audience. My critique, however, went to the heart of the irrational anxiety many of us have about public speaking and she was able to cope with it by FOGGING and completely eliminate it in a real, in-vivo speaking situation. After she extinguished my critical enthusiasm, she asked the audience with a devilish glint in her eye if they would like to take up where I had pooped out. She got no takers.

If you have a problem similar to Sue's (like other novice speakers), you can ask your audience to criticize your talk after you give it—or even before (NEGATIVE ASSERTION!)—to help you improve your speaking style. You then respond to criticism with FOGGING (and perhaps with NEGATIVE INQUIRY if their critique poops out too fast). This method has been used in dry run or mock practice presentations as well as in real talks by learners to reduce public-speaking anxiety with good results. In such a practice, you would have your friends or associates (as many as you can muster) criticize your style and manner of giving your talk while you respond to each criticism with FOGGING, as Sue's dialogue shows.

Setting of the dialogue: Sue had just asked me to criticize her talk up to that point to demonstrate FOGGING to the audience.

ME: (Quite pompously) Sue, I'm glad you asked me

to give you a little feedback. I'm sure it will help you to improve your speaking ability in the future.

SUE: *I'm sure it will.* [FOGGING]

ME: It seems to me that you have difficulty in pronouncing some words. There were times when you mumbled a lot.

SUE: *You're probably right.* [FOGGING]

ME: You should not use words that you really can't pronounce. It makes things hard for the audience.

SUE: *That's true.* [FOGGING]

ME: It makes you seem as if you are trying to impress them or intimidate them; it's just kind of phony.

SUE: *Sure. That does seem phony.* [FOGGING]

ME: And when people can't pronounce words right, it usually means that they really don't understand what they mean.

SUE: *That's true, I probably do use words that I don't fully understand the meaning of.* [FOGGING]

ME: Also your accent. You sound as if you learned English on the streets of South Philadelphia.

SUE: Elkins Park actually, but *I'm sure I do have an accent.* [FOGGING]

ME: Which brings up another thing. The way you come across in speaking, you sound like you have a general lack of confidence in what you are saying.

SUE: *I'm sure I do sound less confident than I should be.* [FOGGING]

ME: You give the impression that you really don't know and understand all the implications and finer points of what you are presenting.

SUE: *You're probably right. It's likely that I don't understand all of the finer points.* [FOGGING]

ME: If you really cared about your audience, all these nice people who came to hear you, you would be better prepared.

SUE: *That's true, I'm sure I could be better prepared.* [FOGGING]

ME: After all, these are reasonable people. They don't mind if you slip up and make a few mistakes.

SUE: *I'm sure they don't.* [FOGGING]

ME: But the amount of sloppiness in your talk is irritating. You ramble. You're not well organized. You're putting them off a very interesting subject.

SUE: *I'm sure I do ramble and could be better organized and the audience may get irritated and bored.* [FOGGING]

ME: If you really cared about what you are doing, you should have declined to speak at all and let people who are good speakers do the job.

SUE: *That's true. If I cared that much, I probably would have declined.* [FOGGING]

ME: If you were a good speaker, you could have bluffed it and carried it off with the force of your personality.

SUE: *If I were a good speaker, I'm sure I could.* [FOGGING]

ME: Instead, you showed that you obviously were afraid of this audience.

SUE: *That's true, I was a bit nervous.* [FOGGING]

ME: Sue, I say this as a friend. So I want you to take it to heart.

SUE: *I'm sure you do.* [FOGGING]

ME: In public speaking, you can get up on the dais and go through all the motions, but frankly, a Winston Churchill you're not!

SUE: *That's true. I'm not a Winston Churchill. I'm a Sue Levine.* [FOGGING]

At this point, the FOGGING demonstration broke up in laughter and Sue sailed through the rest of her talk and the questions from the audience that followed. She was animated, excited, interesting to watch and listen to, and she thoroughly enjoyed herself.

In contrast to Sue's in-vivo public speaking dialogue, the next one deals with the practice of several of the assertive skills in learning how to take charge of a group of people when leading a discussion or presenting a report while coping with comments from the audience.

Dialogue #22
**Ron handles digressive, irrelevant,
pertinent, and critical
comments during the
presentation of a
report.**

Ron is a young graduate student in business administration taking a course in economics. He has great difficulty in getting up in front of a group of people and organizing a discussion or giving a report. Ron's major fear, a common one, is that people in the audience will know more than he about the subject or catch him in an error or say something stupid. Fear of public performance, even a minor one, is for many people quite debilitating and keeps them back in school and on the job, prevents them from expanding their careers, and even limits them socially in volunteer work, clubs, charity organizations, or recreational activities. Just prior to presenting an oral term paper in his economics class, Ron volunteered to have a dry run in his assertive group. To desensitize Ron to his fear of public speaking, the members of the group were coached to interrupt Ron's talk with comments and questions that ranged from the sarcastic and irrelevant to those that were pertinent or insightful. These kinds of responses were selected from a variety that a speaker could expect from different audiences and Ron was coached in assertively coping with them. Although Ron received nowhere near the number of comments in the actual presentation from his classmates as he had to field in the assertive group, he was given as much coping exposure as possible in the practice session to comments that might unnerve him. The following dialogue is a condensation of a lengthy report of over twenty minutes with a sample of the audience comments and Ron's responses which allowed him to take charge assertively and lead the discussion, giving him confidence in his ability to field comments during his actual class presentation.

Setting of the dialogue: Ron is in the middle of his presentation and is interrupted by group members asking questions and making comments.

RON: The next major factor in economic growth is public confidence in the economic process. We can see . . . (interruption)

1ST MEMBER: How about the influence of foreign speculation in European markets?

RON: *Although I'm sure that factors outside the continental U.S. do influence our economy,* in this report I am limiting myself to a discussion of domestic factors. [FOGGING]

1ST MEMBER: Doesn't that leave out discussion of some very important things? This means your report is incomplete, with big holes in it.

RON: *I'm sure it has large gaps in it that we could cover,* but *I'm limiting my discussion to domestic factors only.* [FOGGING and BROKEN RECORD] Now returning to public confidence as a major factor . . . (interruption)

2ND MEMBER: What influence, if any, does Securities Exchange Commission policy have on the economy?

RON: That's a very interesting point. However, *I'd like to discuss that later* in context with other regulatory factors. *I'd appreciate it if you would ask your question again when we come to that area.* [SELF-DISCLOSURE] Any other questions before I continue?

3RD MEMBER: Yes. So far you haven't said anything about the preferential federal tax structure as a potent incentive for economic growth.

RON: *That's true, I haven't mentioned it at all yet,* but *I feel that's a subject worth several hours' discussion. With the limited time we have, I don't think I could do a good enough job to make it a worthwhile topic of discussion.* [FOGGING, SELF-DISCLOSURE, and NEGATIVE ASSERTION] Back to public confidence . . . (interruption)

4TH MEMBER: What about the Keynesian doctrine as an influence in the past thirty years?

RON: *That's a subject my thinking isn't at all clear on*

yet. Perhaps one of the other speakers might care to comment upon it, or if there is enough time at the end of the papers, you might give us the benefit of your knowledge on the subject. [NEGATIVE ASSERTION and WORKABLE COMPROMISE] Any other questions. No? Well, moving right along . . . (interruption)

5TH MEMBER: In your opening statement you said your report would cover the period starting with FDR's Administration in 1936 to the present. He took office in 1934 at the height of the depression. Why start in 1936?

RON: Did I say 1936? *That's an error on my part, of course.* The report covers 1934 to the present. [NEGATIVE ASSERTION] Back to the point of discussion, public confidence . . . (interruption)

6TH MEMBER: Are you still talking about public confidence?

RON: *At this rate I'll never get too far, will I? I'd appreciate it if you will limit your questions until after each section of the report. We might progress faster that way.* Now back to public confidence. [NEGATIVE ASSERTION, SELF-DISCLOSURE, and WORKABLE COMPROMISE]

At the beginning of this mock presentation of his material to a bunch of hostile listeners, Ron was quite nervous. He had trouble both with his presentation of material and in responding to audience comments. Near the end of the practice session, the group began to find it more difficult to question and criticize Ron's material and his presentation; particularly when he began to smile each time someone interrupted him. After he finished, this deliberately hostile bunch of critics gave him a round of enthusiastic applause for learning how to cope with them. After the practice, Ron's report in class was anticlimactic He felt quite comfortable in delivering his paper on important factors in the national economy, as he saw them, and even enjoyed the mild interchange between himself and fellow class members on the subject. Ron specifically commented on his good feelings on learning that he could assertively cope with the two types of manipulative questions which he received from his classmates. These questions are the classical "South of France" and "sandbagging" types. When a listener asks, "But how does that (what you have just said) apply in the South of France," he is prompting the speaker to comment upon areas beyond his expertise. Novice speakers often feel that they must have the answer to any question. The "South of France" is often needlessly guilt-inducing and troublesome if you are not assertive enough to simply say: "I don't know." The "sandbagging" comment or question is put to the speaker by a member of the audience who already knows (or thinks he knows) the answer to it. This is usually a deliberate attempt to either deflate the speaker and/or puff up the questioner's own ego. "Sandbagging" questions are usually preceded by an exceedingly long-winded monologue by the questioner that is intended to show his qualifications to ask the question. Most of the time, you won't even know what the question is and will be in trouble if you, the speaker, hesitate to say: "I don't understand your question. Would you repeat it?" or if you do understand it, to say, as Ron did in his dialogue: "My thinking on that subject isn't at all clear yet. Perhaps you might want to give us the benefit of your own expertise later if we have the time?" If the "sandbagger" then panics and blurts out the answer to his own question immediately, you might simply respond as I did once, by saying: "Thank you. That seems like a good answer to your question," and proceed.

Turning back to a different aspect of authority relationships, in the next set of dialogues, you may see how assertive parents and teachers cope with young children and teen-agers, a behavioral area that many of us have found troublesome.

Dialogue #23
Parents and teachers assertively
deal with the complaints of
small children.

In this common set of situations, a married couple,
Bert and Sara, cope with the complaints of their children, and Barbara, an elementary school teacher, assertively directs her students to follow classroom routines
she has set up.

Bert is a professor of drama at a local college, who
has been married to Sara for fourteen years and has
three children, all girls; one five, one a prepubescent
nine, and the other a young teen-ager. I got to know
Bert and Sara socially over a period of years. We usually got together for an evening of fun, sometimes just
for talk over a bottle of wine. When this relaxed mood
came about, our chat invariably turned to writing, and
Bert and I would swap stories on the human happen-
ings behind the scenes in Hollywood and in academic
and clinical psychology. Both Bert and Sara became interested in what I was teaching people about being systematically assertive. One evening their children kept
coming into the family room on one pretext after another. After the last stern look from Bert had banished
them for the rest of the night to their rooms, he turned
to me and commented: "These kids. They're great, but
sometimes they drive me bananas. They just love to
show off when company is present. Does your assertion
work on them too?" I asked Bert what it was he
wanted them to stop, and he said: "Like now. All
night they keep coming in to see what they are missing.
They always come in with a complaint as an excuse for
one thing or another. Tell them, 'Go back to bed,' and
then they give you an argument. When I send one back
to bed, another one comes out with something else to
complain about. They are okay when we're by ourselves, but when company arrives they act as lonely as
three sailors on shore leave. They know I'm not going
to yell at them in front of company. Until I know

they're asleep, we don't have any privacy. They cramp my style in telling a story or copping a feel from Sara or just getting high on grass. You're the expert. How would you handle them?" Still grinning after hearing Bert's earthy way of characterizing his predicament and his daughters' attention-getting behavior, I told him to try empathic FOGGING—to listen to their complaints, to say something like: *"I understand how you feel, that's rough (unfair, uncomfortable, etc.) to have to be lonely (to be bored, to be wide awake, to listen to our noise, to go to the john, etc.),* but I want you to go back to bed and not come out with the adults again tonight." That suggestion set off a discussion, which lasted all evening, about children, parents, and the sometime strange twists that the authority relationship between them takes.

Several months after that talk about raising children, we got together again and Bert picked up the discussion where we had started it. He pointed out that just empathizing with his youngest girl solved a problem when she came up to him crying over a scraped knee. He did not pick her up or make a big fuss about her complaint, but said simply: "When you cry that much, it must really hurt," instead of: "It's not that bad a scrape, Marcie, you should be a big girl now and not cry over everything." Marcie stopped crying immediately after hearing Bert's first empathic FOGGING response, looked up, as Bert described it, with stunned amazement, and after getting a pat on the head, ran back to play with the other children. The message Bert gave with empathic FOGGING—that Marcie received and acted upon—was that her father understood that she was hurting, he agreed that she was entitled to hurt, but that there wasn't anything he could or would do about it. With his actions and words, Bert was teaching Marcie an important lesson; "Sometimes you get hurt in life. I've been hurt too, so I can understand how you feel, but I can't take the hurt away. If you want to play, you have to learn to suffer the hurt."

Sara was also enthusiastic about being more assertive in coping and told me of a situation with her oldest daughter Katy where use of several systematic assertive verbal skills solved an old problem for her. In this incident, Sara was to meet Katy, at 3:00 P.M. sharp in front of the Contempo Boutique in Westwood Village to go shopping together. At fifteen minutes past the hour, a rushed Sara parked in front of the store and stepped out of her car to face a cold, fishy look from an irritated young teen-ager who had been made to wait too long for her liking. The following is the dialogue between an assertive Sara and a grumbling, bitchy Katy.

SARA: Hi, *I'm late.* [NEGATIVE ASSERTION]

KATY: You sure are! I've been waiting for you for over half an hour.

SARA: *That's irritating when you have to wait. I don't blame you for being mad at me.* [FOGGING]

KATY: What have you been doing to take you so long getting here?

SARA: Nothing. *It's my fault entirely.* I just didn't look at the clock, and made a late start. *Just a stupid thing to do.* [NEGATIVE ASSERTION]

KATY: Well, I wish you would be here when you say you are going to be here. You are always late!

SARA: *I am, aren't I? That's dumb for me to be careless when you're waiting for me.* [FOGGING and NEGATIVE ASSERTION]

KATY: (Silent)

SARA: Where do you want to start first? The U. N. or Contempo?

Sara was delighted in finding a new way to cope with an old difficulty, a different way of coping that accomplished two things for her. First, being more assertive to her daughter made Sara feel better about herself. Her assertive coping made her realize that it was true she had screwed things up, *but so what?* Being fifteen minutes late in that situation did not mean the sky was going to fall down on her head. Second, assertively coping with Katy's grumbles about being late gave Katy an inescapable message of: "You're right, I am late, I did screw things up for you and I can appreciate your feelings about it, but I'm not going to roll over and play dead for you," and Katy responded to it. What before had been at least ten minutes, off and on, of Katy bitching, grumbling, and complaining while Sara was making up one excuse and denial after another was over within less than thirty seconds.

As Barbara, an elementary school teacher in her first year of teaching, found out, children can be just as manipulative and difficult to cope with outside the family situation. At the time Barbara learned to cope assertively with schoolchildren of all ages, she was a student in one of my classes. Barbara brought up the subject of how to cope with children who didn't follow a teacher's orders at school by asking: "What do you do when a child won't take part in a class activity? How do you get him to play with the other kids during sports time?" Upon being assured by Barbara that the boy in question was a healthy, apparently normal six-year-old who passively resisted doing what she wanted him to do, I asked her if she had already tried all the manipulative ploys we all know so well, like external structure—"It's a rule that you have to play"; or threats—"I'll tell your mother (or the principal) if you don't"; or making him feel guilty if he didn't—"Everyone likes to play with the other children"; or making him feel ignorant—"You should learn to play with the other children if you are going to be anything in life"; or even anxious—"If you don't play with the other boys, they may not like you and want to play with you." Barbara said she had tried about everything and nothing worked. I then asked her why in her supervisory-authority relationship with this boy she hadn't persistently told him something like: "I'm the teacher and you're the student. I'm in charge here. When I tell you I want you to play with the other boys, you go out and play with the other boys. You don't have to like it, all you have to do is *do it*." Barbara cast a doubtful look in my direction at this suggestion which implied: "Look, dummy. You may know a lot about assertion but you sure as hell don't know much about teaching a bunch of kids!" Vocally, however, Barbara agreed to give straightforward assertive communication a try. Except for a chance meeting on a coffee break some weeks after the course was over, I could only have guessed at her success in class with this young student and others. Over coffee, Barbara told me quite enthusiastically about the following dialogue with the boy who didn't want to play with others.

BARBARA: Tommy. You still don't want to play with the other kids?

TOMMY: (Walking around in a small circle kicking the ground, silently shaking his head)

BARBARA: *I can appreciate that*, but I'm in charge of you here and I want you to go play ball with the others. [FOGGING]

TOMMY: I don't want to.

BARBARA: *I'm sure you don't, Tommy*, but *I'm in charge, and I want you to play with the others.* [FOGGING and BROKEN RECORD]

TOMMY: (First excuse) My foot hurts. (Starting to limp)

BARBARA: *I'm sure it hurts*, but *I want you to play with the other boys.* [FOGGING and BROKEN RECORD]

TOMMY: It will hurt more if I play with them. (Limping even more)

BARBARA: *Maybe it will*, but *I still want you to play with them. If it still hurts after you are finished playing, I'll take you to the nurse myself.* [FOGGING, BROKEN RECORD, and WORKABLE COMPROMISE]

TOMMY: (Second excuse) I don't like them. (No longer limping)

BARBARA: *It's okay if you don't like them or even like playing with them. I just want you to play ball with them.* [FOGGING and BROKEN RECORD]

TOMMY: (Third excuse) I don't like playing ball.

BARBARA: *That's okay, you don't have to like it,*

all I want you to do is do it. [FOGGING and BROKEN RECORD]

TOMMY: I don't know how to play ball.

BARBARA: *That's okay too. You don't have to know how. I'm a lousy ball player myself. You'll make a lot of mistakes while you're learning and that's going to make you uncomfortable, like I did when I was learning, but I want you to go out there and play ball.* [FOGGING, SELF-DISCLOSURE, and BROKEN RECORD]

TOMMY: I still don't want to.

BARBARA: *Sure you don't want to, but I want you to.* Which would you rather do? *Stay here each play period and talk to me like this or go out there and play with the other kids?* [FOGGING, BROKEN RECORD, and WORKABLE COMPROMISE]

TOMMY: (Walking out onto the playground toward the other children) I still don't want to.

BARBARA: Super! You feel any way you want to. Just play ball.

It became apparent as the details of the interaction between Barbara and Tommy unfolded that Tommy was avoiding playing ball with the other boys because he thought he was a lousy ball player, and I asked Barbara if he was inept or uncoordinated. Barbara replied with a smile, "He fumbled a bit the first week, but whenever I saw him do something well, in my best behavior-modification manner, I praised him afterwards. Now he's just the same as the rest of the boys. He catches some. He drops some."

At the same time Barbara was more assertive to Tommy, she was also changing her behavior toward the other children in her classes when conflict arose over things like learning exercises, behavior during class, etc. Over a period of weeks with repeated assertive confrontations between herself and her students, like the one with Tommy, Barbara found that the children gave her less and less trouble when she told them to do something. As she put it: "Before they didn't say anything about me or what I wanted them to do, but half of them didn't do it. Now when I tell them to do something, they all move together even though they bitch and moan about it. They may not like me or what I tell them to do, but they do it and they do it quick!"

Other teachers have also found that being assertive with their students resolves conflicts in the classroom quickly, even with older students who can be very clever at times. One of these learners, Zeke, used systematic assertiveness to cope with manipulation from his high school students, particularly during test and grading time. Zeke reported that he didn't need to go into long dialogues with his students when they complained or tried to get him to change their grades, but felt very good about responding to their manipulative comments and criticisms of his teaching and testing with "one-liners" such as: "You're right. Some of the true-false questions were ambiguous, but I'm not going to give another test," or "That's true, I could have made that point a bit clearer before you took the quiz, but you still get a 'C'," or "I can see how you feel being right on the cut-off point between a 'B' and an 'A.' That's rough, but you still get a 'B,'" or "Of course it's unfair that you got sick and have to take a different makeup quiz from the other students, but that's the test I'm going to give you." Or even humorously to the whole class: "I'm sure a lot of you feel that you could have gotten a better teacher who doesn't mumble a lot, but you're stuck with me!"

In the next dialogue, you will see how one father learned to begin the process of gradually changing the relationship between himself and his young teen-age daughter from that of a parent and child into that of one adult interacting with another adult.

Dialogue #24
Scotty prompts his
teen-age daughter
to be responsible
for her own
behavior.

Scotty is a thirty-eight-year-old lawyer, married fifteen years to his second wife, Lynn. Scotty has two children, a daughter Bunny, fourteen, and a son, Dave, twelve, by his second wife. His first marriage produced no children and ended in divorce after one year. Scotty's second marriage to Lynn had been satisfying to both spouses until Bunny reached puberty. Lynn's concern for Bunny's well-being during her transition from child to young woman caused her to aggressively place pressure on Scotty. She continually insisted that Scotty deal strongly with Bunny when she broke dating rules, while she herself verbally "fled" and remained silent, communicating little of her personal concern to her daughter.

After discussing his daughter's worrisome habit of not coming home on time, I recommended that Scotty persistently use self-disclosure of his private feelings to Bunny about her dating behavior. Several factors were involved in the decision to deal with Bunny's troublesome behavior through persistent communication of Scotty's personal feelings about his daughter's behavior directly to her. By communicating his personal feelings to Bunny, Scotty would literally force her to deal with him on an adult-to-adult basis. He would be teaching Bunny to realize that if she wanted adult freedom within the family structure, she would have to take on some of the adult responsibilities within that structure; she would have to be responsible for her own behavior. The most important adult responsibility she would have to learn to shoulder would be regulating and placing limits on her behavior within the household through the workable compromise process. It was very important that she learn to function with the adults in the family so that they could *all* reach some agreement on behavior that affected each other. Within this assertive compromise process Bunny would learn that assertive independence is not achieved by angrily alienating or sullenly withdrawing from adult family members. Instead, she had to learn to begin working out some arrangement with her parents that allowed her as much behavioral freedom as was realistically possible while she was learning to cope with this new adult freedom and all the problems it would generate. Bunny, like many teen-agers, would not accept as a basis for self-regulation of her behavior a list of all the troubles she could fall prey to: unwanted pregnancy through rape, seduction, or her sexual willingness; drug dependency or at least a "bad trip" through social peer pressure or experimentation; a police record through a chance arrest because of a dating companion's illegal behavior; physical injury or perhaps even death through a driving mistake on the part of her relatively inexperienced teen-age date; getting involved emotionally before she could cope with it and getting hurt; etc., etc., etc. This fatherly counseling approach was tried in the past and seemed to make no impression upon Bunny, probably due to the unrealistic optimism of her youth. On the other hand, due to their relative age and the problems they experienced, her parents had a more pessimistic but equally unrealistic prognosis for their daughter's success in growing up. Taking into account both viewpoints, optimistic and pessimistic, for every "reason" Scotty could give Bunny as to why she should be careful and more conservative, Bunny could find an equally valid "reason" why she should be more unrestricted. Warnings and logical or statistical reasons for limiting Bunny's behavior, therefore, would have little impact on her. They would, as in the past, prompt her to countermanipulate her parents. The only approach Scotty actually had at his disposal for changing his daughter's behavior, with his relatively weak ability to restrict her physically, was the disclosure of his own feelings as a person, and the persistent asserting of these feelings and their consequences. The most powerful communication he could bring to bear on Bunny to get her to regulate her own behavior was a persistent disclosure of his upset with her behavior whenever it worried him and his consequent "bugging" her, as well as the fact that if she worried him in the future, he would continue to confront her. Scotty needed to make clear to Bunny that keeping her word was the only solution to his worry about her transition from childhood to womanhood, no matter how rational or irrational his worry was. The aim of disclosure of his feelings of worry was not to make Bunny feel guilty but to make her deal with the reality of Scotty's feeling on an adult basis. By using this assertive, persistent self-disclosure of worried feelings and a workable compromise procedure, Scotty was to accomplish three very important things for his daughter and himself.

First, Scotty would communicate to Bunny that she had a problem. She would have to deal with Scotty's worry when she came home late. It mattered little how much Bunny protested about her father's worry being unfair, unreasonable, irrational, illogical, and unwanted. Bunny was to learn that the situation boiled down to the fact that her father worried about her. To avoid being frequently confronted by him, she had to deal with his worry—a *have to* imposed by Scotty, not a *should*. There was no reason for her to feel guilty about her father's worry or her own desire for freedom. The fact of the matter was simply that her father worried when she came home late and she had to deal with this worry, for it would not change; she had to find a solution to this problem.

Second, disclosure of Scotty's true worried feelings about Bunny's behavior would force the relationship between them to change, to move from an authoritarian parent-child relationship to a relationship more in keeping with Bunny's gradual transition into womanhood: less of an a priori structured relationship, more of a closer adult-to-adult equality relationship.

Third, by dealing with Bunny in this new adult instead of fatherly way, Scotty forces himself to examine his unrealistic worries about Bunny and, at the same time, prepares himself emotionally for the eventual separation of Bunny from her family by allowing her more and more adult status and freedom with each repeated assertive confrontation over the years.

To prepare Scotty for dealing with his daughter in this different way, a dialogue rehearsal was set up with a young female member of his assertive therapy group. After the dialogue was rehearsed and Scotty felt prepared to interact with his daughter in this new way, I recommended that he talk to his wife about her taking part in the solution to the problem and that he also prompt her to be more assertive with Bunny.

Setting of the dialogue: In the rehearsed sequence, Bunny arrives home an hour late and Scotty is waiting up for her in the living room.

BUNNY: (Opening front door) Oh . . . Hi, Dad.

SCOTTY: Come over and sit down with me, Bunny. I want to talk with you.

BUNNY: (Feigning innocence and ignorance) What about?

SCOTTY: Did you have a good time tonight?

BUNNY: Oh, yes. We had a lot of fun.

SCOTTY: That's good. What did you do?

BUNNY: We went to the horrorama festival in Hollywood, and afterwards over to Rosalie's house and danced.

SCOTTY: I guess that's why you've come in later than you said you would.

BUNNY: Oh, Daddy. You've lectured to me like this a hundred times already.

SCOTTY: I want to talk about it again.

BUNNY: Do we really have to? I mean right now? Why can't we talk about it later? It'll ruin the whole evening! I had so much fun.

SCOTTY: I understand. *I don't want to spoil your fun, but I do want to talk about it.* [SELF-DISCLOSURE and BROKEN RECORD]

BUNNY: Every time we talk about me, you get mad.

SCOTTY: *That's true,* but this time I'm not going to get mad. *I just want to talk to you about it.* [FOG-

GING and BROKEN RECORD] (Instead of: "Why do you think I got mad? You never obey me and come home on time!")

BUNNY: (Puzzled but defensive) But it's no fun to leave everybody and come home early. The other kids don't have to come home at ten thirty.

SCOTTY: *I know it's no fun,* but when you stay out later than we agreed upon, *I get very worried about you.* [FOGGING and SELF-DISCLOSURE of feelings]

BUNNY: (Angrily and sarcastically) Is that all I can do. . . . Go to a movie and then come home?

SCOTTY: I can see how you feel, but when you're not home when I expect you, *I get very worried about you.* [BROKEN RECORD]

BUNNY: (Exasperated) But there is nothing to worry about!!!!

SCOTTY: *I know it's really stupid,* Bunny, but *I still get worried.* When I get held up at work or on the freeway for an hour or more, your mother worries that I'm in an auto accident. I've never been in an auto accident when I'm late, but your mother still worries about me. I guess because we're close and important to each other. *It's dumb for her to let her feelings rule her when she doesn't know what's happening, but it's the same with me and you. I worry when you don't come home when I expect you.* [NEGATIVE ASSERTION and BROKEN RECORD]

BUNNY: But nothing happened. Nothing ever happened to make you worry.

SCOTTY: I know how you feel, Bunny, and *what you say is true* except that when you don't come home when you say you will, *I get worried.* [FOGGING and BROKEN RECORD]

BUNNY: But that's not mȳ fault ȳou get worried. You should know that nothing will happen.

SCOTTY: *It's not logical,* Bunny. It's just the way I feel. I feel fine when I know that you're out having fun on a date. When you don't show up when you say you will be home, *that's when I start to worry.* [FOGGING and BROKEN RECORD]

BUNNY: No. You shouldn't worry when I'm late.

SCOTTY: Bunny, so far in this discussion, I haven't told you that you shouldn't be late. I'm just telling you what happens to me when you are late. . . . *I get very worried.* [BROKEN RECORD] Is that clear?

BUNNY: Yes, but you shouldn't worry.

SCOTTY: *But I do worry* and that's what you have to cope with. [BROKEN RECORD]

BUNNY: Why don't you stop worrying?

SCOTTY: *It would be a great blessing if I did stop worrying, but the fact is that I do worry* . . . and that's what you have to deal with. [NEGATIVE ASSERTION and BROKEN RECORD]

BUNNY: (Silence)

SCOTTY: Is that clear to you what I'm getting at?

BUNNY: Yes.

SCOTTY: Okay, I don't like it, you don't like it. But it's a fact of life that you have to cope with. When you come in later than you agreed to, *I get worried. When I get worried, you're going to hear about it. Maybe you'll even get restricted.* It's that simple. [BROKEN RECORD]

BUNNY: (Rising to leave)

SCOTTY: Sit down and hear me out, Bunny. I'm not finished yet. When you come in late, *I get worried. When I get worried, I'm going to bug the hell out of you, like now.* That is not negotiable. [BROKEN RECORD]

BUNNY: (Showing interest) What do you mean?

SCOTTY: *I'm unhappy about you coming in late.* You're unhappy about coming in sooner than you want to. *Why don't we try to work something out so we both feel better about it?* [SELF-DISCLOSURE and WORKABLE COMPROMISE]

BUNNY: You could stop worrying.

SCOTTY: That's not what I'm talking about, Bunny. I could say that you should feel happier about coming in at ten thirty. But that's unrealistic. Like you telling me not to worry. I'm not telling you how to feel. Don't tell me how to feel. *I get worried.* [BROKEN RECORD]

BUNNY: Okay . . . but what else?

SCOTTY: You want to stay out later, I want you to come home on time.

BUNNY: We could change the time.

SCOTTY: That could happen, but there are a lot of problems to be worked out first.

BUNNY: (Rising again to leave) I thought you would say "No."

SCOTTY: *Maybe,* but the way I see it, it simply means that if you want to stay out later, *we have to deal with some things first,* like your mother. [FOGGING and BROKEN RECORD]

BUNNY: She never talks to me about it. What can I do about her?

SCOTTY: Why don't you talk to her about it? You do want to stay out later, don't you?

BUNNY: Yes, but she's just like you. I can see she doesn't trust me either.

SCOTTY: Well, how about sitting down with both of us and talking about it?

BUNNY: Will you let me stay out later?

SCOTTY: *If we work out certain things.* [BROKEN RECORD]

BUNNY: What things?

SCOTTY: *Like how your mother feels about it for one thing.* [WORKABLE COMPROMISE]

BUNNY: What else?

SCOTTY: Like me believing in you to keep your word for another thing. [WORKABLE COMPROMISE]

BUNNY: I told you that you felt that way. You don't trust me and treat me like a child.

SCOTTY: Bunny, so far you have made me believe that you will come in late. That's what you do most of the time. *I can't read minds. I don't have any way of knowing you won't stay out till twelve thirty if we change the time.* And then we're right back to the same old thing. *I get worried, you get restricted.* [NEGATIVE ASSERTION and BROKEN RECORD]

BUNNY: But I'll come in at eleven thirty, I will!

SCOTTY: How are you going to convince me of that? Right now, *I have trouble believing you when you say that.* [BROKEN RECORD]

BUNNY: I don't know.

SCOTTY: *How about showing me that you can keep your word?* [WORKABLE COMPROMISE]

BUNNY: How?

SCOTTY: *How about coming in on time for a while?* [WORKABLE COMPROMISE]

BUNNY: All you care about is me getting home at ten thirty!

SCOTTY: *The hour doesn't really mean much to me, Bunny. Your keeping your word does.* [SELF-DISCLOSURE]

BUNNY: Then let me stay out till eleven thirty.

SCOTTY: *I'm willing if I believe you will come home then.* [WORKABLE COMPROMISE]

BUNNY: I will.

SCOTTY: *How can you make me believe that?* [BROKEN RECORD]

BUNNY: I don't know.

SCOTTY: *How about coming home for a while when you said you would.* [WORKABLE COMPROMISE]

BUNNY: Would you believe me if I came home at ten thirty next week?

SCOTTY: *It would take more than one week.* [WORKABLE COMPROMISE]

BUNNY: How long?

SCOTTY: *How about five or six weeks?* If you didn't get me worried by the middle of next month, I would be willing to agree to a new time. [WORKABLE COMPROMISE]

BUNNY: And I could stay out another hour after then?

SCOTTY: If you don't go back on your word in the meantime and *get me worried* again, and if your mother says okay. [BROKEN RECORD and WORKABLE COMPROMISE]

BUNNY: She'd never agree.

SCOTTY: *What have you got to lose by trying?* [WORKABLE COMPROMISE]

BUNNY: Why don't you talk to her?

SCOTTY: I'm going to tell her exactly how I feel

about it. *But you still have to work things out with her yourself.* [WORKABLE COMPROMISE]

BUNNY: I don't know what to tell her.

SCOTTY: *Why don't we all sit down together and talk about it?* [WORKABLE COMPROMISE]

BUNNY: Will you be on my side?

SCOTTY: As far as what we have talked about tonight, yes.

BUNNY: Okay, daddy, let's do it tomorrow.

SCOTTY: It may take longer than just one talk to convince your mother that you will come home on time.

BUNNY: That's what I was afraid of.

SCOTTY: Do you want to give it a try and see what happens?

BUNNY: Okay.

SCOTTY: Good! Give your father a hug and go to bed.

BUNNY: Okay.

Shortly after learning this new way to cope with his teen-age daughter, Scotty finished his assertive therapy and I never found out how well he did in working out a compromise with Bunny. I hope he had as much success in being assertive to teen-agers as the other learners I trained.

In the next chapter, let's look at what Scotty was learning to teach his daughter: assertively working out ways of living with people who are your equals.

10

Everyday equal relationships— working out compromises or just saying "No"

The most difficult situations in which to learn to be assertive are those involving people we truly care about—our equals, like parents, friends, lovers, and mates. An equal relationship has the least a priori structure of any of the interactions you can have with another person. When conflict with an equal arises, how "should" you cope with it? Just suppose that your roommate is gay and you only learn of it after he (or she) puts the make on you, what "should" you do? Where's the book of rules that tells you how to relate to gay friends "properly?" Does Emily Post know? In an even less threatening example, what do you do if your roommate wants you to date a friend of his (or hers) and you just can't work up any enthusiasm for the idea? Or more commonly, what rules do you follow when your friend or roommate keeps bugging you with particular actions? Or if your spouse does the same thing? What are the "proper" ways of coping with such close conflicts? The answer to all these questions is of course that there is no proper, correct, no one-and-only way of dealing with these problems. Even the Bible gives up offering advice after you have been slapped on the second cheek. In these interactions between equals, everything is negotiable; you even have to work on who will take out the trash.

When a conflict arises between your mate and yourself, working out a solution can be difficult if you assume that everything, including how to work out a solution to a problem, must be accomplished by some arbitrary set of rules on marriage and close relationships; husbands "should" not upset wives, and wives "should" always defer to husbands, friends "should" be nice to each other, etc. But arbitrary rules can interfere with saying what you or your mate really want and then working out some compromise that you both can live with. Being assertive in these situations can clarify what both parties really want and a compromise often falls out naturally. It may be as simple as your wanting to wear Levis and a pink T-shirt but only at work and parties, while your wife only gets really upset when you wear such a striking combination when you see her mother. To work out a compromise on this example, it may be necessary first to exhaust all the external nonassertive manipulative "shoulds" like: "You should dress like a grown man and not like a punk kid," or "Don't you care what other people may think?" or "Nobody should wear clothes like that!" before the *I want* or *I don't like* statements that precede a compromise are given in place of the "shoulds." Manipulation used to control your behavior (or that you use to control your mate's behavior) is generally not malicious or malignant, but a result, as we have seen, of our childhood training on how to cope when we feel uncertain. In my clinical experience in treating nonassertive patients who use lots of manipulation to control other people's behavior, I have observed that the manipulator often has hidden anxiety agendas about special things. These anxiety agendas are often recognized by the manipulator, but he or she has no acceptable or "proper" way of dealing with these fears, let alone communicating them to close relations; after all, no one "should" be anxious or afraid or have neurotic hangups, "should" they? For some people, these hidden anxiety agendas are only expressed on the level of their feelings. This type of patient has trouble verbalizing what it is specifically that makes him or her anxious. They can't put their finger on what makes them nervous, what they are afraid will happen if you do a "certain" thing. Therefore they must control and limit your behavior even if they cannot say specifically why it is necessary to do so.

Older patients I have seen in conflict with their adult children often have hidden anxiety agendas about being left alone or financially dependent, especially if their own spouse is physically debilitated or has passed away. These hidden anxiety agendas can sometimes be coped with by the patient, with the help of assertive, emotionally supportive adults like the patient's adult offspring. Many times these hidden anxiety agendas unfortunately are expressed by the most demanding and rigid but "kind" manipulation of children by elderly parents. Younger patients who show manipulative coping with their mates often have their own hidden anxiety agendas centering around their futile dependence upon their mates to shield them from reality and to make them personally happy. These unfortunate people have anxieties about their own sexual attractiveness, anxieties about their mate's love for them and flirting with possible sexual partners, anxieties about being an effective parent, anxieties about their own personal achievement and frustrations, anxieties about their own human limitations, even anxieties about being anxious. In short, the majority of nonassertive people I have seen in clinical settings have a passive or manipulative posture; they are not always cruel bastards or bitches with malignant intent, but mostly anxious, insecure people who are coping the best way they know how.

Because of the possibility of hidden anxiety agendas operating within close relationships, I suggest to learners that they be *assertive with empathy* when dealing with people they care for, with the emphasis on being assertive! You can increase the level of communication with your possibly passive or manipulative partner by using a combination of all of the assertive verbal skills to exhaust any manipulation and prompt your partner to be assertive, to say what he or she wants, in place of passivity or manipulation, even if it is said to you in a very critical manner. By coping assertively yet empathically, you are more likely to express your own point of view without taking away your partner's self-respect, at the same time prompting your mate to examine any hidden desires or anxieties that are interfering with close communication.

Again, I have learners first work on being assertive

to those equals whom they are least close to but see often, preferably on a daily basis: a co-worker or acquaintance. Only when the learner feels sufficiently comfortable in asserting himself without any supportive rules on how he and his equal "should" behave toward each other (perhaps even in the face of strong criticism), do I recommend that assertiveness be used to cope with people about whom great care is really felt.

Let's now turn to the first dialogue in this chapter: a training dialogue dealing with an unstructured conflict between equals—how to cope with a co-worker and then with a close friend who wants to borrow your car.

Dialogue #25
Saying "No" to a friend
when he wants to
borrow your
car

As one of the first training exercises for students or patients to learn to be more assertive with people they presumably have equal relationships with, I have them role-play a situation in which a friend, co-worker, cousin, brother-in-law, etc., tries to borrow their car and uses a lot of manipulation to achieve that goal. Lending something like your car when you really don't want to is a common problem. Many learners complain of their inability to cope in this situation. You also may feel that either you have to lend your car to keep peace or the relationship will be destroyed, or you will have to show some anger before the other person will believe that you won't lend them your car. To extinguish feelings of anxiety in this type of situation, I first have learners practice assertively and empathically saying "No" to a request from an equal, perhaps a co-worker who is an associate but not necessarily a close friend.

Setting of the first dialogue: You are on a coffee break at work and your co-worker, Harry, approaches you and sits down.

HARRY: Boy, am I glad to see you! I got a real problem and I was afraid I couldn't get anyone to help me out.

YOU: What's the problem?

HARRY: I need to use your car this afternoon.

YOU: Umm. *That is a problem,* but *I don't want to lend out my car this afternoon.* [FOGGING and SELF-DISCLOSURE]

HARRY: Why not?

YOU: *I agree you need it,* but *I just don't want to lend out my car.* [FOGGING and BROKEN RECORD]

HARRY: Do you have someplace to go?

YOU: *I may want it myself,* Harry. [SELF-DISCLOSURE]

HARRY: When do you need it? I'll get it back on time.

YOU: *I'm sure you would,* but *I just don't want to lend out my car today.* [FOGGING and BROKEN RECORD]

HARRY: Whenever I asked to borrow your car, you always lent it to me before.

YOU: *That's true, I did, didn't I?* [NEGATIVE ASSERTION]

HARRY: Why won't you lend it to me today? I always took care of it before.

YOU: *That's true,* Harry, and *I can see you're in a jam,* but *I just don't want to lend my car out today.* [FOGGING, SELF-DISCLOSURE, and BROKEN RECORD]

Up to this point, you are simply coping with a manipulative co-worker who wants something you have—a car, some time off, part of your work schedule, the last parking sticker, the newest typewriter in the office, or any one of a hundred things someone may try to talk you out of. In most cases, the co-worker is not malignant in intent but just someone who wants something you have and really doesn't give a damn how you feel: a conflict where most learners have no difficulty in refusing to give reasons to justify or explain their behavior to the other person. Most people, however, have greater difficulty in not giving reasons for what they want to do to their friends, family, etc. To get learners to be able to cope with such anxiety-producing and therefore more difficult situations, I have them change Harry, at this point in the dialogue, from just a co-worker into a good friend and coach them on how to cope with such a friend's manipulation through assertively disclosing their own feelings of worry.

HARRY: Look, I'm a good driver and I've never done anything to your car.

YOU: *That's true,* Harry, *I just worry when I lend my car out, so I don't want to go through that hassle again.* [FOGGING and SELF-DISCLOSURE]

HARRY: You know that I won't damage your car!

YOU: *You won't. I know that and it's dumb for me to feel this way, but I do.* [FOGGING and NEGATIVE ASSERTION]

HARRY: So why won't you lend me your car?

YOU: *Because I don't want to have this worry.* [SELF-DISCLOSURE]

HARRY: But you know I won't do anything wrong.

YOU: *You're right, Harry. It's not you, it's me that's the problem. I just worry when I lend out my car. So I'm not going to lend it out.* [FOGGING and SELF-DISCLOSURE]

HARRY: Well, you should do something about that.

YOU: For instance?

HARRY: See a shrink or something. I don't know!

YOU: Thanks for the suggestion. Maybe I will, maybe not. I'll see.

Many learners report that, for their own self-respect, they want to be able to say "No" to a good friend occasionally and mean it! The difficulty in achieving this expectation with their friends is that they have a near-perfect history of always saying "Yes" to requests; consequently their friends always expect to get the car. Some learners have asked me why not simply go up to Harry, come right out and say: "Look, Harry. You get too pushy at times. Sometimes you can use my car and sometimes you can't. Don't always expect to get everything you want out of me," and let it go at that? The route you take depends, as the Cheshire Cat pointed out to Alice, a good deal upon where you want to go. If you want to change your friend's long-term manipulative behavior, then changing your own behavior toward him over a period of time is probably most efficient. If you want the more immediate satisfaction of venting your irritated feelings upon Harry for his manipulation of you in the past, having it out with him then is the most efficient course. You may not be able to do both: tell Harry off for how shabbily he has treated your feelings in the past, and still keep his friendship—unless he is a very, very close friend. That sort of emotional catharsis works fine in sensitivity groups but typically does not transfer to the real world with our bonafide, everyday relationships—a unilateral sensitivity group doesn't work. Harry has to first want to join your therapy group before he will accept your emotional venting. Another difficulty with coming right out and telling Harry that "Maybe you can have my car and maybe not," is that it will probably confuse the hell out of Harry as well as get him angry. Harry will not have the vaguest notion of what your problem is and will wonder why you are taking it out on him now; after all, he never stole your car, did he? He always asked to use it and you said yes. If you didn't want him to have it, why didn't you say so before, instead of making a big deal of the whole issue now? The problem for most learners, and perhaps yourself if you are like them, is simply this: at times you would feel comfortable in lending something out depending upon the circumstances and other times you just don't want to, no matter what the circumstances. Any other solution to this problem beside changing your own behavior to suit each decision you make borders on trying to control other people's behavior for your own convenience. If you, like most novice learners, have this problem of being assertive to close friends, you need to make up your mind on what you want to give your friends as you go along and assertively cope with the consequences of each decision; instead, for example, of asking Harry to control his behavior for you by guessing beforehand if you will lend him the car or not—making him read your mind! It's your responsibility to make that decision, not Harry's. It's your car. What happens to it depends upon you!

Other alternatives are open to you and your friend Harry besides lending him your car. At the end of the previous dialogue, you might help Harry with his problem in other ways. You could suggest someone else who might lend Harry a car, or even suggest that Harry try again tomorrow or later in the week to see if your car is available then, or a variety of other compromises.

At this stage of practicing to be assertive, most learners ask the obvious question: "Do you mean that I should never give a friend a reason for what I want to do or why I want to do it?" To this question, I give them this obvious answer: "If you and your friend have the same specific goal and are working together on it, two minds are usually better than one in figuring out ways to solve a problem. However, we are covering situations where there is a conflict and there is no apparent common goal. You want one thing and your friend wants something else. Give reasons for what you want and your friend will come up with equally valid reasons for what he wants. Giving reasons during conflict to justify or defend a viewpoint is just as manipulative as giving reasons to attack that viewpoint. Neither of these routes is an honest, assertive *I want* that can lead to a workable compromise of interests to quickly resolve the conflict."

The next short dialogue is about a real-life situation between neighbors where an assertive woman quickly coped with manipulation that took her by surprise, a situation that many learners have difficulties with.

Dialogue #26
**Bobbie copes with a neighbor
who wants her to cut down
her gum trees.**

Bobbie, the suburban housewife whom I described earlier in the chapter on NEGATIVE INQUIRY, also reported the following short dialogue with another neighbor, Dr. Slick, about—of all things; you guessed it!—another swimming pool.

Setting of the dialogue: Bobbie is planting some ivy in her front yard when Dr. Slick drives up in his Marinara Longostino custom sports car. Approaching Bobbie, he introduces himself and speaks:

DR. SLICK: Hello, I'm your backyard neighbor, Stanley Slick. I think you know my wife, Shanda.

BOBBIE: Yes, we often say hello over the fence. How are you?

DR. SLICK: Fine! I wanted to tell you that I am going to put a swimming pool in our backyard right up against your eucalyptus trees and they are going to drop a lot of leaves into it . . .

BOBBIE: My God! *You aren't kidding. They are really going to drop leaves into it. Your gardener must have to rake up three or four bushels of leaves a week now.* [NEGATIVE ASSERTION]

DR. SLICK: (Caught in mid-sentence, hesitates, and changes tack) Well, I don't care about the leaves really, it's just that your trees will cut out the afternoon sun, and that's the only time I can use the pool.

BOBBIE: (Looking back toward the trees) *You're probably right. If you put it right up against them, you are going to have plenty of shade there.* [FOGGING]

DR. SLICK: (Again hesitating while his eyes flash back and forth rapidly between Bobbie and her trees) I noticed that they were overgrown enough to have some workers trim them a few weeks back.

BOBBIE: *That's true.* [FOGGING]

DR. SLICK: Would you cut them down if I paid for the labor?

BOBBIE: No.

DR. SLICK: No?

BOBBIE: No.

DR. SLICK: Oh!

BOBBIE: When are you going to begin construction?

DR. SLICK: Tomorrow.

BOBBIE: *I wish you had talked to me sooner about this.* I had a pool put in my last house and I had an awful lot of trouble with it. *You might have been able to profit from my dumb mistakes.* [SELF-DISCLOSURE and NEGATIVE ASSERTION]

DR. SLICK: Well, it's too late to do anything about it now. I've already signed the contract and approved the plans.

BOBBIE: *Maybe you could get them to move it closer to the back of your house and away from the trees so they cause you fewer problems.* [WORKABLE COMPROMISE]

DR. SLICK: (Walking away toward his car) I doubt it.

BOBBIE: (Empathically) Assert yourself! If you want it changed, you can get it changed. It's your pool and your money!

DR. SLICK: Maybe. I'll talk to them. Thanks.

When Bobbie reported this incident to me, she was quite proud of herself for the way she had calmly, almost routinely, coped with a manipulative interaction she was unprepared for. Dr. Slick came on Bobbie without any warning, without any time for Bobbie to "get herself up for it." I think she did quite well too.

The next dialogue shows how one learner coped with a friend's request for a business loan after he had tentatively agreed and then changed his mind.

Dialogue #27
**Alan and a good friend
who asks for a
business
loan**

Alan is a data processor, in his early thirties, married with no children; he earns a good salary, part of which he and his wife have saved during their marriage as both a security cushion and for possible investment. In addition to their savings, Alan has just received a small inheritance of two thousand dollars from an uncle.

Setting of the dialogue: Alan's good friend Ralph enters his office at work on a coffee break and speaks to him.

RALPH: Alan, you remember that deal with the surplus electronics warehouse I told you about?

ALAN: Yes.

RALPH: Well, I'm ready to swing it, but I need another $1,600.

ALAN: Where are you going to get it?

RALPH: That's what I wanted to talk to you about. You put up the other $1,600, I do all the work, and you get 10 per cent interest.

ALAN: Thanks for the offer, Ralph, but *I'm not interested.* [SELF-DISCLOSURE]

RALPH: But it's a really good deal. We talked it over before. You thought it would make money then.

ALAN: *That's true,* but *I'm not interested in it now.*

RALPH: You can't lose on this deal. You'll get 10 per cent return in six months.

ALAN: *You're probably right,* but *I'm not interested.* [FOGGING and SELF-DISCLOSURE]

RALPH: Why not? You've got the money. You told me yourself last week that you just inherited a couple of thousand.

ALAN: *You're right,* but I've thought it over since then and *decided not to mix business with friendship.* [FOGGING and SELF-DISCLOSURE]

RALPH: Don't worry about that. You know I'm not going to screw you. This is a legitimate deal.

ALAN: *I agree with you that there is nothing to worry about,* but when large sums of money are involved, *I worry about how things are going.* I'd keep looking over your shoulder to see what you're doing with the money. I know I can trust you, Ralph, *I know my worried feelings are dumb,* but *that's the way I am.* [FOGGING, SELF-DISCLOSURE, and NEGATIVE ASSERTION]

RALPH: That won't bother me. Check up all you want to.

ALAN: *I'm sure it wouldn't bother you if I checked on you, Ralph,* but *it would bother me.* I just don't want to operate our friendship that way. [FOGGING and SELF-DISCLOSURE]

RALPH: You know I'm good for the money. I've borrowed money before and always paid it back.

ALAN: *That's for sure,* but this is a business loan, not a loan between two friends. *I'm afraid if we get into business together, the friendship goes down the drain.* [FOGGING and SELF-DISCLOSURE]

RALPH: As far as I'm concerned, it won't.

ALAN: *I'm sure you won't let it affect you,* but *it's me that's the problem.* If I lend you that money, *I know my feelings for you will change. I know it's dumb, I know it shouldn't be that way, but that's me. That's the way I feel about it.* [FOGGING, SELF-DISCLOSURE, and NEGATIVE ASSERTION]

RALPH: Okay, if you feel that strongly about it, I'll try and get the money somewhere else. I don't know where I can get it but I'll try.

ALAN: Let me talk to some people I know. If they're interested I'll have them call you, okay? [WORKABLE COMPROMISE]

RALPH: Okay.

ALAN: Ralph.

RALPH: Yeah?

ALAN: Thanks for asking me first.

Alan tried to help Ralph out after this dialogue by calling several business associates and they all told him that they wanted no part of it and praised his judgment for not getting involved in it himself. Alan liked Ralph and enjoyed his company, perhaps because Ralph could always come up with ideas and interesting schemes that were so different from Alan's lifestyle and way of thinking. But this same quality of novelty that Alan enjoyed in a social sense with Ralph did not overcome Alan's conservative style when it came down to dollars and cents. Alan was worried when it came to money and he did not want this conservative style—perhaps too conservative a style and therefore unrealistic—to interfere with the good feelings he always had with buoyant Ralph, so he assertively told Ralph of his worries and the value of his friendship with him and kept his worries from interfering with his good feelings.

In the following set of dialogues, you can see how some learners coped with a very emotional and anxiety-provoking situation which many of us, perhaps even you yourself, have great difficulty with—parental interference in our lives after we are adults.

Dialogue #28
Sandy gradually changes the relationship
between herself and her parents
from an authoritarian one
to an interaction
between
equals.

In all of my assertive classes and therapy groups, more than half the learners have failed to establish an equality relationship between themselves and their parents. They live away from Mom and Dad, sometimes for many years, yet their parents still keep that mantle of ultimate authority over their children. In most cases, these parents do not tell their children what to do, but somehow reserve the ultimate approval or disapproval of their now-adult offspring. This lack of equality in

dealing with Mom and Dad is not simply a charac-
teristic of my younger students and patients. Many of
these unfortunate people are in their forties and fifties,
and some over sixty years old still have their lives ruled
by an eighty- or ninety-year-old tyrant. Before assertive therapy, many of these learners did not even know
what the problem was; they only knew that somehow,
whenever Mom or Dad was involved, they came out
dissatisfied, humbled; they always had that bitter sense
of impotence, yet accepted this condition as inevitable.
Because of the discomfort this outmoded authority relationship causes many students, I always have them
practice the various assertive skills to cope with their
parents' manipulation in a new way, so that they will
not need to be unwillingly, childishly responsive to parental whims. I have them rehearse a common situation
that was successfully handled by Sandy, one of my
early learners. In this situation, I start out by teaching
these learners how to say "No" to manipulative requests, suggestions, sometimes demands that they visit
their parents more often than they would care to.

At the time Sandy was learning to assert herself in
her very anxious interactions with her parents, she was
twenty-four years old, married to Jay for eleven
months, graduated from college, and substitute-teaching
while Jay was working for a graduate degree in business administration. The main subject of Sandy's assertive practice was her mother. Mom was demanding of
Sandy for attention, but particularly so after Sandy's
older sister and brother married, started families of
their own, and moved away (possibly to flee from
Mom). Sandy's mother was almost a stereotype of a
Yiddishe momma, without being Jewish. The characteristics and manipulative coping toward family members of this classic momma, her blatant or even subtle
arousal of feelings of guilt, ignorance, and anxiety in
others, are not seen only in some Jewish moms within
their restrictive traditional culture. I and my colleagues
in the mental health disciplines have reliably observed
her coping habits again and again in Jews, Arabs, Gen-
tiles, Catholics, Protestants, atheists, Orientals, blacks,

whites, Democrats (both northern and southern) Republicans, independents, liberals, conservatives, male chauvinists and even in liberated women; in short, the more insecure and nonassertive we are, the more we cope as the Yiddishe momma does; only we're much more subtle at it than she is!

Sandy brought this problem up and we discussed how she could cope with her mother's increased level of manipulation without either destroying the relationship or running away from it as her siblings had probably done. Because of her anxiety in dealing with Mom, Sandy required a lot of practice before she began to change her style of responding to her parents' manipulation of her behavior. As things turned out, when she began asserting herself toward Mom and Dad, Sandy went through a half dozen assertive encounters similar to the early parts of this dialogue before she noticed a change in Mom's behavior and attitude. The following dialogue, like some others in this chapter dealing with close (and some not so close) equal relationships, is a condensation and a sampling of the manipulative ploys used by Sandy's parents over a period of several weeks and the assertive statements Sandy used to reduce their manipulation as well as to prompt them to be more assertive to her and her husband. All of Sandy's dialogues took place over the phone. Some were initiated by Sandy; most by Mom.

Setting of the dialogue: Sandy and Jay are seated on the sofa in their apartment watching TV. The phone rings and Sandy answers it.

MOM: Sandra. This is your mother.

SANDY: Hi, Mom. How's things?

MOM: Your father is not feeling too good.

SANDY: Gee. What's wrong?

MOM: I don't know. He just wants to see you this weekend.

SANDY: Is it serious?

MOM: You talk to him.

SANDY: Dad. What's wrong?

DAD: It's just my back again. I think I pulled another muscle trying to prune the trees.

SANDY: Thank God! The way Mom sounded I thought you were dying.

DAD: It's not that bad. It's just that I'm in pain a lot of the time. When can you come over this weekend?

SANDY: *I'm sure your back hurts, Dad. I hope you feel better soon,* but I'm not coming over to see you this weekend. *I've got some other things I want to do.* [FOGGING and SELF-DISCLOSURE]

DAD: What's more important than seeing your mother?

SANDY: *I understand how you feel, Dad,* but *I won't be coming over this weekend.* [SELF-DISCLOSURE and BROKEN RECORD]

DAD: (Showing irritation) This is your father you are talking to!

SANDY: *You're right,* and *I'm sure I sound a bit disrespectful to you,* but *I won't be coming over this weekend.* [FOGGING, NEGATIVE ASSERTION, and BROKEN RECORD]

DAD: You know your mother has already bought the turkey for dinner.

SANDY: *No, I didn't know that.* [SELF-DISCLO-SURE]

DAD: She bought it just for you and Jay. A big one. We can't eat it all ourselves.

SANDY: *No, I'm sure you can't.* [FOGGING]

DAD: If you don't come over for dinner, what is your mother going to do with that turkey?

SANDY: *I don't know.* What can she do with it? [SELF-DISCLOSURE]

DAD: Your mother is going to be very upset about this.

SANDY: *I'm sure she will, Dad,* but *I won't be coming over this weekend.* [FOGGING and BROKEN RECORD]

DAD: (Aside to Mom) Talk to your daughter. She says she isn't coming over.

MOM: Sandra.

SANDY: Yes, Mom?

MOM: What have we done that would make you turn on your father like this? He's a sick man. Ever since he developed that heart murmur last year I've been worried about him. He's not going to be here forever, you know.

SANDY: *I'm sure you are worried since Dad developed heart trouble, and I know it must be lonely for you since Bob and Joan are not around anymore, but I won't be coming over this weekend.* [FOGGING, SELF-DISCLOSURE, and BROKEN RECORD]

MOM: Your brother and sister always came over when we invited them. All we had to do was to suggest it.

SANDY: *That's true, Mom. They did give you a lot of company, but I won't be over this weekend.* [FOGGING and BROKEN RECORD]

MOM: It's not right for you to treat your father this way.

SANDY: (Softly) *What is it I'm doing that's wrong?* [NEGATIVE INQUIRY]

MOM: Not coming over when he wants to see you!

SANDY: *What is it about my not coming over when he wants to see me that is wrong?* [NEGATIVE INQUIRY]

MOM: A good Christian (Jewish, Buddhist, etc.) daughter would come over to see her father.

SANDY: *What is it about my not coming over to see Dad that makes me a bad Christian daughter?*

MOM: If you really loved us, you would want to come and see us.

SANDY: *What is it about my not wanting to see you this weekend that means I don't love you?* [NEGATIVE INQUIRY]

MOM: I've never heard such a thing in all my life.

SANDY: What's that, Mom?

MOM: A daughter talking back to her mother.

SANDY: *What is it about me talking back to you that's so strange?* [NEGATIVE INQUIRY]

MOM: You've never done this before.

SANDY: (Without sarcasm) *That's true, I've never talked back to you before, have I?* [FOGGING]

MOM: You've changed since you married that Jay. I told you before you married him that you would have to watch out.

SANDY: *I don't understand. What is it about Jay that I should have to watch out for?* [NEGATIVE INQUIRY]

MOM: He's changed you, for one thing.

SANDY: *That's true, Mom, he has,* but I still don't understand, *what is it about my changing that is wrong?* [FOGGING and NEGATIVE INQUIRY]

MOM: I know he never liked me. And now he's making you choose between him and us.

SANDY: *I'm sure there is some friction between Jay and you,* but if *I choose not to come over this weekend, it's my choice, not his.* [FOGGING and SELF-DISCLOSURE]

MOM: After all we did for you. Sending you to college. And now this.

SANDY: *That's true, Mom. If it weren't for you and Dad I wouldn't have graduated by now. I still appreciate the money you gave me to go to school.* [FOGGING and SELF-DISCLOSURE]

MOM: If you appreciate it that much, you might show it.

SANDY: How?

MOM: Come over and cheer up your father this weekend.

SANDY: *You're right. If I came over to see him, that might cheer him up, but I'm not going to.* [FOGGING and BROKEN RECORD]

MOM: The way you are talking, I don't think you want to see us.

SANDY: *Not this weekend anyway, Mom.* [SELF-DISCLOSURE]

MOM: Have we done something to make you mad at us?

SANDY: No, not really mad. *You get me irritated sometimes, like now when you keep pushing me after I tell you "No," but that's dumb for me to get annoyed because that's just your way of doing things. Still it*

bugs me. [SELF-DISCLOSURE, NEGATIVE AS-
SERTION, and SELF-DISCLOSURE]

MOM: Well, if I've upset you, I apologize. (Quick
tears flowing) I just want us to be together and not
grow apart from each other.

SANDY: *I know that, Mom. I want us to be close too.
But if I want a life of my own, sometimes I have to put
my foot down and say "No," even to you and Dad. I
don't know any other way to do it. I wish I did . . . but
I don't.* [SELF-DISCLOSURE and NEGATIVE AS-
SERTION]

MOM: You don't have to chop my head off just because I'm concerned about you.

SANDY: *That's true, I shouldn't chop your head off,
Mom, and I'll try not to if you try not to push. Okay?*
[FOGGING and WORKABLE COMPROMISE]

MOM: Does this mean you don't want to see us anymore?

SANDY: *I'm sure I give that impression, Mom, but
I don't mean to. I think this is just something I have to
get out of my system; feeling like I'm still tied to your
apron strings. After a while of not coming over to your
place as much, I'm sure it won't bother me anymore.*
[FOGGING, SELF-DISCLOSURE, and WORKABLE
COMPROMISE]

MOM: (Sniffing) You'll at least call me to let me
know how you are?

SANDY: *I'll call you every week if that will make you
feel better about what I want to do.* [WORKABLE
COMPROMISE]

MOM: That's a promise?

SANDY: *That's a promise I'll try and keep, but re-
member . . . sometimes I forget things. I'm not perfect.*
[WORKABLE COMPROMISE and NEGATIVE AS-
SERTION]

MOM: That's for sure. But you'll try?

SANDY: I'll try. [WORKABLE COMPROMISE]

During the first few encounters when Sandy assertively coped with her mother's demands upon her,

things did not always go smoothly. Several times her mother hung up the phone, and except for once when Sandy immediately called her back to continue asserting herself to her mother, Mom always called back in a few days as if nothing had happened between them. After a number of assertive discussions over the phone, Sandy felt less and less pressure from her parents to do things their way. Her mother even stopped trying to tell her how to be a better schoolteacher. After this change began to be apparent, Sandy felt that both her parents gave her more and more respect for doing things the way she wanted to do them. If the way Sandy wanted to do something, to go shopping, for instance, fit in with Mom's plans, they were both happy; if not, Mom stopped her bitching and nudging and made her own arrangements the way Sandy did. What Sandy found most curious about the results of her asserting her independence as an adult was that even her Yiddishe momma had *adult* worries and fears about being older and alone that an *adult daughter* could help her mother cope with on an adult-to-adult basis.

Although Sandy's predicament with her parents was very upsetting to her before she learned to cope with it, the judgmental power she previously gave to her parents was not based upon any stereotyped sex role; it is not just women who have this problem with their parents, as you can see in the next dialogue.

Dialogue #29
Paul finally stops his father
from interfering with
his marriage and
his work.

Paul had much the same problem with his parents as Sandy in the previous dialogue had with hers until he reached the age of thirty. Before Paul learned to be more assertive in his dealings with his parents, he relied heavily upon them for many things. They, instead of the bride's family, had arranged all the details of his wedding to Connie, ten years previously. They chose the godparents to Paul and Connie's two children. They helped out financially several times when his business was slow, and they capitalized a new business when his first venture went bankrupt. All of this in spite of the fact that Paul's parents were not even financially secure themselves, let alone wealthy. Viewed through clinical eyes, Paul's parents wanted very much for Paul to do things their way, for Paul to be the kind of son that they wanted him to be. All this meddling in Paul's affairs was done in an altruistic "family" way, with the end result that Paul was quite dependent upon his parents, even after he became an adult in a chronological and legal sense. Twice during his ten years of marriage to Connie, Paul had separated from her. Both times, Dad intervened and talked Paul into going back to Connie even though Paul had said he was utterly miserable living with her. Paul and Connie never had any significant marital battles even though there was a lot of conflict between them over money, religion, raising of the children, and how Paul "should" spend his relaxation time—for himself or doing things Connie wanted him to do. Connie's style of controlling Paul was to cut him up manipulatively without getting angry and Paul responded to Connie in the same way that he dealt with his parents; he quietly "argued" back, did not cut Connie up verbally the way she did him, but gave in most of the time. I saw Paul in an assertive therapy setting shortly after his tenth wedding anniversary. At the anniversary party given them by his parents (who else?), Paul got very drunk, and his smoldering anger and resentment—built up over the years by Connie's "pussy whipping"—finally exploded in a drunken act. After two hours of her nagging him to stop drinking so much, he walked over to the buffet, picked up the anniversary cake his mother had baked for them, walked back to Connie, told her: "Go screw yourself," and dropped the cake over her head. Paul then walked out of the party and drove to a motel for the night. When he sobered up the next day, he went home and told Connie that he was sorry he ruined the party, but that if she didn't stop nagging him in the future he was going to "belt her one right in the mouth." After a verbal fight that lasted several hours, Connie told Paul that he was mentally sick and should get treatment. Apparently willing to try anything that might help his situation, Paul consulted with a colleague for a few sessions and was referred to me for assertive therapy. After several weeks of intensive assertive therapy, Paul asked if he could bring Connie in to his sessions with me. After discussing why he wanted Connie to see me, it became apparent that Paul wanted me to be the referee for their interactions. I told Paul that I would see him and Connie together if she was willing to take part in marital counseling, but experience had taught me that it would serve no therapeutic purpose for me to be a referee between them—telling one that this particular behavior was wrong, the other that this behavior is right, etc. Paul agreed that his request was only a manipulative attempt to get me to tell Connie that her behavior toward him was wrong, but he still thought that marital counseling for both of them was a good idea. Paul talked to her about it and Connie agreed to taking part in therapy; I saw them conjointly for a number of weekly sessions. Things went smoothly for the first few sessions with Paul taking the "hot seat," being quite open about his feelings and wanting to explore them with Connie, perhaps because he was feeling less anxious about himself and his behavior after some assertive therapy. When I tried to see how Connie was coping emotionally in her marriage relationship, she balked about getting involved. She resisted specifically the conditions I laid down at our first meeting. I had explained that initially in marital counseling the only goal I would work toward was the exploration of each partner's feelings about the marriage relationship. The exploration was aimed at helping each of them to decide if they wished to continue the relationship, work toward new ways of coping with one another, separate temporarily, or permanently, get a divorce, or whatever other alternative they wished to work out. Once the goal of deciding what to do about the marriage was reached, Paul and Connie could either work in conjoint therapy on new ways of living with each other, or if they chose, I would work with each of them individually to help them cope with the crisis of separation and/or divorce. Connie passively resisted any attempts to allow Paul to come to a decision about the marriage—any decision that is, which differed with her desire: a return to the previous status quo, with Paul "behaving himself" according to Connie's standards. She insisted that Paul was the "identified patient"; he was the one who needed therapy to straighten out his thinking. She was apparently unwilling to explore any new ways of thinking about their common marital problems. In the face of Connie's unwillingness to look at her own contribution to their dilemma, Paul gave up trying and opted for separation leading to a divorce. Connie then disengaged herself from therapy while Paul asked for continued counseling about the habits that got him into trouble, as well as learning to cope with other people. Paul requested specific practice in assertively coping with his dad's manipulation in his marital affairs since he had decided upon divorce twice before and his father had reasoned him out of it. Paul rehearsed being assertive with one immediate goal in mind, one that we both agreed upon as important: achieving independence from his parents' influence without fleeing from them or alienating them, if that was at all possible. After Paul was coached to respond assertively to the same manipulations his father had used before to control his decision about divorce (and also throwing in some he hadn't heard before), he saw his parents, dealt with their objections, but went beyond what we had practiced. The following dialogue is a shortened version of a discussion between Paul and his father that took place over an afternoon.

Setting of the dialogue: Paul doesn't wait for his parents to contact him, but goes to their home to talk to his father about his decision to separate from Connie.

Paul walks into the living room and his father gets up from his chair and greets him coldly.

DAD: I wondered if we'd hear from you. Connie came right over and told us that you wanted a divorce after the last session with the doctor. Sometimes I think you have your head screwed on backward.

PAUL: *So do I, Dad, so do I.* [NEGATIVE ASSERTION]

DAD: You're not really serious about this divorce thing again, are you?

PAUL: *About the divorce, I don't know. About separating from Connie, yes.* [SELF-DISCLOSURE.]

DAD: This is foolish. I expected something better of you.

PAUL: *You're right, Dad, it is foolish and I'm sure you expected me to be different than I am, but I am going through with it* [FOGGING and BROKEN RECORD]

DAD: You've gone through this nonsense twice before and it's lucky I was able to make you see the right thing to do.

PAUL: *You're right again. I tried to do it twice before and you did talk me out of it,* but *not this time. I've had it with Connie.* [FOGGING, BROKEN RECORD, and SELF-DISCLOSURE]

DAD: All you accomplished before by talking divorce was to create a lot of unnecessary trouble and got nothing for it.

PAUL: *That's for sure. Was I wishy-washy about it!* [FOGGING and NEGATIVE ASSERTION]

DAD: You don't want a divorce.

PAUL: *That's true, Dad, I don't want one,* but *I'm through with Connie. Whatever it takes—separation, divorce, whatever.* [FOGGING, SELF-DISCLOSURE, and BROKEN RECORD]

DAD: Look, she's obviously done something that's made you madder than hell or you wouldn't have hit her with your mother's cake. Besides you were dead drunk or you wouldn't have done it. These things blow over. You have to be flexible like you were before.

PAUL: *Dad, she did make me angry and you're right;*

I wouldn't have had enough courage to let her have it with the cake unless I was drunk. It was stupid to act that way instead of waiting until the party was over and then have it out. I spoiled the party, but what can I say? I'm not sorry I did it. I just wish I hadn't upset you two. [FOGGING, NEGATIVE ASSERTION, and SELF-DISCLOSURE]

DAD: Don't worry about us. Your mother just cried a lot. Connie got hysterical and beat the hell out of little Jamie just because he laughed at her with all that frosting on her face. I had to stop her or he would have been hurt.

PAUL: *I didn't know that.* [SELF-DISCLOSURE]

DAD: I didn't think you did. That's why I told you. Connie is all right, but she does get hysterical. That's one reason why you can't divorce her. How do you know the kids will be okay without you around?

PAUL: *I don't. I guess Connie and I will have to talk about that with my lawyer.* [SELF-DISCLOSURE and WORKABLE COMPROMISE]

DAD: You'll never get custody. Not after getting drunk and hitting her with your mother's cake.

PAUL: *Maybe, but my lawyer can figure that one out.* [FOGGING and WORKABLE COMPROMISE]

DAD: Look, Son. We've just been BS'ing up to now. Believe me. Divorce is wrong! You don't want one! You'll be making a big mistake!

PAUL: *Maybe I will make a mistake, but what is it about getting a divorce that's wrong?* [FOGGING and NEGATIVE INQUIRY]

DAD: Kids shouldn't be exposed to such things.

PAUL: *What is it about exposing them to reality like divorce that is bad for them?* [NEGATIVE INQUIRY]

DAD: It will give them a bad outlook on their own lives.

PAUL: *What is it about reality that will give them a bad outlook?* [NEGATIVE INQUIRY]

DAD: Kids have to be protected.

PAUL: *I agree, but only up to a point. I won't argue it with you, but I feel that they'll come to more harm having to live with Connie and me bitching and ar-*

guing every day than knowing that we aren't going to live together. [FOGGING and NEGATIVE ASSERTION]

DAD: You don't want to do this to your kids.

PAUL: *I don't* but *I'm through with Connie.* [FOGGING and BROKEN RECORD]

DAD: How are you going to work this out for them?

PAUL: *I don't know yet.* But I'll do something. [SELF-DISCLOSURE]

DAD: Do you know what this will do to your mother if you go through with it?

PAUL: *No, but I guess she won't like it.* [SELF-DISCLOSURE]

DAD: Paul. Your mother and I have given up a lot of things for you and Connie. Especially for our grandchildren. Don't do this. It makes everything we've worked hard for worth nothing.

PAUL: *You and Mom have done a lot for me, Dad.* I appreciate it because it tells me that you both care a lot. [FOGGING]

DAD: That's what parents are for, Son. To help out when we see things going wrong. That's what I'm trying to do now.

PAUL: *I'm sure you feel that way, Dad.* But *I'm doing what I think is best now, even if it's unpleasant for you and Mom.* [FOGGING and NEGATIVE ASSERTION]

DAD: Well, I tried. I know how your mother is going to take it. Pretty badly, I think.

PAUL: *I don't know,* but *you're probably right.* There's something else I want to talk to you about. [SELF-DISCLOSURE and FOGGING]

DAD: What's that?

PAUL: About the shop. *I want to sell it and pay you back the money you put up for it.* [SELF-DISCLOSURE]

DAD: Why do you want to do that after all the work you did building it up? You're making good money from it now. You don't have to pay me back.

PAUL: *You're right, I know I don't have to re-*

pay the money, but *I want to and it's important to me.* [FOGGING and SELF-DISCLOSURE]

DAD: That's the stupidest thing I've ever heard you say! Everything we have is going to go to you and the kids someday anyway.

PAUL: *I agree 100 per cent with you. It is stupid and doesn't make sense,* but *I've always had the uncomfortable feeling that I was working for you instead of myself.* [NEGATIVE ASSERTION and SELF-DISCLOSURE]

DAD: That's crazy. I never told you how to run your business. No wonder you needed to see a shrink.

PAUL: *It is crazy,* but *it's the way I feel. You never put any pressure on me about how to run things,* but *I've always had a feeling that you worried that I would make a fool of myself again in business and throw away your money.* [NEGATIVE ASSERTION, FOGGING, and BROKEN RECORD]

DAD: If you couldn't make a go of it, that's just one of those things. Your mother and I were glad to let you have the money.

PAUL: *Are you sure you didn't have some doubts about me being able to run it?* [NEGATIVE INQUIRY]

DAD: (Defensively) Maybe a little, but what do you expect with the bankruptcy and everything else?

PAUL: *You hit the nail on the head. I did screw things up before and I don't blame you for how you feel.* But *ever since you bailed me out with that money I felt like I always had to check with you to make sure I was doing things okay.* [NEGATIVE ASSERTION and SELF-DISCLOSURE]

DAD: (Protesting) But . . .

PAUL: (Interrupting) *I know what you're going to say and I agree with you. It's stupid to feel that way,* but *I do! Call it a neurotic hangup. I am going to work on it in psychotherapy,* but *in the meantime I want to change things so I don't feel like a little boy who always has to check with his daddy about things.* [NEGATIVE ASSERTION and SELF-DISCLOSURE]

DAD: (Silent for a few moments and looking at Paul

thoughtfully) I never thought that trying to help you out was a bad thing.

PAUL: (Silently looking at his father) *I don't think it is a bad thing. I appreciate that you were trying to help me, but it makes me feel like an incompetent. Maybe I was; and maybe I still am, but I don't want to feel that way whether I am or not.* [FOGGING, SELF-DIS-CLOSURE, and NEGATIVE ASSERTION and SELF-DISCLOSURE]

DAD: If you feel that strongly about it, why don't you pay me back a little bit at a time instead of selling the shop?

PAUL: *What is it about me selling the shop that worries you?* [NEGATIVE INQUIRY]

DAD: It makes me feel better knowing that you have a good steady income. If something happened to me and I couldn't work anymore, I know I could depend upon you to help your mom and me out. Retirement doesn't go very far, and when I retire, maybe I could help you do things there to keep busy.

PAUL: Dad. If you ever get in a jam, I'll try to help as much as I can. (Choking up) That sounds strange coming from me. Me helping you out. (Silent for a while) How's this sound? *We make out a mortgage note on the business for what I owe you. It's in your name at a bank and I make regular payments with interest to your account there.* That would make me feel a lot better. [WORKABLE COMPROMISE]

DAD: But what about property settlement with Connie when the divorce comes through?

PAUL: The lawyers can work that out. She would get a percentage of the action.

DAD: You won't have to sell the shop and give her half of the money as a settlement?

PAUL: We'll work it out so that doesn't happen.

DAD: Okay with me.

PAUL: Okay except for one thing. When it comes to the shop, even when you retire and work there, I'm the boss! Agreed?

DAD: (Extending his hand to shake Paul's) Agreed!

When Paul and I later discussed his assertive interaction with his father, it became apparent to me that while Paul had accomplished much for himself in that one session, he still had, what seemed to me at least, a problem in relating to his father. The one predominent feeling that Paul's interaction with his dad evoked within me was a heavy sadness; I was touched. I felt sad for Paul because of the type of relationship he had with his father and I also felt sad for his father, who, possibly out of anxiety about a lot of things, had used his son's life to cope with these anxieties. In being touched, I had committed the classic cardinal sin of the therapist: countertransference. I had personally identified too much with the patient's problems. Worse yet, I told Paul about my feelings in the following dialogue.

ME: I think you did super, Paul, but your talk with your father made me feel sad. How do you feel about it?

PAUL: Afterwards, I felt depressed. Not about the divorce. About me and my father.

ME: Have you figured out why?

PAUL: Yes and no. At first I felt good about getting my way. Then I got mad as hell at him. Afterwards I just felt unhappy.

ME: Just a letdown after a conflict?

PAUL: No. I guess it's because I thought he was always on the ball. When he told me he wanted me to help support him if something happened, I wanted to cry.

ME: Do you know why?

PAUL: No.

ME: Do you want to take a risk? You may be hurt trying to find out why.

PAUL: Why not?

ME: Why do you think your father didn't just accept the fact that you were in trouble and wanted a divorce?

PAUL: I don't know. I've been thinking about that myself. He's never accepted it before.

ME: What would it have cost him to just say something like: "I wish you could make a go of it with Connie, but if you think you can't, you do what you think best. I'm sorry for you. If I can help, let me know?"

PAUL: I don't know why. I wish he would have.

ME: What did he say that made you want to cry?

PAUL: When he said he wanted me to help him.

ME: Has he ever said that before?

PAUL: No.

ME: When did he say that?

PAUL: When I asked him what worried him about me selling the shop and wanting to be independent of him.

ME: Has he ever told you that he had worries before?

PAUL: No, that's the first time.

ME: And that made you want to cry?

PAUL: I feel like crying now thinking about it.

ME: Do you want me to stop talking?

PAUL: No.

ME: Why was he worried about you selling the shop?

PAUL: (Looking at me uncomfortably)

ME: You got a hunch running around inside?

PAUL: Yeah, but I don't like to think about it.

ME: Do you know the sound a hammer makes when it hits solid steel? That true ringing sound?

PAUL: Yes.

ME: Does your hunch have the same feeling? That same solid true ring?

PAUL: I think so.

ME: Then say it. Why was your dad worried about you selling your shop?

PAUL: He was counting on me all along if things went wrong to bail him out.

ME: Did he ever tell you that?

PAUL: No, never.

ME: Do you know why he never told you?

PAUL: No.

ME: Why didn't he accept the fact that you were in trouble and wanted a divorce?

PAUL: If I divorced Connie, that would screw the family up and he couldn't count on me.

ME: How?

PAUL: I might split and live somewhere else. Then he couldn't count on me.

ME: What would you have to do first before you could split?

PAUL: Sell the shop. Just like I told him I wanted to do.

ME: And what would worry him about selling the shop?

PAUL: Me and the shop making money was his insurance policy in case he couldn't work or when he retired.

ME: Why do you think he kept bailing you out whenever you got in trouble and doing everything for you instead of letting you learn by taking your lumps like the rest of us?

PAUL: I was his insurance policy and bailing me out was paying his premiums. I owed him! That son of a bitch! He's been doing that all these years!

ME: Do you think your father is a mean man?

PAUL: No.

ME: Then why did you call him a son of a bitch?

PAUL: Because he used me! I tried to get a divorce twice and he stopped me because of his own problems!

ME: Then why did you want to cry when he said he wanted your help?

PAUL: He said he was worried about what might happen if he had to retire.

ME: Did he control you because he was a son of a bitch or because he was worried?

PAUL: I've never worried like that about my future. I've screwed up a lot but I've never worried about what would happen when I got old.

ME: Do you know now why he manipulates you?

PAUL: Yes. I don't like it but I know why.

ME: You know now why I feel sad about your father?

PAUL: I feel sad about it too. The poor bastard.

ME: Do you still feel like a little boy that your father has to keep checking up on?

PAUL: No.

ME: Do you know what to say if you feel like he is checking up on you?

PAUL: I think so.

ME: For example?

PAUL: Dad. Stop worrying about things. I can handle it.

ME: Are you still unhappy about the situation?

PAUL: Yes.

ME: Reality isn't nice sometimes.

PAUL: It sure as hell isn't for me.

ME: (Pompously) Which would you rather be: unhappy and controlled by your father, or unhappy and in charge of your own life and able to change what you want?

PAUL: (Sarcastically) What do you think?

ME: (Dead serious) I hope you've learned everything I've tried to teach you.

PAUL: You're getting to sound like my father!

ME: (Smiling) You're learning fast. May I offer some advice?

PAUL: Sure.

ME: Don't let anybody make your decisions for you, *including me.*

In the next set of everyday life situations, you can see how several people assertively cope with manipulation in a relationship that, thankfully for the survival of the human species, has more promise of good feelings and closeness than the relationship between Paul and his father: the mating of men and women.

Dialogue #30
Dana and Beth cope with
friendly manipulation
from their sexual
partners, and
many a young
co-ed learns
how to say
"No."

In this set of social-sexual dialogues, two young women, Dana and Beth, assertively and successfully

cope with their own mixed feelings about bed and marriage. In the second dialogue, a psychologist demon-
strates to generally unsophisticated young co-eds how
to assertively yet emphatically say "No" (if they want
to say "No") to possible sexual partners who may
manipulatively try to talk them into bed.

Dana is a twenty-seven-year-old merchandise buyer.
She impressed me as a very bright young woman who
could not be classified as either beautiful or homely in
face or figure: interesting and not unattractive. Dana
described her own heterosexual dating lifestyle as that
of a single woman who was required to actively hustle
single men for dates with the qualities of her personality
instead of passively with her physical appearance. As
you might suspect, Dana spent many a night alone or
on a "Dutch treat" basis in singles' bars. During assertive therapy, Dana reported a situation that, for her at
least, was unusual and boosted her ego and self-respect
quite a bit. Several weeks before the incident described
in the dialogue, she met a man who "turned her on"
sexually and whom she was attracted to generally; she
liked John's way of being attentive to her, his intelligence, his physical appearance. Consequently, as a result of both her general low self-confidence and being
attracted to him physically, she went to bed with him
on the first date (they met in a singles' bar) even
though, as she reported later, she really didn't want to
have sex then. This liaison produced no Victorian guilt
for Dana, but made her feel rotten; she had had sex
with someone she hardly knew when she would rather
have not. Not surprisingly, she didn't enjoy herself, although her partner seemed to have a great time. As I
suggested, and Dana identified with, many single
women feel that sexual relations in dating situations are
their admission tickets into a relationship with men;
they are paying a price for not being lonely instead of
mutually sharing something both exciting and tender.
In Dana's case, she operated under a current variation
of our old manipulative structure and belief system,
i.e., that nowadays under the aegis of the sexual revolution, "Everybody's doing it," or "If a woman doesn't

put out, she must have a neurotic hangup," or "She won't get dated again." After dealing with this sometimes painful situation in a more assertive way, Dana found out that such statements about sexual behavior (either from herself or from others) have just about as much truth in them as the manipulative statements many people used to control her behavior in other areas of her life. In clinically working with women of all ages and circumstances, single, divorced, widowed, I have observed that such structured beliefs about the new sexual expectations are used by some of them as an excuse for not getting involved in other meaningful activities—activities which might produce growth and change to make them interesting to new men on other than just a sexual basis. Forming a relationship primarily on the basis of sexual intercourse is a "cheap shot" and quite easy to do. The only difficulty with it is that such a relationship doesn't last very long, at least for the women (and men too!) whom I see clinically. The problem for many of them is that they want an "instant" close relationship and don't want to have to go through the doubt, uncertainty, and hard work of the slow and sometimes painful building of such a close relationship. This, then, was the situation Dana realized she was in, specifically with John, and drifting toward generally with other men. However, she coped with it very well on a second chance meeting with John, using the assertive verbal skills she had learned in other situations without specific practice applied to social-sexual behavior.

Setting of the dialogue: Dana is seated with an old friend, Jan, whom she has not seen in several years. Seated in a booth in a Redondo Beach singles' bar that Dana visited often in the past, they are excitedly chatting about old times and friends (gossiping) when John comes in, sees Dana, walks up to the two women, leans over their table and speaks:

JOHN: Hi, Dana, how are you?

DANA: Hello, I'm fine. Yourself?

JOHN: (Looking straight at Jan) Okay. Who's your cute friend? I don't think we've ever met before.

DANA: (To Jan) Jan, this is Johnny. (To John) Jan is an old friend I haven't seen for years. We just ran into each other a few minutes ago.

JAN: Nice to meet you, Johnny.

JOHN: (To no one in particular) I've got a great idea. Why don't the three of us have a few drinks here together and later I'll get one of my friends to join us.

DANA: (Without consulting with Jan) *That would be nice, Johnny,* but *I'd like to just sit and talk to Jan for a while.* [FOGGING and BROKEN RECORD]

JOHN: That friend I spoke about. He's a great guy, Jan would really like to meet him.

DANA: *I understand how you feel,* but *I'd just like to be alone to talk to Jan for a while. Afterwards . . . ?* [SELF-DISCLOSURE, BROKEN RECORD, and WORKABLE COMPROMISE]

JOHN: We had such super vibes last time, Dana. I'm sure Jan would understand and you two could talk later.

DANA: (Smiling) *That's super you remembered, and I understand how you feel,* but *I just want to sit and talk to Jan for a while.* [SELF-DISCLOSURE and BROKEN RECORD]

JOHN: Dana. You don't think I'm going to let two groovy foxes who really turn me on sit alone here!

DANA: *I understand how you feel, Johnny,* but *I just want to sit alone with Jan for a while* [SELF-DISCLOSURE and BROKEN RECORD]

JOHN: But there is no one else in this whole place worth being with except you two. Do you want to ruin my whole evening? Would you refuse a glass of water to a man dying of thirst?

DANA: *You may be right,* but *I still want to talk to Jan for a while.* [FOGGING and BROKEN RECORD]

JOHN: Last time was so great, I've been hoping to run into you again.

DANA: (Again smiling and beginning to enjoy herself) *I understand how you feel,* but *I just want to talk to*

Jan. Tell you what, though. *I'm free on Friday night. Why don't we get together then?* [SELF-DIS-CLOSURE, BROKEN RECORD, and WORKABLE COMPROMISE]

JOHN: (Taken aback for a moment) Oh? ... Okay ... Here?

DANA: How about dinner first and then here or somewhere else?

JOHN: Okay. What if I pick you up at seven?

DANA: Why don't you give me a call at work before Friday and we can work out the details? (Writing her work phone number on a napkin)

JOHN: Okay ...

JAN: Nice meeting you, Johnny. See you around.

JOHN: Same here.

Dana's experience in asserting her independence from a social-sexual partner without resorting to hostility or blaming John for her own mixed feelings about being talked into bed was a delight to her. Not only was Dana able to cope with John's "make" without telling him to go to hell, but she had begun the process of assertively renegotiating the basis of their future relationship. I asked Dana what happened afterwards and how she felt about it.

ME: Why did you want him to call you at work?

DANA: I wanted us to go out on a regular date instead of meeting him in a bar for drinks.

ME: So?

DANA: So, I wanted him to call me. To make some effort. To hustle me for a change.

ME: And what happened?

DANA: He called on Thursday afternoon and guess what he said: "Would you still like to go out to dinner tomorrow?"

ME: And?

DANA: And I said "Yes" and we worked out the details. He asked if I had any preference in restaurants and I said I didn't like Chasen's or Frascatti's; they were too expensive.

ME: (Smiling) And he breathed a sigh of relief!

DANA: No. He was straight up about it and said he wanted to go to a place in the Valley he liked. So I said okay.

ME: And?

DANA: And we went and I really enjoyed his company.

ME: And?

DANA: And we went just for drinks afterwards and talked.

ME: And?

DANA: And nothing! Pete, you've got a one-track mind!

ME: You're probably right, Dana, but what happened afterwards? Was it a repeat of the first time?

DANA: No. After dinner, I told John that I liked him very much, but I had gone to bed with him just because I thought he wouldn't have been interested in me if I hadn't. And I didn't like what I did.

ME: And how did he take it?

DANA: It didn't faze him at all. He said that he was sorry that I didn't enjoy myself then and if I felt that way to say so.

ME: So?

DANA: So I told him that I was very unsure of myself with him even though we have fun together ... probably because I liked him so much.

ME: In your best negative assertive manner?

DANA: Yup.

ME: Do you have another date with him?

DANA: He said he would call me again soon.

ME: What's that mean? He likes you ... or a brush-off?

DANA: I don't know. That's up to him. If he doesn't call next week, I'll call him and suggest we go to lunch and see what happens.

ME: And how do you feel about the whole thing?

DANA: Pretty good.

ME: Even though you don't have a lock on him through your body?

DANA: A guy like John can get laid any time he

wants to. I don't want to compete on that basis. If he's
interested in me as Dana and wants to continue the
relationship, that's good enough for me.

At last report, Dana was still seeing John occasionally, dating several other men, and, most importantly,
was more comfortable with her role as an assertive, selective sexual partner and no longer felt like a piece of
meat on the butcher's block to be haggled over and
bargained for.

In their interaction, Dana communicated her problem to John and he supported her attempt to cope with
her own mixed feelings about their relationship. If on
the other hand, John was not John but somebody else
less mature and less sure of his own personal machismo
(sexual masculinity), he might have ignored Dana's request for an exploration of their relationship based on
other things besides sex—common interests, intellect,
personality styles, long-term personal goals, likes and
dislikes, etc. If he were less sure of his ability to attract
women sexually, John might have tried to verbally
manipulate (seduce) and titillate Dana into bedding
down again in spite of her mixed feelings about it. If
that were the case, Dana could have assertively coped
with this sexual manipulation in the same way she
learned to cope with manipulation of her behavior in
other areas. She could have coped in a systematic assertive way that was demonstrated to hundreds of UCLA
co-eds in introductory psychology classes by Dr. Aaron
Hass, a colleague, a friend, and one of my former graduate students whom I trained in systematic assertiveness
at the UCLA Psychology Clinic. Then-Doctoral Candi-
date Hass and a lovely female graduate student he
recruited made the rounds of the large psychology
classes to show young co-eds (and their future mates)
with little or no sexual sophistication how to assertively
say "No" to a partner bent upon seduction using
manipulation varying from "hurt" ploys or guilt to
ignorance-inducing statements or accusatory remarks.
Although Dr. Hass pointed out that most males are not
as intent upon getting a woman into bed as his demon-

stration portrayed, he felt it was important to show how being assertive can be used even in an extreme case where a frustrated male shows anger toward his date. The following dialogue on this situation is one that my colleague. Ms. Susan Levine, and myself demonstrated at a professional workshop on systematic assertive therapy. The manipulative ploys that I used in the dialogue were similar to those used by Dr. Hass at UCLA. The assertive responses to this manipulation are those Ms. Levine chose to demonstrate the use of several assertive verbal skills in coping with an attractive but obnoxious seducer.

Setting of the dialogue: Sue and I are sitting on a table at the head of the class which simulates the couch in her living room. We have just returned to her apartment after a movie date and she has invited me in for a drink. After some wine, I lean over for a kiss and she pulls away.

ME: What's wrong?

SUE: (Smiling a friendly smile) I don't feel like making out tonight.

ME: But I thought we really had a nice time tonight.

SUE: *You're right. I did have a great time tonight.* [FOGGING]

ME: Then what's wrong?

SUE: I don't understand. *How come my not wanting to make out is wrong?* [NEGATIVE INQUIRY]

ME: Why not? I thought you liked me.

SUE: *I do, but I'm just not up for sleeping with you tonight.* [FOGGING and BROKEN RECORD]

ME: I think it would really be nice.

SUE: *Yeah, it might be,* but *I don't want to get in bed with you tonight.* [FOGGING and BROKEN RECORD]

ME: I think it would be a fantastic experience for both of us.

SUE: *Once again, you may be right,* but *I just don't want to.* [FOGGING and BROKEN RECORD]

ME: What's wrong with enjoying ourselves?

SUE: *Nothing that I know of.* [FOGGING]

ME: Then why don't you?

SUE: *I don't know. I just don't want to go to bed with you tonight.* [SELF-DISCLOSURE and BROKEN RECORD]

ME: I think it's a really natural thing to do when people get close and enjoy each other.

SUE: I don't understand. *What's unnatural about me not wanting to go to bed with you?* [NEGATIVE INQUIRY]

ME: We could just flow with our good feelings and get to know each other much better in bed.

SUE: *We could do that. I want to flow with our good feelings but not if it means going to bed with you.* [FOGGING and WORKABLE COMPROMISE]

ME: We get along ... the vibes between us are special and right.

SUE: *You're right. I do like to talk to you.* [FOGGING and SELF-DISCLOSURE]

ME: Think of how much better it would be in bed with those good feelings we have for each other.

SUE: *I understand how you feel,* but *I don't want to go to bed with you.* [SELF-DISCLOSURE and BROKEN RECORD]

ME: What's wrong with me?

SUE: *If I don't go to bed with you, how come that means there has to be something wrong with you?* [NEGATIVE INQUIRY]

ME: Well, I'm not turning you on.

SUE: (With amazement) *That I really don't understand. How come my not going to bed with you means you're not turning me on?* [SELF-DISCLOSURE and NEGATIVE INQUIRY]

ME: I thought you liked me.

SUE: *I do like you,* but *I don't want to go to bed with you tonight.* [FOGGING and BROKEN RECORD]

ME: How much do you like me?

SUE: *I'm not really sure.* [SELF-DISCLOSURE]

ME: If you really cared how I feel, you would want to go to bed with me. (Note: the cheapest of all possible shots.)

SUE: *Maybe you're right, if I cared for you more, I would go to bed with you* [FOGGING and BROKEN RECORD]

ME: I'm a lonely guy . . .

SUE: (Just a silent smile)

ME: You don't care for my feelings. Is there something wrong with you?

SUE: *There's a lot wrong with me.* [NEGATIVE ASSERTION]

ME: Do you have a problem with sex? Lots of chicks do.

SUE: *I'm sure they have. What am I doing that tells you I have a problem with sex?* [FOGGING and NEGATIVE INQUIRY]

ME: You seem like you have a hangup over going to bed.

SUE: *I'm sure it seems that way.* [FOGGING]

ME: I could help you get over it if that's your problem.

SUE: *Maybe, but I don't want to go to bed with you.* [FOGGING and BROKEN RECORD]

ME: For someone who says they care for other people, you don't seem to be what you say.

SUE: *You may be right, I do come on like a phony sometimes.* [FOGGING and NEGATIVE ASSERTION]

ME: All night we talked about how superficial most people are when they relate to each other. They don't get into something meaningful. I ask for a more meaningful level of understanding between us and you are copping out.

SUE: *I probably am copping out.* [FOGGING]

ME: Is this a game you play with all the guys?

SUE: *I don't understand.* [SELF-DISCLOSURE]

ME: I think you were leading me on.

SUE: *How was I leading you on?* [NEGATIVE INQUIRY]

ME: I think you played a number on me tonight . . . giving good vibes about really enjoying me and then asking me up to your apartment afterwards.

SUE: (Absolutely without sarcasm) *It's obvious that I*

gave you the wrong idea by asking you to come up to my apartment. That was dumb of me. [NEGATIVE ASSERTION]

ME: There's a name people use for girls like you.

SUE: *What's that?* [NEGATIVE INQUIRY]

ME: A prick tease.

SUE: (Walking to the door, opening it, and standing outside) *It was a mistake for me to invite you up here. Please leave.* [NEGATIVE ASSERTION and WORKABLE COMPROMISE]

Although the demonstration was carried to the worst possible extreme for any future dating relationship, you can see that if the possible male sexual partner had listened to his date's assertive but empathic "No" earlier in the piece, he might have been in a position to date her again and see if she had changed her mind. We kept out of the demonstration any flattering seductive ploys, such as "I think I love you," "You turn me on so much I can't study thinking about you," "You have such a sexy smile and personality that I just have to kiss you to let you know," "You and your body are so fascinating that my hand trembles when I think of touching you!" Such flattery is, of course, outrageous nonsense offered up as arousing and titillating verbal foreplay in the sexual spirit of the occasion; where both partners have given either verbal or innate signs of being sexually interested in one another.

After the demonstration, I asked Sue why she walked to the door and opened it and stood outside the classroom. She turned to the workshop members and replied: "Look at the difference in our sizes. At that point, which would stand me a better chance—fight or flight?"

In contrast to the first two situations in this set of dialogues, the next one deals not just with sexual relations and dating, but with one assertive young woman, Beth, who coped with a marriage proposal from a young man whom she felt she loved, but had some doubts and reservations about as a lifetime partner. I met Beth as a result of a staff development and communication consultation for a public agency. I gave these people systematic assertive instruction and Beth was included in one of the first groups I ran. Already having a less than average quota of "shoulds-shouldn'ts" in her portfolio as a result of her up-bringing, Beth took to assertive training like a duck to water. We became good friends and maintained the relationship, however infrequent our chance meetings after the staff development program was finished a year later. On one of these meetings, Beth told me of her experiences with Ted, the young man she cared very much for, his proposal of marriage, and the workable compromise she negotiated with him. The following dialogue is a shortened version of many such interactions Beth and Ted engaged in over a period of several weeks.

Setting of the dialogue: Beth is seated in the living room of Ted's apartment on a hot Saturday afternoon and he walks out of the kitchen with a pitcher of wine, crushed ice, and fruit to take down to the pool with them. Ted speaks first.

TED: Why don't we just sit here for a minute before we swim? I want to talk about you and me.

BETH: Sounds serious. *Have I done anything to upset you?* [NEGATIVE INQUIRY]

TED: (Smiling) Not yet, but you may if you don't do what I ask you.

BETH: Shoot.

TED: You're the nicest, most exciting girl I've ever met, Beth. I think you feel like that about me. How much do you love me?

BETH: A lot!

TED: Enough to get married?

BETH: *I don't know.* [SELF-DISCLOSURE]

TED: Why not? We've been going together for close to a year. That should be enough time to find out.

BETH: *Maybe,* but *I just don't know.* [FOGGING and BROKEN RECORD]

TED: We get along together, don't we?

BETH: *Sure we do,* but getting along part of the time, dating, isn't like getting along twenty-four hours a day when you are married; *at least to my way of think-ing it isn't and that's what worries me.* [FOGGING and SELF-DISCLOSURE]

TED: How are we going to know if we don't try it? We could go on forever dating like this.

BETH: *That's true,* but I don't understand. *What is it about dating and not marrying that's wrong?* [FOG-GING and NEGATIVE INQUIRY]

TED: There's nothing wrong with it. I just want to marry you, that's all.

BETH: *Is there something about our sleeping together without being married that's bothering you?* [NEGA-TIVE INQUIRY]

TED: No, not really. It's just that the more I think about it, the more I want to marry you.

BETH: Ted. *That's really sweet to say that and I think it's a great way of saying you love me,* but *I still get the feeling that you are unhappy about something. Are you sure something isn't bothering you about the way we do things now?* [SELF-DISCLOSURE and NEGATIVE INQUIRY]

TED: Somehow I feel less secure about us just dating. I'd feel a lot better about how much you cared for me if we were married.

BETH: I don't understand. *It sounds like you're saying that I don't care enough about you to marry you and that's making you uneasy, is that it?* [NEGATIVE INQUIRY]

TED: It's making me uptight.

BETH: *Do you want me to stop asking you questions about us?* [NEGATIVE INQUIRY]

TED: No.

BETH: Okay. *I've noticed something that's bothering me. I think you're a bit jealous of the other guys who talk to me at the pool. Am I right?* [SELF-DIS-CLOSURE]

TED: (Defensively) Why should I be jealous?

BETH: *I don't know why. Are you?* [SELF-DIS-CLOSURE]

TED: Just a little, but what do you expect with the way you are built and the way you talk to them?

BETH: *You're right, Ted, I am a bit of a flirt, but that's me. That wouldn't change if we were married.* [FOGGING and NEGATIVE ASSERTION]

TED: (Silent, looking a bit hurt)

BETH: If we got married, you would still be jealous, *because I like to flirt and that's part of me. But it doesn't mean that I'm hot to go to bed with them.* [NEGATIVE ASSERTION and SELF-DISCLOSURE]

TED: How am I supposed to know that?

BETH: *I don't know. I guess the same dumb way I have to make up my mind about you* [SELF-DISCLOSURE and NEGATIVE ASSERTION]

TED: (With some finality) So you don't want to marry me.

BETH: *I don't know.* [SELF-DISCLOSURE]

TED: (Sarcastically) How long do you think it will take you to know?

BETH: *I don't know that either.* [SELF-DISCLOSURE]

TED: So what do I do? I don't want to tell you to shove it because I love you so much. But I don't want to keep feeling uneasy about you caring for me.

BETH: *Why don't we live together?* [WORKABLE COMPROMISE]

TED: How is that going to be any different? What kind of answer is that? We almost live together now!

BETH: *That's almost true,* but *I think it would make a difference.* Right now we are both as free as we can be, but living together we have responsibilities for each other. [FOGGING and SELF-DISCLOSURE]

TED: We can't live together!

BETH: I don't understand. *What is it about living together that's wrong?* [NEGATIVE INQUIRY]

TED: What if the neighbors found out?

BETH: *What is it about the neighbors finding out that upsets you?* [NEGATIVE INQUIRY]

TED: Nothing I guess. Probably half of them aren't married either.

BETH: *Okay, but we can get a new apartment if you want where no one knows us.* [WORKABLE COMPROMISE]

TED: No, I'd rather stay here.

BETH: Let's move my stuff in next weekend. We have a lot to do.

TED: What do I tell Mom and Dad?

BETH: *What is it about us not telling them that's so terrible?* [NEGATIVE INQUIRY]

TED: They'll find out.

BETH: *So we handle that when it comes up.* Your mom and I get along okay. Do you want to use my brass bed or your twins? [WORKABLE COMPROMISE]

Although Ted was more manipulative than this dialogue shows, this shortened version simply summarizes the interaction that took place over the several weeks it took to work out the compromise of living together to see how compatible Beth and Ted really were. As it turned out, Beth's doubts about Ted as a long-term life partner were proved true. After six months of living together, both Ted and Beth mutually decided to separate and go their own ways. As you might have guessed from Ted's responses in the dialogue, their separation was an amicable one, based upon genuine differences in personality styles that became difficult to reconcile while they were living together. What could have been a very messy emotional and legal situation was avoided at the start by Beth listening to her own inner feelings and thoughts and then assertively acting upon them. Part of these feelings were doubts based upon Ted's hidden agenda for proposing marriage; being married to Beth was supposed to give him the "right" to make her stop flirting with other men. Beth's flirting was a behavior which activated Ted's self-doubts about his own sexual attractiveness to women and his ability to keep Beth sexually interested in himself. In dialogues to come, you can see how learners cope with these hidden agendas in their mates, assertively prompting them to bring their anxieties about themselves or the close relationship they share out into the open in order to work out possible remedies for these hidden fears.

11

Really close equal relationships —sex and assertion

After assertive learners are no longer novices, after they have a lot of practice in using their assertive verbal skills in class (or in group therapy) and in their everyday lives, I turn their attention to the many problems that Beth alluded to in the last dialogue: the problems that you and I have to cope with when we live with another person day in and day out.

I start them practicing in situations where they can learn how to be assertive to the people who really count, those whom we most care about, whose opinions are genuinely important to us—our mates and lovers, wives and husbands. To quicken the pace of learning in this most important equal relationship, I suggest that they start practicing (at least in class) in a particular behavior area, one which has an innate, psychophysiological guarantee to arouse and capture our attention and interest—*sex!* I start learners in practicing to verbally assert their own sexual wants or fantasies simply because sexual matters do command an intense interest from most people. When I first talk in class about the basis of sexual problems and how being assertive can help in resolving these problems, occasionally I stop and look for feedback from the students. Every eye is riveted on me and it's often so quiet that I can hear the students breathing. This same intense interest is carried over into the assertive role rehearsal of sexual wants and I put this interest to work for them. Because of the way we are built, because of our psychophysiology, it is impossible to be anxious about something and deeply interested in it at the same time. If any of our ancestral cousins could accomplish this psychophysiological feat, they are now extinct. Those who could just stand there, intensely fascinated, while the beautiful saber-toothed

tiger charged are gone. . . . Those poor souls found out
the hard way why it would have been better for their
interests—and other good feelings—to be overcome by
their fears. In the same way that intense fear can overcome your enjoyable feelings of fun and interest, so can
intense interest and other good feelings overcome some
of your anxiety. Since close relationships are those in
which students experience the most anxiety when learning to be assertive, I try to give them an edge, to set up
the odds in their favor, to give them a slight advantage
in coping with these anxieties by having them first
practice in a situation that is innately interesting and
also fun! A second benefit that typically occurs in
working with sexual material is that the student learns
that if he can cope with these potentially embarrassing
(in spite of the so-called sexual revolution) personal
wants comfortably, can his other wishes be so difficult
to express? The teaching format I follow then is to talk
about sexual behavior, sexual wants, sexual problems,
and the interaction between sex and assertion. After exposure to this material, I have learners begin practicing
to be assertive sexually and when they are comfortable
when expressing their sexual wants, to change the topic
and assert themselves with their practice partners over
any of the common marital conflict situations: getting a
job, use of leisure time, taking care of the kids, use of
family money, buying a new home, etc.; the list is end-
less. After learners become more comfortable in practicing to be assertive with their mates generally, I suggest
that they turn back to the area of sex and assertion to
examine for themselves the links between nonassertion,
manipulation, coping poorly with marital conflict, and
sexual difficulties. As a last exercise in class, I suggest
they practice being assertive to a hypothetical partner
who has a sexual difficulty in order to help that person
overcome it. As you may see in the following discussion, many sexual problems have their roots in the
passive, nonassertive, or manipulative style of the sexual partner.

One of the closest and most meaningful ways we can
communicate is the sharing of a sexual experience with

someone we care for. Many experiences you share with this person and others you are close to are equally important to your well-being, to your feeling good about yourself, but sexual communication as an act of love is special. While sex is only one link in the chain of communicating with your mate (it is basically primitive behavior and in large part, mechanical), it is different from the other links. Its disruption is not only a loss in itself but can complicate the mutual working out of problems that have nothing to do with sex. If close sexual activity is often disrupted or falters because of pressure from external problems or because of difficulties with the sexual act itself, a unique, private way of communicating with your mate may be lost. We, as members of *the* cortical species, who praise ourselves on the accomplishments of our intellect, would be greatly surprised, I suspect, if we knew the true survival benefits to mankind from the number of conflicts settled between the sheets after a satisfying sexual experience. My humble guess is that the results of these nocturnal negotiations far outweigh the gains of all the Metternichs, Kissingers, and Chamberlains of our species, who throughout history have brought us "peace in our time." Unfortunately, many couples in equal relationships have difficulties with this natural anxiety-reducing outlet, an outlet producing a climate of closeness which can help in working out conflicts through true mutual compromise. The experience and research of myself and my colleagues who have studied a human sexual functioning in the clinic and the laboratory have taught us a number of things about sexual difficulties and how they can compound problems in other areas of a close, equal relationship. Thankfully, not only have we learned how to treat many sexual difficulties with relative speed to ease the patient's psychic pain, we are also beginning to learn that being assertive with a sexual partner may not only aid in eliminating the sexual difficulty itself but can help in resolving the problems of living together that cause certain sexual difficulties. To understand the relationship between nonassertiveness and sexual difficulties, let's briefly examine some of the types of sexual problems we can clinically isolate and treat, the three basic psychotherapeutic treatment models of these difficulties, and then see where and how being assertive with one's mate may help in overcoming them.

The three basic treatment models for sexual problems and the therapists most associated with their use are: the *anxiety model* (Dr. Joseph Wolpe, Temple University, Pennsylvania; Dr. Zev Wanderer, the Center for Behavior Therapy, Beverly Hills, California), the *anger model* (a host of traditional "talk" therapists), and the *mixed model* with elements of both the anger and anxiety models (Dr. William Masters and Ms. Virginia Johnson, Reproductive Biology Research Foundation, St. Louis, Missouri; Dr. William Hartman and Ms. Marilyn Fithian, the Center for Marital and Sexual Studies, Long Beach, California). As you can see from the descriptive titles, our primitive coping patterns of fear-flight and anger-aggression rule us all when we get into trouble, even sexual trouble.

The anxiety model assumes that if you (or anyone else) are in good physical and neurological condition but have *certain, specific sexual problems consistently,* you have acquired a conditioned or learned anxiety response triggered by sexual stimuli that interferes with your sexual performance. In plain language, the anxiety model says: "You aren't built to enjoy yourself sexually and worry about things like your income tax return at the same time!" If you are a male, these specific sexual problems are premature ejaculation, and lack or loss of erection; and if you are a female, vaginismus (involuntary contraction of the vaginal opening preventing intercourse), lack of orgasm with a specific partner where no problem existed with him or other partners previously, or the lack of orgasm with any male (or female) partner when orgasm occurs regularly in another context such as solitary masturbation. Treatment given under this model assumes that these difficulties are conditioned or involuntary, learned *phobic* or fear responses (generally called erotophobia or any of a half dozen other frightening labels) and are the same as any other phobia, for instance, fear of heights (acrophobia) or fear of enclosed places (claustrophobia).

Like most phobic conditions, learned sexual anxiety responses generally have a history of specific trauma (anxiety shock) associated with them. Some patients were physically or psychologically punished through guilt for masturbation as teen-agers, or were not reassured emotionally or helped by their first sexual partner when they were too anxious to perform that first time (a common occurrence). Most often, patients with sexual phobic reactions report that for a variety of causes, physical tiredness, upset over other problems, general stress, excessive demands by their mates, etc., there was a definite period of time when they did not perform well sexually in the opinion of either the patient or the sexual partner, but the patient was not reassured by the sexual partner of its relative unimportance. During this time, the typical patient anticipated further failure, and, in being sensitive to the slightest sign of failure during the next sexual act, induced further anxiety in him or herself, thereby producing the complete failure he or she was looking for (a self-fulfilling prophecy!). In cases where their sexual partners were quite unsympathetic with such failure and put pressure on them to perform adequately, the patient's own worries made the initial anxiety even more intense and guaranteed failure. Eventually, after a number of sexual failures caused by worrying about sex in and out of bed, no matter what the initial stimulus-reason for the anxiety was, almost any sexual stimulus becomes something to make the patient nervous—a trigger stimulus for debilitating anxiety during sex. To illustrate the involuntary physiological characteristics of sexual arousal to my students in class, I take a $20 bill out of my wallet and make them an offer: "If you can command yourself to be sexually aroused, to control your sexual physiology, to command an erection or engorged vaginal tissue, I'll give you $20! Take thirty seconds. That's not enough? You want a minute? You got it!" No one has ever picked up my $20 bill. The important point, of course, is that willpower—commanding yourself to feel sexy—

doesn't work; any more than commanding yourself not to feel anxious in other phobic situations alleviates the anxiety.

Again, as with the other phobias, the sexually conditioned anxiety response may generalize to all sorts of other stimuli associated with the sexual act to the point of producing a general avoidance or flight response. When this extreme conditioning takes place, the unfortunate sexually phobic patient may avoid any contact that has even a low possibility of leading up to sex, such as just talking to possible sexual partners (let alone dating them!). Contrary to some archaic and moldy, but still popular professional beliefs, sexual phobia is not a sign of a twisted personality or some deeply hidden incestual, homosexual, or psychotic conflict but, like the other phobias, is learned and can usually be "unlearned" in relatively short order (several weeks to several months) with behavioral treatment methods.

Unlike the anxiety model with all its diagnostic clues indicating a psychophysiological inability to have successful sexual relations, sometimes with very rapid onset, the *anger model* has only one clear indication that a sexual difficulty exists—a gradual decrease in frequency of sex with a spouse over a long period of time, several months to several years. Although sexual frequency in couples with a sexual problem described by the anger model often reaches zero for significant periods of time, frequency invariably bounces back and forth between periods of no sex and periods of low-frequency sex. During these periods of low-frequency sexual intercourse, none of the types of sexual difficulties described in the anxiety model is observed. The male "patients" have no significant problems with lack or loss of erection or other anxiety-produced difficulties, although they often report lack of ejaculation. Some of the female "patients" report they are "just lying there going through the motions," totally disinterested; some even contemptuous and therefore usually nonorgasmic.

The anger model assumes, unlike the anxiety model, that the low frequency of sexual intercourse is a result of problems between spouses outside the bed. Typically one of the sexual partners holds many "hidden" grudges against the other; he or she has a lot of unexpressed anger against the spouse. The anger may be denied, the fact that a sexual problem exists may even be denied. The other partner is typically willing to show anger and does, and is usually manipulative as well as angry in dealing with his or her "passive" mate. In my clinical experience in treating this problem, one mate is *always* too tired or not in the mood or has a headache, or is too busy, or feels a bit ill, or has something more important to do, or has to get up early and go to work tomorrow. And this is the mate who directly causes the drop in sexual frequency by avoidance of sexual contact—not out of fear, but out of dislike and unexpressed anger of the spouse's everyday living behavior toward him or her. Clinical experience with this type of problem is common, and a common observation—made by other therapists as well as myself—is that the withdrawing partner is not only withdrawing in bed, he or she is withdrawing from intimate contact and sharing in all areas with the sexual partner. The withdrawal of the passively angry partner is a result of having no effective outlet for communicating his anger. He seems, clinically, to be either unable or unwilling to show his anger toward his mate as one way of putting down strong limits on what he will and will not tolerate as well as effectively venting this uncomfortable emotion and clearing the air between them. In addition, and perhaps even more important than the lack of open, angry communication by the withdrawing mate, in the clinical cases I see with this problem, the withdrawing partner, without exception, is not assertive to his or her mate. He does not seem to be able to express his own likes to her, or she is able to manipulatively block him from acting on his own wants. In addition, he seems dreadfully lacking in the ability to calmly, or even not so calmly, tell his spouse of his displeasure with the way she behaves toward him. Without effective assertive communication, or even generally ineffective angry communication, available to him, he withdraws. He does not willingly share any close intimate contact with his mate—his worries, his hopes, or even his joys—in anticipation of being impotent to cope with her ability to make him feel guilty or anxious if she does not like what he says. Consequently, over a period of time, as resentment and dislike for her manipulative behavior toward him build up, the frequency of his sharing anything intimate with her goes down, including sexual love.

The generally accepted treatment for this sexual problem involves getting the withdrawing sexual partner to be able both to express appropriate anger toward his mate when she takes away his self-respect as well as to be more assertive on an everyday basis concerning what he wants for himself, what he is willing to give her, what he will not tolerate, and what compromises they can work out in living together. When I first presented my work in developing the concepts and verbal skills of systematic assertive therapy at the 1972 meetings of the American Psychological Association in a symposium entitled "New Directions in Psychotherapy," one of the co-participants, Dr. Harold Segal, made a witty comment on the preferred treatment of this sexual problem that was understood immediately; "First assertion, then insertion."

The *mixed model* of treatment for sexual dysfunction assumes that both anxiety and anger components are involved in the history of the problem. For instance, a withdrawing spouse may be coerced into having sexual intercourse without really wanting to, without really being interested in close communication with his (or her) mate; he isn't aroused enough sexually to either maintain an erection during intercourse, or perhaps even during foreplay. If he is not assertive enough to say: "I just don't want to have sex with you now," he is likely to be talked into at least giving the appearance of wanting to go to bed. After several failures due to disinterest, his manipulative spouse is likely to give him a strong message that either makes him feel guilty or anxious; in some cases, this is done quickly and efficiently right in bed, an *in vivo* phobic conditioning procedure. At other times his mate may express her sexual displeasure other ways, sometimes silently, but in any case, a message is eventually given and received that sexual failure is not surprising; it is only one more item added to the already great list of frustrations in this manipulative-passive relationship where both spouses are angry with each other—one actively—one passively.

In treating sexual problems having elements of both anger and anxiety in their development, it is generally a waste of time to (1) do sexual anxiety deconditioning without resolving the anger produced in this manipulative-passive relationship; or (2) to simply teach the couple how to effectively live with each other without treating the anxiety-produced sexual failure. If one is done without the other, it is likely that the anger component will induce further sexual failure, starting the whole process over again, or the untreated sexual anxiety component may preclude future sex; a condition likely to reevoke rational angry feelings from both partners over sexual frustration that may be very difficult to cope with without destroying the marriage. Using the mixed model, it is imperative to treat both components of the sexual problem, feelings of anger from and about the spouse, and feelings of anxiety about sexual performance.

Some therapists, like Dr. Masters and Dr. Wolpe, point out that it may be impossible to treat the sexual anxiety component in such cases without dealing first with the anger component if it is very pronounced. Using descriptions like lack of caring and sabotage of sexual therapy to talk about the anger component, their experience in such cases parallels my own, and I agree with their warning. Conjoint sexual therapy using a mixed model is difficult, if not impossible to do without replacing under-the-table manipulation with straightforward assertive communication, without replacing hidden anger with nondefensive, assertive statements of emotion.

With this prologue, let's turn to the teaching of assertiveness in sexual matters to show how being assertive can help in coping with sexual naïveté and sexual problems, but also to show that the assertiveness used in working out sexual conflicts in close relationships is basically no different from the assertiveness used to resolve other problems in that same relationship.

In teaching people to openly and assertively talk to their mates about what they want sexually and to evolve some compromise between them, I give them several actual examples to work with. These are sexual problems that other learners (or patients) have dealt with previously—we discuss how these often delicate and sometimes embarrassing problems can be handled. Some of these learners were married, some living together, some unattached and only dating or having extramarital affairs. In all of these actual conflict situations, one partner of each pair was dissatisfied with the sexual relationship and the other had either manipulatively or passively resisted any change in the sexual status quo. For some of the "satisfied" sexual partners, there were hidden anxiety agendas which prompted them to resist change. These resistant sexual partners were probably like many people I see in sexual therapy—anxious that any change would expose some sexual "weakness" in them such as sexual ignorance about techniques to please their partners (and themselves), or fear that if their mates who wanted a change expanded their sexual horizons, who knew where such appetites might lead! And could they satisfy these appetites? What were they letting themselves in for? Could they cope if their mates suggested something far out, such as a trio? What would that "kinky" twist do to their own already dimly sensed feelings of jealousy and insecurity when they observed their mates flirting in response to overtures from other possible sexual partners? Would such a change signal the end of their own established sexual relationship—one perhaps not quite yet dull, but certainly secure and ordered? The actual difficulties in expanding sexual horizons with one's mate that I have observed in both clinical and teaching settings are probably not statistically representative of the general population; even so, these examples (a few of

which are presented here) provide assertive learners
with a sample of situations that they can use to practice
being more assertive when communicating their sexual
wants.

In describing the sexual wants that many couples
have trouble communicating about, I lump all the difficulties together as if I were talking about only one pair
of unfortunate hypothetical lovers, Jack and Jill, who
have a host of complaints about their sex life. As always, I have learners start out with the simplest sexual
request such as wanting a variation from the "missionary" position, and then given the examples of actual
complaints, to build upon them by letting their imagi-
nations run wild with the most erotic fantasies. I suggest this learning procedure to them as a way to
provide some "safe" experience and social exposure
that may help reduce their anxieties by talking about
their sexuality and sexual wants first with someone they
are not close to and have no great personal investment
in. This procedure also produces tears of laughter for
some learners, a condition in which anxiety-induced in-
hibitions wither away and die. As you can see in the
following dialogues, a request for sexual change is
linked exclusively to neither male nor female sexuality.
During the assertive verbal rehearsals, I have the learners make Jack the dissatisfied mate who wants some
things changed in his sexual relationship with Jill, who
then manipulatively resists because of her feelings of
sexual insecurity. Alternatively, in another conflict situation, I have the learners make Jill the assertive prompt-
er and Jack the resister. The following dialogues are
short, edited versions of rehearsals between assertive
learners communicating their sexual wants to each
other. Not surprisingly, these practices produced some
of the same end compromises worked out by previous
learners in reporting their own real-life experiences.
Note that in these close, equal relationship dialogues,
late in the training of learners, the stereotyped language
of the assertive verbal skills, which was stressed in earlier dialogues, has been adapted to fit the learner's own
speaking style. Although quite a bit of "regular" lan-

guage goes on to give information to one another, the verbal skills, however personalized, are still used when conflict arises in the situation.

Dialogue #31
A husband (or wife) assertively tells his (or her) mate that their sex is routine and seeks some change.

In the first dialogue of this set of learning situations, the role of either Jack or Jill as the assertive person or the manipulator is interchangeable. In either case, only the details of physiological prerequisites need to be rearranged to suit the sex identification. In this situation, for instance, Jack, married to Jill eight years and having two children by her, feels that life somehow is slipping by him. There is a lot going on outside his marriage that he hears only bits and pieces about during coffee breaks with his male friends. One of the areas of his life that seems to give him less and less reward as the years roll by is his sexual relationship to Jill. Something seems missing. The excitement he always felt with Jill during the early years of their marriage is fading away to routine. He wants to regain it in their lovemaking but doesn't know exactly what it is or how to get it. He has some ideas, but up to now he didn't know how to try them out or how Jill would receive them.

Setting of the dialogue: Jack and Jill are in bed after making love and talking about sex.

JACK: I've been thinking about us lately. About our sex life. It's not the same as it used to be.

JILL: What do you mean? It's the same as it always was.

JACK: That's exactly what I mean. It's always the same, but it's not like it used to be.

JILL: What are you trying to say? Is it the same or isn't it?

JACK: *I really don't know what I'm trying to say. It's not as exciting to me as it used to be.* Maybe because we always do the same thing. [SELF-DISCLOSURE]

JILL: (Irritatedly) Have you been talking about what we do in bed to those guys at the office again?

JACK: *No, that was a dumb thing for me to do before and dumber yet to tell you about it.* [NEGATIVE ASSERTION]

JILL: Last time you started talking this way was when that new guy was hired and we met his wife. All she has is a body with big boobs. She hasn't a brain in her head, but all you could think about was what he told you about how great she was in bed.

JACK: *I've gotta admit that. I sure listened to him.* [FOGGING]

JILL: Look, there's nothing wrong with the way we make love. Everybody thinks the grass is greener on the other side of the fence.

JACK: *Yeah, that's true. I feel that way myself sometimes,* but *I still can't get over the feeling that we could get more fun out of making love to each other if we tried something different.* Remember how it was when we were first going together. [FOGGING and BROKEN RECORD]

JILL: You mean in the back seat of the car? What's gotten into you?

JACK: *You're right, maybe I am freaking out.* But *I'd like to experiment.* I had a couple of ideas. When we make love we always do it with me on top of you or you on top of me. *I think we would have more fun if we tried something different.* [FOGGING and BROKEN RECORD]

JILL: (Showing some interest) What ideas do you have.

JACK: *I don't think either of us knows much about sex and we could learn something new.* [NEGATIVE ASSERTION]

JILL: You want to get some books and read them together?

JACK: *That's not a bad idea,* but *what I really want is for us to go to someplace like Backbone Ridge in*

Malibu Canyon and see if we can learn anything.
[FOGGING and WORKABLE COMPROMISE]

JILL: Backbone! That's the nudist colony where they have free sex and orgies. My God! What if my mother saw me there?

JACK: *That's possible . . .* if she's there, the first thing we could do is ask: "Where's Dad?" [FOGGING]

JILL: Don't be silly. What if one of the girls I work with saw me there?

JACK: *One of them may be there. . . . What's so wrong about someone seeing us go to Malibu to learn some more about sex?* [FOGGING and NEGATIVE INQUIRY]

JILL: I'd have to face her the next day.

JACK: *You would,* but *what about seeing her the next day would upset you?* [FOGGING and NEGATIVE INQUIRY]

JILL: What would she think about me?

JACK: *I don't know.* What do you think? [SELF-DISCLOSURE]

JILL: She would probably think I was a sex freak.

JACK: (Smiling) *Like her?* [NEGATIVE INQUIRY]

JILL: Okay . . . but what if she told someone else? What would they think?

JACK: *She might. . . .* You'd have to work that out yourself with them, but *I'd still like to go.* [FOGGING and BROKEN RECORD]

JILL: But they would know that we were undressed.

JACK: *Sure,* but *what's so awful about being nude or even if someone knew about it?* [FOGGING and NEGATIVE INQUIRY]

JILL: All those other people at Malibu would see us.

JACK: (Smiling) *They would,* but *I still want to go and learn something.* [FOGGING and BROKEN RECORD]

JILL: You mean you wouldn't care if other men looked at me? Looked at everything?

JACK: *I don't know,* but *I still want us to go.* [SELF-DISCLOSURE and BROKEN RECORD]

JILL: I don't like it. The whole idea upsets me.

JACK: *Okay. . . . That's not surprising,* but *what is it specifically about my wanting us to go out to Malibu that you don't like?* [FOGGING and NEGATIVE INQUIRY]

JILL: I'll bet that new guy at work told you about Backbone . . . and you listened to him.

JACK: *You're right, I did.* But *what is it about my wanting us to go there and improve our sex life that upsets you?* [FOGGING and NEGATIVE INQUIRY]

JILL: You'd probably hope to meet his wife there and see what's underneath those tacky tight dresses she wears.

JACK: (Smiling) *You may be right. They may be there and I wouldn't mind seeing what she's got,* but *what is it about my liking to see nude women that upsets you?* [FOGGING and NEGATIVE INQUIRY]

JILL: You're married to me.

JACK: (Only a bit sarcastically) *That's true,* but *what is it about us being married that makes my looking at nude women wrong?* [FOGGING and NEGATIVE INQUIRY]

JILL: How would you like it if I wanted to see what other men looked like?

JACK: *What is it about you wanting to see what other men look like that's wrong?* (Instead of: "You have! In the back seat of Harry Schwartz's car before you met me. Only he didn't have much to see!") [NEGATIVE INQUIRY]

JILL: (Sarcastically and biting) Would you like it if other men turned me on?

JACK: *I don't know,* but *I'd still like us to go and see if we could learn something.* [SELF-DISCLOSURE and BROKEN RECORD]

JILL: You mean you think we should get turned on by other people to spice up our own sex life?

JACK: *What is it about other people turning us on and spicing up our sex life that's wrong?* [NEGATIVE INQUIRY]

JILL: Are you saying that I don't turn you on enough now?

JACK: *You do turn me on,* but our sex is routine.

I want us to go to Malibu to see if we can learn something new. [FOGGING and BROKEN RECORD]

JILL: (Either angry or a few tears falling) I thought I was sexy enough for you.

JACK: *You are,* but *I want us to go to Malibu to see what we can learn.* [FOGGING and BROKEN RECORD]

JILL: Can't we just read some books?

JACK: *We can,* but *I still want us to go to Malibu. What is it about our going there that's wrong?* [FOGGING, BROKEN RECORD, and NEGATIVE INQUIRY]

JILL: Nothing, I guess, but it worries me.

JACK: *I can see that. . . . How about talking about what's worrying you? Okay?* [FOGGING and WORKABLE COMPROMISE]

JILL: Okay.

JACK: *What is it about us going to Malibu that upsets you?* [NEGATIVE INQUIRY]

JILL: I don't know, I just get nervous thinking about it.

JACK: *What is it you think about that makes you nervous?* [NEGATIVE INQUIRY]

JILL: The bare asses.

JACK: (Reassuringly) Okay. *What about a bunch of asses being bare makes you nervous?* [NEGATIVE INQUIRY]

JILL: Our bare asses.

JACK: I'm beginning to understand where you're at. *What is it about our asses being bare that makes you nervous?* [NEGATIVE INQUIRY]

JILL: It's just wrong to walk around in front of a bunch of people bare-assed.

JACK: *What is it that's wrong about us walking around in front of others without any clothes?* [NEGATIVE INQUIRY]

JILL: I never met anybody who did it.

JACK: *We probably never have,* but *what is it about meeting a different kind of people who like to walk around in the nude that's wrong?* [FOGGING and NEGATIVE INQUIRY]

JILL: Some of them might be really weird.

JACK: *I'm sure some of them are,* but *what is it about meeting some nude weirdos that's wrong?* [FOGGING and NEGATIVE INQUIRY]

JILL: It's not wrong. . . . I've met weirdos before, but not without my clothes on.

JACK: *What's different about you meeting some weirdos without your clothes on?* [NEGATIVE INQUIRY]

JILL: I'd just feel exposed to them!

JACK: *You would be exposed,* but *what is it about being exposed that worries you?* [FOGGING and NEGATIVE INQUIRY]

JILL: What would they think of me? Bare-assed and running around a sex colony!

JACK: *You're right. They probably would think you're there for the same reason they are.* [FOGGING]

JILL: But then they would try and put the make on me!

JACK: *I'm sure they would.* But *what is it about them trying to put the make on you that upsets you?* [FOGGING and NEGATIVE INQUIRY]

JILL: I'll feel phony . . . because my ass will be saying one thing and my mouth will be saying no.

JACK: *That's true. . . . We'll both be doing that . . . and maybe we will be playing games with some of the people up there. . . . . I'm not ready for group sex,* but *I still want us to go up and see what happens.* [FOGGING, NEGATIVE ASSERTION, SELF-DISCLOSURE, and BROKEN RECORD]

JILL: (Thoughtfully) What happens if the women put the make on you? You'd like that!

JACK: *Of course I would,* but *being phony doesn't bother me.* [FOGGING and NEGATIVE ASSERTION]

JILL: But what if you don't want to leave?

JACK: *Maybe I won't want to leave until we learn something.* [FOGGING]

JILL: What happens if I get really nervous? I might want to leave right away.

JACK: *How about if we go for a two-hour mini-*

mum. After that, we leave if you get real nervous.
[WORKABLE COMPROMISE]

JILL: But what if they start to screw or God knows what in front of us?

JACK: *God-knows-what is exactly what I'm hoping we'll see.* [FOGGING]

JILL: But what if you like it?

JACK: (Grinning) *You mean I shouldn't get an erection?* [NEGATIVE INQUIRY]

JILL: Exactly what I was thinking.

JACK: *I was thinking about that too. How about if I hide it behind you?* [WORKABLE COMPROMISE]

JILL: Well, I'll be wanting to hide behind you.

JACK: So what do we do?

JILL: How about this. If you get in trouble, you hide behind me, if I get in trouble I'll hide behind you.

JACK: Okay . . . how about going?

JILL: I'll go if we just look and we don't do anything.

JACK: *We just go there to learn.* [WORKABLE COMPROMISE]

JILL: I don't know . . . something still bothers me.

JACK: *What's that?* [NEGATIVE INQUIRY]

JILL: What if we meet someone we know?

JACK: *We may. What would you like to do if that happens?* [FOGGING and WORKABLE COMPROMISE]

JILL: I don't know. God! That would be embarrassing.

JACK: *Yeah,* but *what would you like to do if that happened?* [FOGGING and WORKABLE COMPROMISE]

JILL: (Thinking aloud) I wonder if they would feel the same way? (Giggling) It would be kind of funny seeing Harry and Jane from down the street there. I bet he looks different without his Gucci shoes. Maybe it would be kind of fun . . . but I won't go unless you promise we go together, we stay together, and we leave together.

JACK: That's a deal, luv.

JILL: And you won't make a play for anyone?

JACK: *Only you after we leave.* [WORKABLE COMPROMISE]

JILL: Okay.

This practice dialogue is only one of the real-life situations learners have dealt with by being assertive with their mates and working out sexual compromises that they both can feel better about. These compromises are as simple as sharing sexual position preferences within one act of intercourse or alternating them on different occasions. Sexual compromises that patients and learners have worked out often include mutual "turn-ons" such as increased foreplay, mutual fondling and masturbation, cunnilingus (vaginal kissing), fellatio (giving "head"), anal intercourse, "Wesson oil" wrestling, or as radical as swinging, group sex, "Cops and Robbers," and separate lovers. Most of the learners in assertive training classes use a variety of these topics as hypothetical end goals in their role rehearsals. During the last eighteen months, only one learner out of three hundred reported that such classroom practice made her quite anxious . . . and her anxiety was a great surprise to her. She thought herself quite sophisticated sexually, and she was. She had experience in many of the more exotic sexual behaviors talked about. She had thought herself "liberated" sexually and found she wasn't. She was "liberated" only if someone else did the "liberating"; in class she had great difficulty in practicing requesting what she wanted sexually and when she tried it with her mate, she was astonished to find she had even greater difficulty with him than with a relative stranger—a classmate—even with someone of the same sex. In reality, she was quite nonassertive in this area and needed much more practice than the classroom limits afforded. At this writing, she is specifically working on this area in private therapy. Most learners, happily, have no great apparent difficulty in coping with this sensitive conflict area—not after eight weeks of assertive practice and outside homework in other situations. In fact, the great majority enjoy it and say so verbally or by their behavior in the practice sessions. One woman student in her early forties came up to me during the coffee break following this practice and said: "Pete. If you had told me eight weeks ago that tonight I would have been talking about my sex life and fantasies to a stranger and then asking him what he was going to do about them, I would have said: 'You're crazy!' But that's what I did and I really learned something about myself and other people tonight." After observing her behavior in class for eight weeks, I would hazard a guess that she was not in desperate need of systematic assertiveness to cope with her sexual wants. Nevertheless, what amazed her was her ability to calmly play her hand in this game of psychological strip poker. She learned that if she and others could cope in this high personal risk area with very little anxiety, it took no imagination to see what they could do in the more mundane behavioral realms. Several months later she saw me in Santa Monica. After we exchanged the usual pleasantries, she introduced me to her fourteen-year-old daughter, and said: "This is the Pete Smith who teaches that assertive class I keep telling you about. The class I hope you will take when you're old enough to go to UCLA." Apparently this middle-class Brentwood matron felt strongly that her teen-age daughter could benefit from learning to be assertive—perhaps sexually assertive, although she probably had in mind the more mundane conflicts that her daughter would have to learn how to cope with in living with a future mate.

The following dialogue shows how such a learner can assertively cope with a mate's manipulation—his attempts to keep her at home while she wants to expand the horizons of her own lifestyle beyond that of mother and housekeeper.

Dialogue #32
A wife tells her husband
that she wants
to get a
job.

This is a shortened version of an assertive sequence between spouses developed by my colleague, Ms. Susan Levine, and myself, and demonstrated at a recent professional training workshop. The content of the dialogue is a sampling of situational and manipulative material we have observed clinically when seeing couples for marital problems

Setting of the dialogue: After the children are put to bed, the assertive wife approaches her husband and brings up her desire to change her lifestyle.

SUE: I was thinking about getting a job. The kids are gone a lot and I have a lot of time on my hands.

ME: The house sure doesn't look like you have a lot of time on your hands; it's a regular mess.

SUE: *Yeah, that's true. The house isn't the neatest but I'd still rather get a job out of the house.* [FOGGING and BROKEN RECORD]

ME: Well . . . that seems pretty stupid to me. Especially since you don't have any marketable skills.

SUE: *I agree with you.* In fact I've been thinking about that myself. I don't have any specific skills, but *I still want to look around and see if I can find a job.* [FOGGING and BROKEN RECORD]

ME: (Trying a new tactic, but gentler) The idea seems pretty screwy to me. . . . I mean, by the time you pay a babysitter to watch the kids while you're gone, you won't have any money left. So what's the use of working if you don't have anything to show for it?

SUE: *You know, I've thought of that. You're probably right about me not making much money . . . especially at first . . . but I figure I have to start somewhere and I'm ready to give the working world a try.* [FOGGING and BROKEN RECORD]

ME: You know your parents never thought I could support you in the way they raised you, and now when they see that you're out working they're going to look down on me even more. They'll say I couldn't support you and you had to work.

SUE: *They might . . . but, really . . . what's so terrible if they look down their noses at you?* [FOGGING and NEGATIVE INQUIRY]

ME: You're a lot of help. What's so terrible? Don't get smart ass with me.

SUE: *I'm probably not much help in this, and maybe I was a little smart ass then, but I don't mean it. Really . . . what upsets you so much about them looking down at you?* [FOGGING, SELF-DISCLOSURE, and NEGATIVE INQUIRY]

ME: You want me to spell it out?

SUE: Yes, please.

ME: Well, when your folks look down at me it makes me feel uneasy . . . your dad makes me nervous, I feel kind of inferior, like a young punk sometimes when I talk to him. He's been a bastard to me at times . . . the real problem is that I respect him too. For a bastard, he's made some sharp deals and a hell of a lot of money.

SUE: *Yeah, he is really good at some things,* but when it comes to how to act toward us I don't think everything is kosher. . . . *I think it's a crappy way to treat you, but I also think we make them uncomfortable because we use our own bread and don't rely on them.* [FOGGING and NEGATIVE ASSERTION]

ME: Maybe I could handle your father's digs about your working, but what about the kids? I mean, those kids need you when they come home from school!

SUE: *I'm sure they would like me to be there when they come home.* In fact I like to see them when they come home . . . but I can't be home and go to work too. *I want to get a job.* [FOGGING and BROKEN RECORD]

ME: Remember you can't work and take Josh to his music lesson at the same time.

SUE: *You're right. I figure if I can't make the 3:00*

P.M. *pickup at school and still get a job, I'll choose the job over picking up the kids.* All of us will have to work out some adjustments to a new schedule. I don't know what, but I want to do it that way. [FOGGING and BROKEN RECORD]

ME: (Thinking out loud) That's one thing I always missed as a kid. Both my mom and dad worked when they had the restaurant. When I got home from school I even had to make my own supper and eat it alone. I missed my parents when I was our kids' age. I always envied my cousin Sonny. When I used to get really lonely, I went over to his house after school and Aunt Cody would just add another plate. They never had much money, and I didn't like lamb stew but I liked being with the family. She was always home and when Uncle Spencer wasn't working he would be there too. He even tried to teach me to play the guitar.

SUE: I'm glad you could go over to Aunt Cody's when you felt like that. *But that's still rough.* You never told me that before. [FOGGING]

ME: I know. I never felt like talking about it before.

SUE: I think now I know why you are worried about me working.

ME: Yeah, but who's going to take them out to Little League and the Girl Scouts like you do now? They get something important out of things like that.

SUE: *I couldn't agree with you more,* and right now . . . this minute, *I don't know the answer,* but we'll work something out. Besides that, *what else about me working worries you?* [FOGGING, SELF-DISCLOSURE, and NEGATIVE INQUIRY]

ME: Josh I'm not so worried about. Boys can take care of themselves, but Jenny is an advanced twelve-year-old, or haven't you noticed?

SUE: (Smiling) I've noticed.

ME: And she is always having that slimy little Larry Bisque over. I don't trust that little jerk.

SUE: *That's a point we're going to have to look out for. The kids will have more freedom when I'm working,* and it worries me too. [FOGGING]

ME: I can't believe you want to go to work and leave your daughter alone at home with that creep.

SUE: *You're right. I don't want to worry about that, but I do want to work. How do you think we could handle this . . . so we don't worry about the kids being home alone with their friends?* [FOGGING, BROKEN RECORD, and WORKABLE COMPROMISE]

ME: I don't want you to go to work.

SUE: (With empathy) *I hear you, but how can we work this out so we don't worry about the kids?* [FOGGING and WORKABLE COMPROMISE]

ME: (Thinking) Maybe we could sit down with them, explain the problem and set down some rules . . . like no friends in the house when we aren't here.

SUE: *That sounds good and I could ask Judy down the street if the kids could call on her if they needed something when we weren't here.* [FOGGING and WORKABLE COMPROMISE]

ME: Okay. I don't like the idea of you working but a little bit of being on their own now won't hurt the kids. Hell, I had to take care of myself ever since I was eight years old. But how are you going to work and still run the house? You're tired enough now and if you get a job you'll collapse on me when you get home.

SUE: *I probably will get tired, but what's wrong with me collapsing on you when I get home?* [FOGGING and NEGATIVE INQUIRY]

ME: You know what I mean. The house will go to hell and I'll feel guilty because you are doing two things, working and cleaning up, and I'm doing only one.

SUE: *It could be hard on both of us, but I still want to do it. Will you work with me on it?* [FOGGING, BROKEN RECORD, and WORKABLE COMPROMISE]

ME: How?

SUE: *I don't know exactly what we will have to work out right now. Do you have any ideas?* [SELF-DISCLOSURE and WORKABLE COMPROMISE]

ME: I could do the marketing in the evening. I don't mind that at all. And Jenny and Josh could help more with the house. A little more responsibility won't hurt them. Maybe we can swing it.

SUE: I hope so. . . . What else do you think we can do. . . .

The whole point of this dialogue was to demonstrate that being assertive and saying what you want in a marital conflict does not require a lot of bickering and arguing, or even shouting and screaming. As cotherapists for many married couples trying to work out their problems, Sue and I observed that, aside from blowing off emotional steam due to the general frustrations that none of us can avoid, much of the anger and frustration in marital situations is due to unrealistic fears of *what might happen if . . .* , and manipulation-countermanipulation used to cope with these anxieties. We have observed how being emphatically assertive in telling your mate what you want, in spite of *what might happen if . . .* minimizes mutual manipulation, that awesome stumbling block to close communication and compromise.

In the next training dialogue, I have the women learners practice assertively coping with a sexual difficulty often reported in clinical settings—an act of love without much loving. Women patients often complain of mates who simply have intercourse with them, but nothing else. Although this behavior could be an expression of complete indifference of the husband toward his mate, or ignorance of her wants, the "quick start" habit is also a frequent pattern of sexual behavior of male patients who are clinically treated for difficulty in maintaining an erection over an extended period of time. Many of them have a history of losing their erection during extended foreplay resulting in an inability to penetrate when requested by their partner. After such a sexual fiasco, they have some anticipation of embarrassing failure again. Many of these patients also report that their sexually naïve partners, while not putting them down, also did nothing to re-arouse their sexual excitement level during extended foreplay. Typically not being assertive enough to request some type of sexual teasing or titillation when premature detumes-cence occurs, they prefer quick foreplay and maximum sexual stimulation as soon as possible to avoid failure. While indifference to one's mate may be a result of re-pressed anger or sexual ignorance, I suggest to my women students that they assume initially that this diffi-culty is due to a "hidden anxiety agenda" about per-forming poorly during foreplay which their mate has dif-ficulty in assertively requesting help with. Although the male partner may not like his mate probing into this embarrassing area, my clinical experience in treating this problem has indicated that the sexually hurried husband is more likely to *passively resist* his mate's probing into his sexual performance and *not manipu-late* her into accepting the status quo. I have seen coun-termanipulation by the husband, however, if his mate manipulatively (instead of assertively) tries to get him to do what she wants sexually.

Dialogue #33
A wife tells her mate
she wants more
foreplay in
sex.

In learning one way to cope with this potentially emasculating problem, I have my students assertively practice their verbal skills in the following situation.

Setting of the dialogue: Jill has good relations with Jack, but she feels something is lacking in the way they make love. Typically, if she or he initiates the sexual act, Jack penetrates and begins sexual intercourse very quickly. After his climax, he makes relatively little physical or verbal contact with Jill and usually drops off to sleep. After dinner, Jill sits down with Jack on the sofa and speaks to him.

JILL: Can we turn the TV off, honey? I want to talk to you.

JACK: Sure. (Gets up and switches the set off) What is it?

JILL: *I really don't know how to start talking about this. I guess I should know,* but *it's a bit uncomfortable for me to talk about.* [SELF-DISCLOSURE and NEGATIVE ASSERTION]

JACK: Okay, what is it?

JILL: I really love you, Jack, but *there is something about our sex life that bothers me.* [SELF-DISCLOSURE]

JACK: Our sex life is perfectly normal.

JILL: *Of course it is,* but *there is still something about it that bothers me.* [FOGGING and BROKEN RECORD]

JACK: (Silent for a few moments) Do we have to talk about it right now?

JILL: *No,* but *I'd like to. Do you want to talk about it after you watch the news?* [FOGGING. BROKEN RECORD, and WORKABLE COMPROMISE]

JACK: No.

JILL: Okay. When we make love, *I would like it better if we spent more time fooling around before and having fun instead of just jumping into it. I think I would get turned on more that way. Maybe I'd even come more.* [SELF-DISCLOSURE]

JACK: We don't just jump into it. You make me sound like someone who only cares about his own pleasure.

JILL: *Maybe I do,* and *you're right; we don't just jump into it.* Still, *I think if we had more foreplay and fooling around than we usually have now, I would enjoy it more.* [FOGGING and BROKEN RECORD]

JACK: We used to do that and both of us were usually late for work in the morning.

JILL: *Now that you mention it, I remember we did oversleep a lot.* But we used to spend a lot of time making love in the middle of the night when we were just married. [FOGGING]

JACK: I'm not superman. I have to work the next day you know.

JILL: *You're right, I don't want you to have to be superman,* but *is there some way we could ar-*

range things so that we have more foreplay and you don't get so tired? [FOGGING and WORKABLE COMPROMISE]

JACK: I don't get tired, just sleepy.

JILL: *I know it makes you sleepy,* but *are you sure there isn't something about foreplay that you don't like or would make you tired?* [FOGGING and NEGATIVE INQUIRY]

JACK: There were a few times when we were first married when I was too beat to have sex. You remember?

JILL: *You're right. We did have trouble then. Am I pushing you too much on this? Would you rather talk about it later?* [FOGGING, NEGATIVE INQUIRY, and WORKABLE COMPROMISE]

JACK: No, I'm fine.

JILL: *Is there something about my wanting more foreplay that would make you feel beat?* [NEGATIVE INQUIRY]

JACK: Well, when I was tired before, I couldn't get it up, remember?

JILL: *If we had more foreplay like I want, do you think that would happen again?* [NEGATIVE INQUIRY]

JACK: I don't know. It may.

JILL: *If you lost your erection, what's so terrible about me getting it back up for you?* [NEGATIVE INQUIRY]

JACK: (Looking worried) How?

JILL: (Smiling a Masters-and-Johnson smile) *You want a demonstration now?* [WORKABLE COMPROMISE]

JACK: (Smiling now himself.)

JILL: *If we have more foreplay and you lose it, would you like me to get it back for you?* [WORKABLE COMPROMISE]

JACK: Sure! (Getting serious again) But how about getting to work in the morning if we spend all night making love?

JILL: *Why don't we try it more in the evening like*

now? I think we'd recover by morning. Don't you?
[WORKABLE COMPROMISE]
    JACK: Right on!

If time is short in my classes because other areas of
close conflict are covered in greater detail, I may only
demonstrate this type of assertive dialogue as a way of
coping with the mate who avoids foreplay. I do this
with the help of a woman colleague or one of the better
learners in the class. One of the questions that invariably is asked by some students after the demonstration
(or practice) is: "How does the woman help her mate
maintain his erection during foreplay?" If you are won-
dering about this same question, I suggest that you, like
these students, read the sections of Masters and Johnson's *Human Sexual Inadequacy* (Little Brown, 1970)
dealing specifically with fear of loss of erection and
then any of the popular "how to do it" sex books published in the last five years, particularly Dr. Alex Comfort's *The Joy of Sex* (Crown, 1972) and *More Joy*
(Crown, 1974).

When teaching people to assertively communicate
their wants to their mates, I suggest that as an excellent
learning exercise in dealing with all sorts of conflict in
marriage, they practice coping with that most difficult
of all marital sexual problems, a gradual decrease in
frequency of sexual intercourse over a period of months
or years. After some time, it becomes apparent from
the most casual inspection that one of the partners
never initiates the lovemaking or always has an excuse
on why he or she is not in the mood. Although this
pattern of sexual avoidance is clinically observed in the
repertoire of both sexes, it has been the experience of
both myself and my colleague, Dr. Zev Wanderer, that
the male patient is much more ready to deny that there
is a problem than the female patient. The women we
see are generally more open and willing than men
to admit they are having difficulty with sex. In this particular instance, I am talking about the male partner
who retreats from his mate sexually and has no apparent, reliable signs of conditioned phobic impotence. He

does not frequently lose his erection or have difficulty being aroused sexually by other women, and he shows no signs of premature ejaculation. His behavioral history fits more with the anger model than with the anxiety model or mixed model of psychotherapeutic treatment. This sexual problem, then, is more a matter of what is going on outside the marriage bed than in it. The withdrawal process I am talking about is not short-term—what may happen over a weekend. I don't know one married couple that I have seen clinically or have known socially on a long-time basis that have not told each other to go to hell occasionally and refused to have sex for a short period because of anger. In contrast to this occasional tiff, I am describing a typical clinical history pattern of gradual withdrawal of one mate from the other over a period of many months or even years. The obvious treatment of this condition under the anger model is to train the "identified patient," the reluctant, withdrawing mate, to be able to be more assertive with a life partner about what is displeasing, or at least to show some anger about things and "blow off steam" occasionally to clear the air between them. But how to do it? That's the important question, particularly in the case of the reluctant male. He is likely to deny there is any sexual problem, let alone allow someone to instruct him on how to change his personal style of coping with his wife. In some cases in a clinical setting where a wife has come in for personal psychotherapy and complained of this problem, I have given these women intensive training to make them more assertive; in particular, I stressed FOGGING, NEGATIVE ASSERTION, and NEGATIVE INQUIRY to allow them to cope with both manipulative and valid criticism from their sexually reluctant husbands. When they are sufficiently nondefensive about themselves and their former manipulative style, I have them approach their mates and prompt personal criticism from them about themselves and how they live with each other— personal criticism that their mates are reluctant to communicate to them spontaneously, prompted personal criticism that allows the withdrawing mate to say what he doesn't like about his wife and what she does that, in part, is causing the sexual withdrawal, prompted criticism that gives the reluctant male a radical new message about his spouse; she is not the fragile, easily hurt, very dependent, sometimes smothering woman he thought he had a realistic picture of. For some of these women, however, the effort to find a solution to the dilemma is, to their way of thinking, harder to put up with than the problem of a withdrawing mate. For these unfortunates, coping with some of the complaints of the spouse means changing much of their personal lifestyle, becoming more confident of themselves, developing their own ways of being happy, being less dependent upon what their mates can (or will) give them, being less manipulative and taking charge of investigating and executing their own portfolio of wants and aspirations, assertively examining their own negative feelings and worries and accepting them as part of themselves, or working out compromises with their mates to cope with these worries instead of manipulating their spouses into conforming with structured routine that would protect them from facing these personal insecurities. As I see it from a clinical viewpoint and not a political one, they don't want to make the effort to be "liberated." In my experience, these unfortunate patients view therapy as either a place to get a sympathetic ear to listen to how terrible their mates are and how unfair life is, or as a place to get a clever little set of tricks on how to change their mate's behavior without changing themselves or without any work on their own part. The number of patients (both men and women) with this point of view is relatively small compared to those who are willing to sweat out developing new personal behaviors and ways of coping with the difficulties of living with someone else. The following dialogue illustrating some of the assertive skills which these women used to cope with their mate's withdrawal is again a composite, shortened, and edited version drawn from classroom rehearsals and therapy sessions. The critique prompted by the assertive spouse is a sample of spontaneous criticisms given in rehearsals by hundreds of learners. Their critique, probably drawn from their own experiences, covered just about everything that could go wrong with a marriage, at least from their point of view. The critique is not a male-vs.-female battle. Many times when we had more women learners than males in classes or in therapy sessions, two women would practice with each other and much of their criticism of their hypothetical mates was the same as that given by male learners practicing with women, and when they reversed the roles of asserter and withdrawer, again the criticisms were similar. The language and the details were different, but the male and female criticisms were about the same things. Many, but not all, of the frequent criticisms from these learners (as well as from patients in therapy) are included in this dialogue. Even though the learners practicing this assertive way to cope with sexual conflict may not have a mate who withdraws from them sexually, you can see from the dialogue that the initial sexual problem is used as an interesting training vehicle for teaching people how to change poor coping in close marriage situations.

In the real-life experiences of patients, this problem situation took from several weeks to several months of repeated, noncritical, nondefensive encounters with their withdrawing mates to work out compromises and changes in behavior toward each other. For some, it improved their sexual relationship; for others, it improved their living with each other through open, assertive communication to the point where they could evolve alternate lifestyles that were more satisfying to both of the partners.

Dialogue #34
**A previously manipulative wife (or husband)
assertively prompts her (or his) mate
to say what is wrong with their
marriage so both of
them can work
on it.**

Jill has been married to Jack for three years. During the first eighteen months of their marriage, their sex life was satisfactory, but after that initial period, their love-making gradually declined through the following year to a very low ebb and then for the past four months to zero. Jill still loves her spouse and wants the closeness they had when first married and courting. Jill has learned to be assertive, has practiced diligently to de-sensitize herself to becoming anxious and defensive about herself. She has, after much practice, learned that she is truly her own ultimate judge; she does some things well, others horribly, can evaluate her own success as well as her mistakes and failures, and knows she is ultimately responsible herself for making any changes she wants in her life situation.

Setting of the dialogue: Jill speaks to Jack on a Sunday morning after they are through reading *The Times*. (Jack could just as easily be the assertive initiator of this dialogue instead of Jill. In the dialogue, I have tried to indicate the mood and emotional state of actual couples in therapy sessions using the nondefensive, assertive communication process.)

JILL: Jack. I've been thinking. *Whether we like to admit it or not, we've got a sex problem.* [NEGATIVE ASSERTION]

JACK: Not again. We've been over this so many times. Do you have to bring it up now when we were in such a good mood?

JILL: *You're right. I nagged and cried and got mad at you in the past to get you to make love, but I don't want to nag you now. I just want to see things from your viewpoint.* [FOGGING, SELF-DISCLOSURE, and WORKABLE COMPROMISE]

JACK: (Sarcastically) That's a switch.

JILL: *It is, isn't it? When something like this happens I feel like we are drifting apart from each other.* We haven't had sex now for close to four months. [FOGGING and SELF-DISCLOSURE]

JACK: (Defensively) I love you, but I've been just too beat and tired lately. With all that overtime at work and everything I'm just not in the mood lately.

JILL: *I'm sure you are pooped lately, Jack* (instead of: "For four months!" or "How come you are working overtime so much lately?"), but *it seems to me that something else is happening too. I think I am doing something that is turning you off having sex with me.* [FOGGING SELF-DISCLOSURE, and NEGATIVE ASSERTION]

JACK: You don't turn me off. You're super in bed.

JILL: *Maybe I'm okay once we get to bed but I think we are drifting apart in a lot of ways, and I think I'm doing things that turn you off me generally, outside of bed.* [FOGGING. BROKEN RECORD, and NEGATIVE ASSERTION]

JACK: (Turning back to his paper) Naa, you're fine.

JILL: *I probably am in a lot of ways you can think of, Jack,* but *aren't there some things that I do that really bug you?* [FOGGING and NEGATIVE INQUIRY]

JACK: (Still defensive) Nobody's perfect. All married couples don't like things about each other.

JILL: *I'm sure other couples have problems too,* but *are there some things I do, even little ones that don't mean much, that get under your skin and irritate you a little?* [FOGGING and NEGATIVE INQUIRY]

JACK: Well . . . (thoughtfully) there are a couple of things that you do that annoy me.

JILL: *What is it that I do that annoys you?* [NEGATIVE INQUIRY]

JACK: It's kind of hard to be specific. . . . Just little

things . . . like you asking me if I put out the trash late at night after you reminded me to do it at six o'clock.

JILL: *Anything else?* [NEGATIVE INQUIRY]

JACK: Yeah. Like when I help you with the house-cleaning, you always come along afterwards and find something wrong.

JILL: (Astonished) *Do I do that . . .?* (Slow smile) *Yeah . . . I do that . . . anything else I do that bugs you?* [NEGATIVE INQUIRY, NEGATIVE ASSERTION, and NEGATIVE INQUIRY]

JACK: (Getting in the spirit of it) Yes. It's not even like you don't trust me to do things. It's more like you are looking for things to pick on.

JILL: *It's beginning to sound that way to me too . . . what else am I doing that makes me look like I'm trying to find fault with you?* [NEGATIVE ASSERTION and NEGATIVE INQUIRY]

JACK: Isn't that enough?

JILL: *That's a big chunk of things for me to think about, but I'd still like to hear more of what I do that upsets you.* [FOGGING and SELF-DISCLOSURE]

JACK: Okay, you remember when we had only one car?

JILL: Yes.

JACK: Whenever I was late picking you up, you bitched and moaned for twenty minutes on how you were abused.

JILL: *That was stupid of me to take my frustrations out on you, wasn't it?* (Instead of: "What did you expect? You were always late and never remembered!") [NEGATIVE ASSERTION-INQUIRY]

JACK: (Silent, with his jaw clenched)

JILL: (Prompting from where Jack left off) *I guess I didn't give you much leeway then, did I? That was a crappy way to behave.* [EMPATHIC NEGATIVE INQUIRY and NEGATIVE ASSERTION]

JACK: (Getting angry) You sure as hell didn't. It makes me mad as hell even now just thinking about it. And that's another thing. Whenever you started bitching and moaning and getting mad, I was just sup-posed to sit there and take it.

JILL: *How did I screw up there?* [NEGATIVE INQUIRY]

JACK: You could get mad whenever you wanted. That was okay for you to do. But when we were first married and I got mad back at you, you started crying and screaming and ran away into the bedroom and cried for hours until I came in and apologized.

JILL: (With empathy and maybe some embarrassment) *I did, didn't I? That was a bitchy thing to do. I could get mad, but you weren't supposed to. I tell you what. Let's make a pact. If I get mad, so can you and vice-versa, and nobody has to apologize afterwards, okay?* [NEGATIVE ASSERTION and WORKABLE COMPROMISE]

JACK: (Cautiously) Okay . . . but why not apologize?

JILL: 'Cause that makes it like it's wrong to just get mad and blow off steam.

JACK: Okay, but I think I might be getting the short end of the stick on that.

JILL: *How am I giving you the short end of the stick?* [NEGATIVE INQUIRY]

JACK: You get mad at me an awful lot more than I get mad at you.

JILL: *I think that's true too . . . so I tell you what we can do. I'll try not to pop off at you for every little thing that irritates me if you let me have it when you get mad at me. How's that?* [FOGGING and WORKABLE COMPROMISE]

JACK: Isn't that going to make you frustrated just like it did me?

JILL: *Maybe . . . but I've got a good memory. I can bring it all out later and blast you with it.* [FOGGING and WORKABLE COMPROMISE]

JACK: That's another thing. You always bring up things where I screwed up. . . . Where you think I screwed up . . . again and again and again. Why don't you just say what you don't like and then drop it? It's like you are trying to punish me. I'm no little kid you are trying to potty-train, I'm a grown man.

JILL: *I guess I do that, don't I? It's awful hard for me to look at some of the shitty things I do to you, Jack.* [NEGATIVE ASSERTION-INQUIRY and SELF-DISCLOSURE-NEGATIVE ASSERTION]

JACK: (Sympathetically) Do you want to stop?

JILL: (Confused) *I don't know. I guess I want to continue,* but *it's hard for me to look at myself like this.* [SELF-DISCLOSURE]

JACK: (Silent again)

JILL: I feel like crying ... but if I cry now, I'll screw everything up like I did before. That's my cop-out all the time. (Long pause) How about some more coffee until I feel better, okay?

JACK: Okay. (After coffee) What do you want to do?

JILL: It's still hard for me, but is it okay if we still talk about it?

JACK: Sure, if you really want to.

JILL: I do and I don't, you're going to have to help me.

JACK: What do you want me to say?

JILL: I wish you were my therapist and you could tell me what to say.

JACK: (Angrily) Did he tell you to do this?

JILL: He suggested it. But it makes sense to me if it can clear the air between us. I think I've been chopping you down whenever you did something I don't like. I want to see if I can handle what you don't like without flinching so much. If I'm not so damned uptight when you feel like bitching maybe we can start sharing things again.

JACK: (Fleeing) Now I want some coffee! (Comes back in after a few minutes looking angry and lights a cigarette)

JILL: *What is it about me doing this that upsets you?* [NEGATIVE INQUIRY]

JACK: I don't like being a guinea pig for you and your psychologist's experiments.

JILL: *I can understand that. How about coming in and talking to him with me?* [FOGGING and WORKABLE COMPROMISE]

JACK: No.

JILL: Do you want a divorce?

JACK: Of course not.

JILL: If we keep on like this and things don't get better between us, then I don't know what to do. *I'd like to work things out right here like this if we could. If you don't want to come in for counseling and you don't want to try something like this, what can we do?* [WORKABLE COMPROMISE]

JACK: I don't like it.

JILL: *You don't have to like it. All I want you to do is try it with me.* [FOGGING and WORKABLE COMPROMISE]

JACK: This is just like before. I'm the dumb shit and you've got all the answers!

JILL: *What am I doing that makes you feel like a dumb shit?* [NEGATIVE INQUIRY]

JACK: It's like you're screwing around with my mind.

JILL: *Do you want to stop talking about it?* [WORKABLE COMPROMISE]

JACK: No. You and that goddamned shrink have pissed me off.

JILL: Okay. *What have we done that pisses you off?* [NEGATIVE INQUIRY]

JACK: You make me feel like I'm the patient, not you. You're just coming on with this assertive therapy crap he taught you.

JILL: *That's true, I am. I don't know any other way to get through to you, but I'm not going to do it if you don't want me to.* [FOGGING, SELF-DISCLOSURE, and WORKABLE COMPROMISE]

JACK: Why can't you leave well enough alone?

JILL: I don't want to. *Maybe I want us to be like we were before, or better or different ...* (Frustrated) *I don't know exactly what the hell I want.* [SELF-DISCLOSURE]

JACK: Well, I feel like you are pulling a sneaky trick on me.

JILL: *I probably am, but I don't know what else to do. What can I do? Do you really want to go on like this?* [FOGGING, SELF-DISCLOSURE, and WORKABLE COMPROMISE]

JACK: What's wrong with the way we are?

JILL: (Angry and slipping back to her old style)

Plenty! Do you want me to list all the stupid things *you* ever did?

JACK: That's what's wrong. You and your big mouth.

JILL: (Still angry) This is exactly what I'm talking about. All we do is fight or I bitch and you shut up. I don't want to live like this anymore.

JACK: (Exasperated) Neither do I!

JILL: Then give it a try for Christ's sake! It won't kill you!

JACK: (Exhausted) What do you want us to do?

JILL: (Recovering her composure and silent for a few minutes) *Nothing if you really don't want to.* [WORKABLE COMPROMISE]

JACK: I don't like this.

JILL: *I can buy that,* but *will you give it a try? If you say "No," we don't do it.* [FOGGING and WORKABLE COMPROMISE]

JACK: If it gets too heavy, we stop?

JILL: *It's up to you.* If you don't want to do it with me, it would just be a waste of time . . . like me bitching at you before. Just to get you to do what I want instead of working together to see what each of us wants. [FOGGING]

JACK: Okay. (Note: At this point, without Jack's consent, further close communication does not exist.)

JILL: *Do you want to do it later? Tomorrow or next week?* [WORKABLE COMPROMISE]

JACK: Let's try it again.

JILL: Where did we leave off?

JACK: I'll be damned if I know. I was pissed off at you trying this on me.

JILL: Okay. Let's start there. *Can you put your finger on what I was doing that pissed you off?* [NEGATIVE INQUIRY]

JACK: You made me feel like you had all the answers.

JILL: *How did I do that?* [NEGATIVE INQUIRY]

JACK: You were so damned cool and slick.

JILL: *Like I was pulling a fast one?* [NEGATIVE INQUIRY]

JACK: Yeah!

JILL: *What was I doing that made you feel like I was pulling a fast one?* [NEGATIVE INQUIRY]

JACK: Like everything I was saying went right by you. You didn't blink an eye . . . at least until you started crying.

JILL: *I thought I was copping out then.* [SELF-DISCLOSURE]

JACK: It wasn't the same kind. When you cry and run off, I can tell you are mad at me. This time you were just crying.

JILL: *What is it about my crying and being mad at you that's different.* [NEGATIVE INQUIRY]

JACK: When you cry like that, I get pissed off at you and then I feel guilty.

JILL: *How do I make you feel guilty?* [NEGATIVE INQUIRY]

JACK: I don't know. I know for sure that what you are doing is pure bullshit, but you still make me feel guilty . . . and then I want to apologize even when I'm still pissed at you.

JILL: *That's a cop-out on my part. . . . I shut you off and make you swallow your anger when I cry and run off. . . . Like I'm saying: "What a rotten, slimy bastard you are for treating me so bad. Poor defenseless me."* [EMPATHIC NEGATIVE ASSERTION]

JACK: When you do that it confuses the hell out of me. I hate your guts and I still kiss your ass. Christ, what a mess.

JILL: *Do you want to stop?* [WORKABLE COMPROMISE]

JACK: (Still angry) Hell no!

JILL: *What else?* [NEGATIVE INQUIRY]

JACK: When that happens, I really feel like a snot-nosed kid who needs his diapers changed.

JILL: (Prompting from where Jack leaves off) *I make you feel like a little kid and not a grown man?* [NEGATIVE INQUIRY]

JACK: Yeah.

JILL: *What other things do I do that make you feel that way?* [NEGATIVE INQUIRY]

JACK: Just little remarks you make like "I have to do everything around here!" or "You never do what's important. You only do things you are interested in!"

JILL: *I do say things like that. I guess I'm just bitching in general, but when I say it that way it sounds like I don't respect you, is that it?* [FOGGING, SELF-DISCLOSURE, and NEGATIVE INQUIRY]

JACK: That's exactly the way it sounds.

JILL: *Can you ignore me when I do that?* [WORKABLE COMPROMISE]

JACK: I try to, but I just burn inside.

JILL: *Then how about blasting me when I say those things and telling me to shut my stupid mouth.* [WORKABLE COMPROMISE-NEGATIVE ASSERTION]

JACK: Come back at you?

JILL: Absolutely.

JACK: (Depressed) Sometimes I just get so fed up with you I don't even want to fight.

JILL: *Yeah, you do that and I accuse you of sulking. I'm not going to stop bitching, but if you blast me when I get way out of line like that even if you don't feel like it, it may help.* [FOGGING NEGATIVE ASSERTION, and WORKABLE COMPROMISE]

JACK: (Cautiously) Okay. I'm not promising anything, but I'll try.

JILL: *What else is it that I do that turns you off me?* [NEGATIVE INQUIRY]

JACK: If anything goes wrong, everyday normal things, I always get the feeling that you blame me for them.

JILL: (Curious) That I really don't understand. *What is it that I do that makes you feel like I'm blaming you when things go wrong?* [NEGATIVE INQUIRY]

JACK: I don't know how it happens. If you don't like something about the apartment and bitch about it, somehow I feel that it's my fault. I should have been more careful in looking at the apartment before we leased it.

JILL: (Prompting from where Jack left off) *It sounds like somehow I dump the responsibility for everything that happens on you, is that it?* [NEGATIVE IN-QUIRY]

JACK: Yes. It's like I'm responsible for every little thing that happens. They're not big things, but after three years there are an awful lot of things that go wrong, and that's tiring. Sometimes I feel like I don't want to come home at night because something else is going to happen that I'm responsible for.

JILL: I understand. *What else do I make you feel responsible for?* [NEGATIVE INQUIRY]

JACK: I don't know. A lot of things. Like if you get bored, I feel like I'm responsible for you getting bored.

JILL: (Prompting where Jack left off) *I make you feel like you are responsible for entertaining me. Is that it?* [NEGATIVE INQUIRY]

JACK: Exactly. It's like I have to watch what I say or do in front of you so you don't get upset, or I can't be myself and just flop down and relax. I always have to worry about you and are you okay.

JILL: (Prompting from where Jack left off) You're saying that I'm too dependent on you for things. (Thoughtfully) *It's probably true. What else am I doing that makes you feel like you're responsible for me?* [FOGGING and NEGATIVE INQUIRY]

JACK: Sometimes I feel like you can't do anything on your own without me. I always have to be involved. If I really don't want to do something and tell you how I feel, you give me the cold, silent treatment. I'm not supposed to dislike things you want to do. It's like I don't have a life except with you. You would bitch if I did anything without you except go to work. I think you would go to work with me if you could find a reason to do it. Sometimes I even feel like this is not a marriage but another job and I work for you. Even about sex. . . . Sometimes I feel like I owe you it instead of wanting to make love, and I resent it! Do you realize that in the three years we have been married, I haven't been out for an evening of fun with my friends except to go fishing and you always bitch when I do that?

JILL: (Losing her cool and a bit exasperated) God, do we have a problem!

JACK: That's exactly what I'm talking about. I tell you how I feel, and you don't listen to what I'm telling you. You just throw up your hands and dump it all on me.

JILL: (Lighting a cigarette and thinking for a moment) *I see your point.* (Smiling a queasy smile) *I'm not doing this very well, am I?* [EMPATHIC FOGGING and NEGATIVE ASSERTION-INQUIRY]

JACK: (Defensively) You asked for it.

JILL: Please, Jack. *You're right. I'm having trouble when you really let me have it,* like now, but *don't give up on me.* [FOGGING and WORKABLE COMPROMISE]

JACK: Well?

JILL: (Recovering and picking up from where Jack left off) *I guess I have been just too damned dependent and demanding, haven't I? What can we do about it?* [EMPATHIC NEGATIVE ASSERTION-INQUIRY and WORKABLE COMPROMISE]

JACK: I don't know. You can say: "Go out and have fun," but if you are sitting home alone and resenting it, I'd still feel guilty and responsible for you. Just saying it won't work.

JILL: *That makes sense. I don't think it would work either.* Let's see what we've got. I want us to be closer and share more. The problem is that I shut you off when you share the bad things, the things you don't like about us. And the worst thing about it is the way I shut you off (tears falling). Jack ... I'm sorry. [FOGGING]

JACK: (Staying where he is) I'm sorry too.

JILL: I guess being close for me only meant good things. I couldn't cope with the crap you gave me too.

JACK: (Smiling and rescuing her) What crap? I'm perfect!

JILL: (Smiling) *Sure you are.* [Friendly, sarcastic FOGGING]

JACK: I guess if I had more balls I would have told you to shut your mouth when you got really bitchy.

JILL: *Maybe . . . I want you to stick to it when you really want something, even if I give you a bad time.* [FOGGING and WORKABLE COMPROMISE]

JACK: All this is easy to say, but how do we do it?

JILL: *We could talk more like this to clear the air and see where each other is coming from?* How's that? [WORKABLE COMPROMISE]

JACK: Okay, but I want you to cut out some of the things that make me feel like I'm a hired hand just to keep you happy.

JILL: *What things?* [NEGATIVE INQUIRY]

JACK: The things we just talked about.

JILL: *Okay . . . but keep telling me them when I do them.* [WORKABLE COMPROMISE]

JACK: That's not going to get you from hanging around my neck.

JILL: *What else can I do?* [NEGATIVE INQUIRY]

JACK: How about getting involved in something besides just staying home. Go to school. Learn a trade. A job. I don't know.

JILL: *You're right. I've got to get some things going in my own life, without you. That's always been hard for me to do,* but *maybe when you want to get out on your own, I can do one of my own things then.* [FOGGING, NEGATIVE ASSERTION, and WORKABLE COMPROMISE]

JACK: When do we start?

JILL: How about right now?

JACK: How about after lunch. I'm starving.

JILL: You're on!

Learners have observed from experience, and, as this dialogue points out, being machine-like or a "verbal karate expert" is not necessary when asserting yourself to another person. They report that little harm is done if they have trouble communicating what they want, or get angry, or say something stupid, or get flustered, or say something they didn't really want to say, or make a commitment they don't want to give. Nothing is lost but some time. They simply start again as if nothing had gone on before and continue to say what it is they want—a specific material goal, a behavioral change in themselves or their partner in conflict, or better communication, as in this dialogue.

In Summary

Interacting and coping in the nondefensive, non-manipulative way that the last dialogue points out gives the person you assert yourself to a very important message. It is the assurance that you will not interfere with his or her decision-making process; most importantly, you will not interfere even if you do not like what you hear. This assurance allows conflicts in wants or dislikes to be worked out with mutual compromise, if compromise is at all possible. Behavior compromise worked out between two people is not behavior control. Behavior control takes place when someone gets "inside" that unique, individual part of you that you call "me." That part of all of us where we are independent of God, Mom and Dad, the Law, Morals, and Other People; the part of us where we decide what we want; where we weigh up the benefits and consequences of what we want to do, sometimes in spite of reality. Even in psychotherapy, the psychologist asks permission to enter that private part of the patient's life, for without permission psycho*therapy* (psycho*service*) is not possible. If the therapist intrudes without consent, either the service relationship ceases or psycho-dependency takes place and the patient becomes unhealthily dependent upon the therapist to make any decision for him. Luckily, this dependency does not happen too often. Therapists soon grow weary of phone calls at three in the morning asking: "What should I do?" The therapeutic intent in sharing the patient's decision process is to help the patient clarify *his* wants, emotions, and the actions resulting from them, to use technical expertise to help the patient solve his own problems and not to solve them for him, to help the patient do what he wants to do, not what the therapist wants him to do!

None of us who profess to be therapists is presumptuous enough to assume that beneficial changes in behavior and thinking between two people occur only in our offices or with our advice. What we really see (at least initially) in our offices are the coping interactions that don't work very well between people. We don't see the productive interactions between people which they work out on their own . . . and they do work out their conflicts without our help. With apologies to those more sensitive souls in our professional ranks, even though we therapists do help and really earn our keep, we are not absolutely essential or indispensable for the process of healthy behavior change to take place. The sum of all my personal and professional experience tells me that two people can cope with the common everyday conflicts that they cause for each other, and cope well with them. The major stumbling block for coping well with our conflicts in living with each other is set up when we interfere with another person's decision-making process, when we routinely manipulate our fellow man's wants by making him feel anxiously threatened, guilty, or ignorant. If you find yourself coping poorly in conflict, particularly with someone you care for, you might try asserting your wants in place of being manipulative, asserting your wants without taking away the dignity and self-respect of your equal and then see what happens.

Some learners, both from the lay and professional ranks, have been intrigued with the idea of projecting what implications, negative and positive, being systematically assertive might have for society in general, implications for how we live our lives or even for how we relate to things like General Motors (or Rolls-Royce). They ask what could happen to society and the way it currently operates socially, politically, economically, legally, if large numbers of people become more assertive and stop being responsive to manipulation of their behavior. While feeling quite comfortable in saying "I don't know," I can also emphasize that my only concerns within systematic assertive training and therapy lie at both end points of human society—the individual and the species. As a psychologist I am truly concerned only with the relations in conflict between two people, the smallest social unit, and at the other end of the continuum with the state of mankind as a dynamic, still evolving species. Everything in between these polar points is arbitrary and negotiable, and probably of no consequence one way or the other for mankind in the long run. If through politics, religion, affluence or excess, we overpopulate, we will automatically be regulated. Nature allows us no choice but to suffer the consequences of our actions. If through pollution, the pill, prejudice, war, famine, or disease, we depopulate our environment, we will automatically regrow as we have in the past. I have implicit faith in our *tried and tested* genetic heritage for the survival of our species, but little faith in my own survival except in how I choose to cope with other individuals. I have faith in mankind, but not in other individual men to make decisions concerning my well-being. I am my own judge. You are your own judge. You decide. If you want to.

Suggested Technical Readings

ALBERTI, R. E., and EMMONS, M. L. *Your Perfect Right.* San Luis Obispo: Impact, 1970.

BATES, H. D., and ZIMMERMAN, S. F. "Toward the Development of a Screening Scale for Assertion Training." *Psychological Reports, 28* (1971), pp. 99–107.

EDWARDS, N. B. Case conference: "Assertive Training in a Case of Homosexual Pedophilia." *Behavior Research and Therapy, 3* (1972), pp. 55–63.

HEDQUIST, F. J., and WEINHOLD, B. K. "Behavioral Group Counseling with Socially Anxious and Unassertive College Students." *Journal of Counseling Psychology, 17* (1970), pp. 237–242.

KRUMBOLTZ, J. D., and THORESEN, C. E., eds. *Behavioral Counseling: Cases and Techniques.* New York: Holt, Rinehart and Winston, 1969.

MCFALL, R. M., and LILLESAND, D. B. "Behavioral Rehearsal with Modeling and Coaching in Assertion Training." *Journal of Abnormal Psychology, 77* (1971), pp. 313–323.

———, and MARSTON, A. R. "An Experimental Investigation of Behavior Rehearsal in Assertive Training." *Journal of Abnormal Psychology, 76* (1970), pp. 295–303.

MACPHERSON, D. L. "Selective Operant Conditioning and Deconditioning of Assertive Modes of Behavior." *Journal of Behavior Therapy and Experimental Psychiatry, 3* (1972), pp. 99–102.

RATHUS, S. A. "An Experimental Investigation of Assertive Training in a Group Setting." *Journal of Behavior Therapy and Experimental Psychiatry, 3* (1972), pp. 81–86.

RUBIN, R. D., FENSTERHEIM, H., LAZARUS, A. A., and FRANKS, C. M., eds. *Advances in Behavior Therapy, 1969.* New York: Academic Press, 1971.

SAGER, C. J., and KAPLAN, H. S., eds. *Progress in Group and Family Therapy.* New York: Brunner-Mazel, 1972.

SALTER, A. *Conditioned Reflex Therapy.* New York: Farrar, Straus and Giroux, 1949.

WOLFE, J. "The Instigation of Assertive Behavior: Transcript from Two Cases." *Journal of Behavior Therapy and Experimental Psychiatry, 1* (1970), pp. 145–151.

———. *The Practice of Behavior Therapy.* Oxford: Pergamon Press, 1969.

————. *Psychotherapy by Reciprocal Inhibition.* Stanford: Stanford Univ. Press, 1958.

————, and LAZARUS, A. A. *Behavior Therapy Techniques.* Oxford: Pergamon Press, 1966.

YATES, A. J. *Behavior Therapy.* New York: Wiley, 1970.

Glossary of Systematic Assertive Skills

BROKEN RECORD

A skill that by calm repetition—saying what you want over and over again—teaches persistence without you having to rehearse arguments or angry feelings beforehand, in order to be "up" for dealing with others.

Clinical effect after practice: Allows you to feel comfortable in ignoring manipulative verbal side traps, argumentative baiting, irrelevant logic, while sticking to your desired point.

FOGGING

A skill that teaches acceptance of manipulative criticism by calmly acknowledging to your critic the probability that there may be some truth in what he says, yet allows you to remain your own judge of what you do.

Clinical effect after practice: Allows you to receive criticism comfortably without becoming anxious or defensive, while giving no reward to those using manipulative criticism.

FREE INFORMATION

A skill that teaches the recognition of simple cues given by a social partner in everyday conversation to indicate what is interesting or important to that person.

Clinical effect after practice: Allows you to feel less shy in entering into conversation while at the same time prompting social partners to talk more easily about themselves.

NEGATIVE ASSERTION

A skill that teaches acceptance of your errors and faults (without having to apologize) by strongly and sympathetically agreeing with hostile or constructive criticism of your negative qualities.

Clinical effect after practice: Allows you to look more comfortably at negatives in your own behavior or personality without feeling defensive and anxious, or resorting to denial of real error, while at the same time reducing your critic's anger or hostility.

323

NEGATIVE INQUIRY

A skill that teaches the active prompting of criticism in order to use the information (if helpful) or exhaust it (if manipulative) while prompting your critic to be more assertive, less dependent on manipulative ploys.

Clinical effect after practice: Allows you more comfortably to seek out criticism about yourself in close relationships while prompting the other person to express honest negative feelings and improve communication.

SELF-DISCLOSURE

A skill that teaches the acceptance and initiation of discussion of both the positive and negative aspects of your personality, behavior, lifestyle, intelligence, to enhance social communication and reduce manipulation.

Clinical effect after practice: Allows you comfortably to disclose aspects of yourself and your life that previously caused feelings of ignorance, anxiety, or guilt.

WORKABLE COMPROMISE

In using your verbal assertive skills, it is practical, whenever you feel that your self-respect is not in question, to offer a workable compromise to the other person. You can always bargain for your material goals unless the compromise affects your personal feelings of self-respect. If the end goal involves a matter of your self-worth, however, there can be *no* compromise.

ABOUT THE AUTHOR

Clinical-experimental psychologist MANUEL J. SMITH is the author of *When I Say No, I Feel Guilty*, which has sold over 1 million copies. A therapist in private practice and assistant clinical professor of psychology at UCLA, Dr. Smith has done research in social psychology, learning, phobic states, psychophysiology and sexual functioning. His work has appeared in various professional publications including *The Journal of Experimental Psychology, Psychology Report, Current Research in Human Sexuality,* and *Experimental Methods and Instrumentation in Psychology*. He is a member of The American Psychological Association, The Society of Psychophysiological Research, The Western Psychological Association and the California State Psychology Association, and has lectured widely in his field. Born in Brooklyn, New York, in 1934, Dr. Smith received both his B.A. (1959) and M.S. (1960) degrees from San Diego State College, and his Ph.D. from the University of California at Los Angeles (1966). He and his wife live in Los Angeles.

WE DELIVER!

And So Do These Bestsellers.

Bantam
On Psychology

☐	12196	**PASSAGES: Predictable Crises of Adult Life,** Gail Sheehy	$2.75
☐	10492	**HOW TO SURVIVE THE LOSS OF A LOVE,** Colgrove, Bloomfield, et. al.	$1.95
☐	11865	**THE GESTALT APPROACH & EYE WITNESS TO THERAPY,** Fritz Perls	$2.25
☐	11656	**KICKING THE FEAR HABIT,** Manuel J. Smith	$2.25
☐	12878	**THE BOOK OF HOPE,** DeRosis & Pellegrino	$2.50
☐	12109	**THE PSYCHOLOGY OF SELF-ESTEEM: A New Concept of Man's Psychological Nature,** Nathaniel Branden	$2.25
☐	12331	**WHAT DO YOU SAY AFTER YOU SAY HELLO?** Eric Berne, M.D.	$2.50
☐	10470	**GESTALT THERAPY VERBATIM,** Fritz Perls	$2.25
☐	12367	**PSYCHO-CYBERNETICS AND SELF-FULFILLMENT,** Maxwell Maltz, M.D.	$2.25
☐	10537	**THE FIFTY-MINUTE HOUR,** Robert Lindner	$1.95
☐	10562	**AWARENESS: Exploring, Experimenting, Experiencing,** John O. Stevens	$2.25
☐	12217	**THE DISOWNED SELF,** Nathaniel Branden	$2.25
☐	11756	**CUTTING LOOSE: An Adult Guide for Coming to Terms With Your Parents,** Howard Halpern	$2.25
☐	12725	**BEYOND FREEDOM AND DIGNITY,** B. F. Skinner	$2.75
☐	12553	**WHEN I SAY NO, I FEEL GUILTY,** Manuel Smith	$2.50
☐	11519	**IN AND OUT OF THE GARBAGE PAIL** Fritz Perls	$2.25

Buy them at your local bookstore or use this handy coupon for ordering:

Bantam Book Catalog

Here's your up-to-the-minute listing of over 1,400 titles by your favorite authors.

This illustrated, large format catalog gives a description of each title. For your convenience, it is divided into categories in fiction and non-fiction—gothics, science fiction, westerns, mysteries, cookbooks, mysticism and occult, biographies, history, family living, health, psychology, art.

So don't delay—take advantage of this special opportunity to increase your reading pleasure.

Just send us your name and address and 50¢ (to help defray postage and handling costs).